D0909702

SIMPSON

IMPRINT IN HUMANITIES

The humanities endowment
by Sharon Hanley Simpson and
Barclay Simpson honors
MURIEL CARTER HANLEY
whose intellect and sensitivity
have enriched the many lives
that she has touched.

Mountain against the Sea

Mountain against the Sea

Essays on Palestinian Society and Culture

Salim Tamari

UNIVERSITY OF CALIFORNIA PRESS
Berkeley · Los Angeles · London

University of California Press, one of the most distinguished university presses in the United States, enriches
lives around the world by advancing scholarship in the
humanities, social sciences, and natural sciences. Its activities are supported by the UC Press Foundation and by
philanthropic contributions from individuals and institutions. For more information, visit www.ucpress.edu.

University of California Press
Berkeley and Los Angeles, California

University of California Press, Ltd.
London, England

Library of Congress Cataloging-in-Publication Data

Tamari, Salim.
    Mountain against the Sea : essays on Palestinian so-
ciety and culture / Salim Tamari.
        p.   cm.
    Includes bibliographical references and index.
    ISBN: 978-0-520-25129-8 (cloth : alk. paper)
    1. Palestinian Arabs—Intellectual life—20th cen-
tury.   2. Palestine—Social life and customs—20th
century.   3. Palestine—Civilization.   I. Title.

DS112.T36   2008
956.9405—dc22   2008021097

Manufactured in the United States of America

17   16   15   14   13   12   11   10   09   08
10   9   8   7   6   5   4   3   2   1

This book is printed on Natures Book, which contains
50% post-consumer waste and meets the minimum
requirements of ANSI/NISO z39.48–1992 (R 1997)
(*Permanence of Paper*).

For Anton Shammas

Contents

Illustrations

Acknowledgments

Many of the ideas discussed in these essays on the modernity of Palestinian culture owe a great deal to debates I had with Anton Shammas. My main critic has been Rema Hammami, who keeps reminding me of my own limitations. For their critical reading and insights on several earlier drafts, I am indebted to Issam Nassar, Beshara Doumani, George Giacaman, May Jayyusi, Lisa Taraki, Samah Salim, Penny Johnson, Hasan Khader, Albert Aghazarian, Rochelle Davis, Suad Amiry, Ahmad Khalifeh, Fawwaz Tarabulsi, Elias Khoury, Lila Abu-Lughod, Tim Mitchell, Zach Lockman, Mark LeVine, James Gelvin, Zakaria Muhammad, Rashid Khalidi, Rasha Salti, Suha Khamis, Ted Swedenburg, Rebecca Stein, and Linda Butler. I am also thankful to Joseph Zernik, Abigail Jacobson, Shlomo Hasson, Hanan Hever, Arnold Band, and Yehouda Shenhav, who made available to me their rich knowledge of the life of Ishaq Shami and the history of Sephardic communities in Palestine and the Arab world. Niels Hooper and Kate Warne, from University of California Press, have been most helpful in bringing this book to fruition. I am especially grateful to Sharron Wood for her outstanding editorial work, which resulted in a much more readable text.

An Arabic version of this book was published by Muwatin as *al Jabal Didd al Bahar* (Ramallah, 2005). Shorter versions of chapters 4 and 5–11 appeared in *The Jerusalem Quarterly* (Jerusalem). A French version of "From Emma Bovary to Hasan al-Banna" appeared in *Peuples Mediterranean* (Paris, 1995); and a version of "A Musician's Lot" appeared as "Wasif Jawhariyyeh, Popular Music, and Early Modernity in Jerusalem," in Rebecca Stein and Ted Swedenburg, eds., *Palestine, Israel, and the Politics of Popular Culture* (Durham, NC: Duke University Press, 2005).

CHAPTER I

Introduction

Palestine's Conflictual Modernity

The chapters in this volume address two main themes. The first part of the book provides an interpretation of social changes common to contemporary societies of the eastern Mediterranean. These changes include the emergence of a cultural divide between mercantile coastal communities and mountain-dwelling smallholder peasants. This divide became more tangible precisely when the two regional economies became more capitalized and more integrated with European and Mediterranean trade networks, thus enhancing the cultures' difference. The book also addresses the relationship between village communities and the urban centers that have dominated them in the recent past through absentee landlordism; the ethnography of protonationalism; and the emergence of a small-town milieu as a backdrop to a reactive ideology of particularistic localism and a more recent ideology of religious triumphalism. This religious ideology emerged after the military encirclement of the PLO in Lebanon in the 1980s, and since then it has begun to replace the tradition of urban liberalism that emerged with the Ottoman reforms and during the British Mandate period, and the secular nationalism that marked Palestinian and Arab political culture for most of the twentieth century.

The second part of the book contains biographies of members of the Jerusalemite intelligentsia at the turn of the twentieth century. These illuminate a critical watershed in the modern social history of Palestine, and indeed the whole Arab East, the moment when the reading public, through mass literacy, public schooling, and the daily press, articulated the ideas of the Arab enlightenment of the late nineteenth century. Most of these biographies are of a number of public intellectuals who left their mark on the way Palestinians thought about themselves and their relationship to the patrimony of a disintegrating multinational state. Virtually all of those intellectuals were males, as well as members of a rising professional and mercantile class that acquired national prominence during the Mandate period. Each whose biography appears here exemplifies an aspect of Palestine's (and, in a few cases, Arab) modernity in an unanticipated manner. The radical pedagogue Khalil Sakakini revolutionized the study of Arabic and its grammar in a way that made it accessible to new generations of children trained in public schools. Already in his 1907 journalistic writings he had created a language that had begun to erode the gulf between the spoken and written language. It was crisp, intimate, and free from the ornamental elaborations of nineteenth-century Arabic, which had confined the written language to a small circle of literati and state functionaries. Omar Saleh al-Barghouti bridged the two eras of Ottoman decentralization and Arab independence movements. His *History of Palestine,* published on the eve of the Mandate (1921), utilizes a historical vocabulary and a current geography in which the country was still half anchored in greater Syria. Alone among his contemporaries, he saw World War I as an instrument of modernity and emancipation. Tawfiq Canaan, a doctor-turned-ethnographer, compiled a massive inventory of peasant lore as a prelude to the study of protonationalism. To him and his circle, Palestine's modern culture was a synthesis of Can'anite, Jebusite, Hebraic, Nabatean, Hellenic, and Arabo-Islamic traditions that were personified in the life of the village community. In his view, the European "contamination" of Levantine urban life, particularly in the coastal regions, should not blind us from the nature of this native hybridity. The apparent "purity" of peasant culture was the product of the impurity of its layered cultural traditions. More than any of his contemporaries, Wasif Jawhariyyeh the musician and bon vivant, was a witness to his age. His career as a soldier, musical performer, and state functionary in the Land Registry provided him with a platform to observe the great transition introduced by the British to colonial Palestine. As an entertainer, he was the shrewd observer par excellence, moving smoothly from the company of the Ottoman and British officer corps to the companionship of common soldiers, and from the mansions of the Jerusalemite aristocracy—his patrons—to street ceremonials and festivals. Daily life, as it appears in his memoirs, was an ongoing carnival.

Ishaq Shami embodies what was later to become a rare species: the native Arab-Jew. His fictional characters were exclusively Muslims and Sephardic Jews who inhabited a Palestinian and Damascene landscape that was soon to be transformed by colonialism and Zionism and enter an era of uncompromising nationalism that separated the Arab-Jew into an Arab and a Jew. Finally, the Bolshevik agitator Najati Sidqi introduces us to the placement of Palestine in its European context. As a functionary of the Comintern, his task was to Arabize Palestinian communism, transforming it from an ideology of Eastern European Jewish immigrants into a doctrine of Arab socialism. His clandestine career took him from the heated debates of Moscow in the 1920s to the ranks of the international brigades of Republican Spain, and from the prisons of Mandatory Palestine to the struggle for Syrian and Lebanese independence. Although he was betrayed and deserted by his comrades, he never lost his firm belief in the goodness of humanity, which he eventually expressed in his literary career as a novelist. The absence of a female voice among these pioneers is largely due to the fact that none of the leading female writers of the period left an accessible diary or memoir. The private papers of many of these women writers, such as Hind al Husseini and Zuleikha Shihabi, are not available to the public. Only later, during the second war and after, do we begin to see public memoirs by women writers, such as those by Samira Azzam, Anbara Salam, and the poet Fadwa Tuqan.

These two major themes, biography and social history, are connected by the issue of an unfulfilled modernity. A wide spectrum of major ideas that have engulfed the Arab East since the demise of the Ottoman Empire is manifested in the biographies of the landlords, professionals, artists, pedagogues, and revolutionaries whose work and writings are discussed here. The figures treated in this book were intellectual activists with a social vision whose lives crossed newly created colonial boundaries and had an impact on a much wider arena than one would expect considering their narrow social milieus. Curiously, they belonged to a community—and sometimes to intellectual circles such as the Vagabond Party—that brought them into intimate association with one another, even though they held highly divergent views about the future of Palestine. One has to recall here the size of this group: not only in the capital city, but in the country as a whole, the intelligentsia consisted of only a few score of writers and cultural workers in a country of fewer than a million inhabitants.

The unfulfilled modernity of Palestine is seen here as the product of the disintegration of pre-1948 society, the result of war and displacement rather than a result of underdevelopment. In this regard, Palestine's modern history diverges from that of the rest of the Arab East, Turkey, and Iran. The first part of the book describes the social features of this exceptional development: the loss of a cosmopolitan coastal culture, the thwarted growth of metropolitan areas, the hegemony of a small-town normative ethics, and so on. However, Palestine was, and continues to be, part of a much larger social and political formation. Its culture and political environment are defined as much by its territorial conflict with Zionism and the Israeli state as by affinities it continues to have with major currents in the Arab East. At the risk of sounding like a cultural nihilist, I would hold that Palestine's cultural contributions are not specifically distinct from those of neighboring Arab countries. What sets the country apart, rather, is that early on, in 1917, it was forcibly separated from that context. It is this physical separateness and its consequences that necessitate that we look at the main contours of the social transformations that have engulfed the country in this momentous century.

PALESTINE'S RUPTURE FROM GREATER SYRIA

Although the twentieth century saw the reemergence of the country as a separate administrative entity, nineteenth-century Palestine was, in terms of its cultural and social patterns, an extension of the Syrian provinces of Ottoman western Asia.[1] It shared with the Syrian provinces similar ecological patterns, similar land tenure and cropping arrangements, a contrast in habitat between coastal regions and highland townships, urban-rural dichotomies, and a relatively autarkic village economy. In common with Anatolia, Syria, and Mount Lebanon, Palestine was dominated numerically by an autonomous peasantry, implemented a tax-farming system (which had replaced the earlier mode of feudal *timars,* or military fiefs), and displayed a distinct differentiation between an urban mercantile culture and the rural communal organization of agricultural production. Social organization and social consciousness, judging from the few narratives that have survived from that period, were distinctly localized and bound by kinship. Cities and villages, on the other hand, were bound by ties of patronage and other feudal alignments.

The entry of Palestine into modernity—its integration into the global economy and its intensive exposure to European technological innovation—has been variously dated to the Napoleonic invasion at the turn of the eighteenth century, to the Egyptian military campaign of Ibrahim Pasha (1831–40), and more specifically to the introduction of the Ottoman administrative reforms of 1839 and the commoditization of land under the Land Code of 1858. But these historical markers merely represent administrative intrusions into social and economic networks that predated these state interventions. In his study of land and mercantile relations in central Palestine, for example, Beshara Doumani suggests that relations of patronage between landlords and peasants persisted despite imperial decrees.

Toward the end of Ottoman rule, the Palestinian village, seemingly immobile, had gone through important transformations that affected its physical characteristics, as well as its relations with the holders of power in the cities. The turn of the nineteenth century heralded the control of nomadic incursions on the peasantry, substantial demographic growth in the countryside, and the establishment of an effective—though rudimentary—network of transportation that linked the village to regional centers and the demands of external markets. Structurally, the period saw a radical reorganization in the land tenure system and the modes of agricultural production, from communal ownership of the land to ownership by absentee landlords, and from subsistence farming to monetization, commodity production, and the export of agricultural yield.

The village remained the source of revenue and power, but it was no longer the seat of authority. Its big landlords, tax farmers, government functionaries, artisans, merchants, and notables all relocated to the four or five major urban centers, where they constituted a privileged elite that established its hegemony over Palestine. Yet despite these hierarchical cleavages and disparities in wealth, Palestinian society was still divided by lineage units and other forms of kinship and quasi-kinship identification in which class formations were hardly visible. And although the city-village dichotomy permeated the consciousness of Palestinians when they reflected on groups outside their local community (as evidenced in the folkloric literature), it was nevertheless a consciousness mediated through other identifications that they believed to be primary, mainly regional loyalties, religious affiliations, and clan affiliations. Throughout the first half of the nineteenth century, with minor exceptions, the peasantry of Palestine was divided into factions based on clan alliances and relations of patronage with urban landlords and notables.

THE DECLINE IN RURAL AUTONOMY

An immediate result of Ottoman reform in nineteenth-century Palestine was a decline in rural autonomy. This was a consequence of a series of administrative decrees (beginning with the Land Code of 1858) aimed at the regulation of landownership, which facilitated the dissolution of the communal *musha'* (shared rotating possession of agricultural plots) and ownership of village lands by the peasants and the rise of absentee landlordism. The reforms aimed at increasing agricultural productivity had other stabilizing results as well, including increased security in the countryside from outside pillagers, substantial growth in the urban population, and the integration of the region into a network of transportation routes, including a railroad system.

Ottoman administrative reforms also contributed to the separation of the *sanjak* (district) of Jerusalem (which included, at that period, the bulk of the Palestinian population within post–World War I boundaries) from the northern *sanjaks* of Akka and Nablus (which contained the best agricultural lands). Jerusalem differed from the main urban centers of Palestine in that it was detached from its rural hinterland. Its elite, in the main, were not absentee landlords, nor was there any organized form of political interaction between Jerusalem and the rural population.

The administrative separation of Jerusalem in the second half of the nineteenth century had two effects on factional politics that should be noted here. First was the relative independence of, and possibly privilege accorded to, the Jerusalemite notables by virtue of their direct relationship to the Sublime Porte in Istanbul. This independence was doubtlessly influenced by the interest in the holy city by the European powers, which demonstrated undisguised imperialist ambitions. This relative autonomy, however, had a marked negative effect on general political life in southern Palestine, resulting in the weakening of local voluntary associations for the advancement of education and social welfare—in contrast with the northern districts and Damascus, where such associations were vigorous. The weakness of these associations flowed from the marked dependence of Jerusalem on the central government. In terms of its social economy, Jerusalem could be characterized as having at that time a "parasitic" social structure, as it was dependent on religious endowments, international charities, and weak organic links with the rural base.

The other consequence of administrative separatism was the intensification of factional rivalry between Jerusalem-based and Nablus-based clans. The roots of these conflicts predate the administrative reform. Northern notables traditionally complained about the way their fates were tied to "the whims of the Jerusalem effendis," as the Nablus historian Ihsan al-Nimr put it. This hostility persisted even after the unification of Palestine under the British Mandate. Several decades later, when al-Istiqlal, the only mass-based pan-Arabist party, began to mobilize Palestinian Arabs around an anti-Zionist and anti-imperialist program, it invariably encountered factional opposition from the Jerusalem clan–based parties of the Husseinis and Nashashibis. Those difficulties were due in no small degree to the fact that the leader of al-Istiqlal, Awni Abdul-Hadi, belonged to a family of big landowners in the Jenin (Nablus) area, but they were primarily a result of the fact that the platform of al-Istiqlal was critical of clan-based parties. But the two main leaders of al-Istiqlal, Abdul-Hadi and Muhammad Izzat Darwazeh, who wrote what are arguably the most profound memoirs of this period, continued to believe in Palestine's identity as a component of the greater Syrian homeland.

The social basis of clan power seems to have been associated with two interrelated features. The first was the number of men that clan notables could mobilize on their side in factional struggles—a factor that was dependent, as far as peasants were concerned, on the amount of land under control by the clan head and the intricate system of patronage he maintained with his sharecroppers and semiautonomous peasants, which in turn was influenced by his ability to act as their creditor in an increasingly monetized economy. The second feature was the access that the clan head and his relatives and aides had to public office, and thus his ability to extend services to his clients in return for their support in factional conflicts (including votes in municipal elections, which became a major arena of rivalry under British rule).

Power over the peasantry resulting from this system of patronage and the power resulting from holding public office reinforced each other. Influential village patriarchs who succeeded in consolidating large estates for themselves after the dissolution of the *musha'* system would soon send a few of their capable sons or relatives to establish themselves in the regional center or acquire a public post themselves. It has been suggested that the power of those potentates can be observed in the transition of residence from their rural base to the district center.

Landownership under semifeudal conditions (in other words, the ability to lease land to sharecroppers through the *wakil*, the landlord's agent) was not always necessary as a basis for factional power. In some cases in Palestine, a clan's power was rooted mainly in the holding of public administrative office—that is, on its ability to organize its members' skills in the service of the state—and landownership and mercantile activities played only a marginal role. This seems to have been the case with the Nashashibi clan, whose members became important contenders for the leadership of the nationalist movement after the Husseinis.

The challenges posed by the Zionist movement and its success in creating modern and independent Jewish institutions, as well as the inability of the colonial government to accommodate Palestinian nationalist
aspirations, all compelled the machinery of factional politics to perform
a role to which it was thoroughly unsuited. While the Arab leadership
was capable of effectively mobilizing the masses against the British colonial presence and for independence, dislodging the Jewish colonies
would have required a radically different strategy. Such a strategy would
have involved the nationalist movement in a protracted struggle and
forced the formation of class alignments, which in all likelihood would
have eroded the system of patronage on which the movement's very
power was based.

The expanded role of the colonial state apparatus after the Great War
paradoxically strengthened the role of the leading families of Palestine,
since alternative institutional mechanisms of intermediate power were
absent. Members of these families became the mediators between the
state and the rural masses and urban poor, as well as their representa-
tives to the central authorities. Both the limitations and strengths of the
factional system were demonstrated in the response of the traditional
leadership to the 1936 revolt.

The spontaneous peasant uprisings that marked the initial period of
the revolt compelled the two main nationalist parties—the Arab Palestinian Party, representing the Husseini faction, and the National Defense
Party, representing the Nashashibis—to merge under the auspices of the
Arab Higher Committee. Both clans represented the same class (if that
term can be used here), and both stood to lose their privileges if independent peasant politics were to prevail, even temporarily. However, the
Husseini faction's stronger links to the land, al-Haj Amin's role as the
mufti of Jerusalem, and the National Defense Party's past record of collaboration with the British authorities all ensured that the Nashashibis
would play a secondary role in the Arab Higher Committee.

In that merger we observe what appears to be the defactionalization
of factional politics. What happened, however, was simply the temporary suspension of factional politics at the national level, while the institutional linkages of the hierarchical, vertical alliances remained intact.

THE EMERGENCE OF NEW ELITES

While the old regional divisions in Palestine—based on administrative
zones under Ottoman and British rule—began to lose their original

significance, there began to emerge new divisions reflecting the integration of the region's economy into the European capitalist market. Colonial penetration also contributed to the development of a modern infrastructure, largely for reasons related to military strategy. By the First World War, Palestine had the greatest quantity of railroad track per capita in the Middle East, although the economic impact of modern transportation here was not as dramatic as it was in Egypt. The building of the Jaffa–Jerusalem railroad line (later the Jerusalem–Haifa line, which was linked to the Hijaz railway), the growth of citriculture and its European market, the proliferation of wage labor related to the British war efforts, and the employment of Palestinians in the government bureaucracy all led to the decline of subsistence agriculture and the semifeudal relations that hinged on it.

Many absentee landlords who resided in the main cities, and a few state functionaries whose wealth was not dependent on land, began to reinvest their agricultural surplus in the import-export trade and in light industries. A Royal Commission report prepared during the revolt year of 1936 challenged the predominant picture of a vigorous Jewish industrial economy dwarfing an Arab sector that was presumed to be based on craft production. "Arab industry," the report states, "is also diversified (as is Jewish industry) and consists of some large undertakings and numerous small ones that, in the aggregate, form an appreciable contribution to the industry of Palestine." The main urban industries in the Arab sector included soap manufacturing, flour milling, and manufacturing textiles and construction materials. Agrarian capitalism, based on citrus plantations in Jaffa, Gaza, and the Ramleh-Lydda regions, also flourished during the Mandate. Olive oil extraction was the main form of manufacture in the rural sector and the industry in which wealthy peasants and landlords invested their capital, although the process tended to remain primitive in its technology.

Thus a new class of merchants and manufacturers was growing in the coastal cities of Gaza, Jaffa, and Haifa, the three cities that constituted Palestine's Mediterranean outlets to Europe. This growth of a coastal bourgeoisie was accompanied by important demographic changes; the population of towns in general, and the coastal cities in particular, increased substantially. The city of Jaffa had the fastest rate of growth, even before the Mandate. Its size quadrupled between 1880 and 1922 as it became the economic and cultural nerve center of Arab Palestine. The 1930s also saw the beginnings of large-scale migration from rural to urban areas, which reflected both an increase in opportunities for employment in the cities and an increase in the agricultural labor surplus. A new regional dichotomy was emerging between the main coastal cities, which were centers of trade, newspapers and literary magazines, and urban Jewish migration, and the inner mountain cities (Nablus, Safad, and Hebron), which were the seats of conservatism and traditional leadership. This was not, however, a class dichotomy between the bourgeoisie and the landed classes, for, unlike the landed elites, the Palestinian bourgeoisie did not behave as an integrated class during this period. This ambiguity resulted from the composition of the mercantile and manufacturing entrepreneurs in Palestine.

As in the neighboring Arab countries, the Palestinian bourgeoisie had strong kinship and social bonds linking it to the landed classes. Those entrepreneurs who were not landlords either had patronage relationships with them, or were related to them by marriage. Furthermore, most landlords found it convenient to invest their agricultural surplus either in real estate transactions, in construction, or in "buying" posts for their sons (through marriage bonds, for example). In each of these cases, their investment constituted a nonproductive activity.

This process of differentiation did not generate the growth of a significant manufacturing class. The urban elites, the class of landlords and urban notables, did not have control over the colonial state apparatus, and because of the intense competition from the autonomous Jewish sector (which, except for the period of the boycott, had unhindered access to the Arab consumer market), the external condition for the growth of the Arab bourgeoisie did not develop. A very small percentage of the agricultural surplus was invested in manufacturing enterprises. Those landed businessmen who did invest in manufacture (such as the al-Masri family, of the Nablus soap industries) were few, and together they were not capable of generating enough employment for the masses of dispossessed peasants, peasant workers, and urban laborers who were looking for jobs. These entrepreneurs were also too closely linked to the landed elite to develop their own distinct sensibilities. Nevertheless, recent research about Palestinian investments in coastal enterprises indicates that in the 1940s a vigorous urban entrepreneurial class was growing, a class that had significant links to Lebanese, Syrian, Egyptian, and European establishments.

FLIGHT AND DISMEMBERMENT

The consequences of factionalism became evident when the collision between Zionist and Arab forces finally came to a head in 1948. The vertical segmentation of Palestinian society, on which its political fabric prevailing in the 1930s and '40s was built, was shattered from without. The result was the physical dislocation of both the agrarian and urban communities. The city of Haifa, for example, had its Arab population reduced from eighty thousand to a few thousand in only one week due to the outflow of Arab refugees.

During the initial period of communal clashes between Jews and Arabs, which extended throughout the latter part of 1947 and early 1948, the Palestinian elite (landlords, businessmen, and professionals) constituted the bulk of the tens of thousands of Palestinian Arabs who fled the country. Given the absence of an extragovernmental body in Palestinian society (equivalent, for example, to the Jewish Agency) that could coordinate the Palestinian resistance and provide basic services to a community steadily being deserted by its elites, the dissolution of its political will was unavoidable. Coupled with the intensive bombardment faced by cities like Jaffa, Lydda, and Ramleh, this exodus was a decisive factor in the collapse of the social fabric of Palestinian society and the mass desertion of towns and villages by their inhabitants.

It is important to look to different categories of analysis to understand the major dislocation that affected Palestinian society after 1948 and the disappearance of relations of patronage upon which factional politics rested. Although most Palestinians remaining in Palestine still dwell in rural districts (in the Galilee, the Triangle, and the West Bank—but not Gaza), as a group they can no longer be characterized as a peasant society, that is, as a society that derives its livelihood primarily from agriculture and in which the family farm constitutes the basic unit of social organization. This is especially true of the Arab rural sector in Israel, which was progressively incorporated into the Jewish economy as former Arab peasants began to participate as wageworkers. To the extent that factional politics persisted in the Arab village, it was due to the external manipulation by Israeli political parties of a traditional clan structure that was losing its viability and coherence. In the 1990s, however, we observed a reemergence of clan politics in parties that were ostensibly nationalist and socialist (in the Arab Democratic Party and the Democratic Front, for example).

As a consequence of the war of 1948, the peasantry of Palestine was uprooted, dispersed, and reconfigured in three different social formations. Approximately 25 percent, constituting an underclass of peasant workers, remained in the state of Israel. Another 40 percent, constituting a reserve labor pool in the periphery of the major urban centers of the host countries (Amman, Nablus, Gaza, Beirut, Damascus, Jericho, and Ramallah), became refugees in neighboring Arab states and the remaining regions of Palestine. Finally, approximately a third of the peasantry remained in their villages in those parts of Palestine that were appropriated by Jordan and Egypt in 1948, the West Bank and Gaza. The social fabric of this group was altered as a result of being incorporated into the new social formation, although in a different manner from that of the refugees.

The urban refugees, composed predominantly of artisans, professionals, landowners, and the traditional working class of colonial Palestine, were successfully integrated, at least at the economic and occupational levels, into the Arab host countries—most notably in Jordan, Kuwait, the Gulf States, and, to a lesser extent, Lebanon. Emerging from their ranks was a Palestinian intelligentsia, unable to assimilate itself politically into these new regimes and soon to become a staunch proponent of pan-Arab nationalism, and later of Palestinian nationalism. Over this intelligentsia lurks an eminently successful Palestinian bourgeoisie whose members were reconstituted from the sons of the dispossessed landed elite of old Palestine, and whose fortunes were accumulated in the new diaspora of the Gulf states. Today they are found among the most prominent bankers, import-export merchants, ministers, government advisors, company managers, and urban planners in every state in the Arab Persian Gulf. Their less fortunate kinsmen swell the ranks of the professional and semiprofessional groups in these states.

PALESTINIANS DECLASSED IN ISRAEL

Whether substantial class differentiation has occurred among Israeli Arabs remains the subject of some controversy. There seems to be a consensus, however, that the quantitative integration of the Arab underclass—mainly rural laborers and peasants who commute daily from their villages to Jewish urban centers—has led to a qualitative change in the relationship between Arab and Jewish society. In formal terms this change can be described as the transformation of Arab and Jewish societies from two parallel social structures into a single hierarchical social structure. What is still in need of empirical substantiation, however, is the amount and character of the social differentiation that took place within Arab society concurrent with its progressive subordination to Jewish society.

Several early ethnographic studies on the fate of Arab villages in Israel, such as those conducted by Nakhleh, Rosenfeld, Kana'ana, Haidar, and

Cohen, illuminate the changing social and political trends among the Palestinian population inside Israel. These studies describe the manner in which the Israeli state, through limiting the options for political affiliation open to Palestinian villagers, and by tying votes for the Zionist parties with material inducements such as jobs, reinforces faction-based conflicts in villages, especially those with a strong religious base. Thus factionalism persists here, but it exists in a context that is clearly different from the one prevailing prior to 1948: patronage today is related to access to privileges afforded by the Israeli state to the Arab population through the Zionist parties. It has become a means for Zionist legitimization in the Arab sector.

Since the early 1980s we have witnessed a diversification in the occupational structure of Israeli Arabs. While maintaining their village-based dwellings and sometimes their plots of land, they have nevertheless succeeded in joining the ranks of the self-employed (in construction subcontracting, retail sales, etc.), gaining professional employment, and producing a militant intelligentsia (trained in large part in Israeli universities) that openly identifies itself with Palestinian nationalism. Rosenfeld describes a policy of "de-territorialization," based on land confiscation and aimed at maintaining the Palestinian population as a subordinate underclass, as having backfired as a result of changes emanating from the work process itself. This process has objectively diminished the class and ethnic cleavages that previously separated Jewish and Arab social structures within the Israeli state, and that now have to be reinforced at the political level by the state.

Reviving interfamily rivalries is not the only means of maintaining the diminished social cleavages between the Arab and Jewish populations. It is also achieved instrumentally by prolonging the physical backwardness of the Arab villages, where a majority of Palestinians continue to live. While the restrictions on village development result in the migration to Jewish urban areas of those intent on self-improvement, village backwardness guarantees the continued reproduction of the peasant-worker underclass.

This process by which structural (socioeconomic) and institutional (political-administrative) mechanisms reinforce each other in ensuring Israeli-Jewish hegemony over the Arab minority is not, however, self-perpetuating. Ian Lustick has suggested that such a system of control is composed of three levers: 1) segmentation, or the internal fragmentation of the Arab community, which prevents its members from participating in united political action; 2) dependence, or the reliance of Arabs on the Jewish economy for its sources of livelihood; and 3) co-optation, or the selective manipulation of Arab factionalism, especially at the village level, by Zionist parties and institutions. Although these three components of control operate simultaneously to ensure Arab quiescence at the political level, they are not foolproof, as evidenced by the increasing claims made by the Arabs for national and local representation in the country's political system. Aziz Haidar has suggested recently that the normalization of relations between Israel and the Arab countries after the peace agreements of 1995 led to the emergence of demands for equality that are atomized and based on a desire for individual self-enhancement by the new professional class, rather than on the goal of equal citizenship for the Arab minority as a whole.

EXILE AND DISPERSAL

The population of refugee camps in Arab exile constitutes the core of Palestinians dispersed in 1948 and again in 1967. Unlike the camp refugees in Gaza and the West Bank, those living in Jordan, Syria, and Lebanon do not reside on the periphery of a relatively dynamic and expanding capitalist economy in constant need of cheap labor, as was the case in Israel. The construction boom in Jordan in the mid-1970s, enhanced by the influx of rich refugees from the Lebanese civil war, changed the situation there, but it did so only temporarily. In general, it may be said that the camp refugees (a majority of Palestinians in Lebanon and Syria, and almost a third of the Palestinians in Jordan) act as a reserve army of the unemployed for the host economies.

The fate of those refugees has been described succinctly by Elias Sanbar as "expulsion for the means of production." Until 1982, when the Israeli invasion of Lebanon shattered the social fabric of the Palestinian community, wage labor in the refugee camps supplemented funds from the United Nations Relief and Works Agency (UNRWA) and money provided by migrant relatives. Together with Kurdish and illegal Syrian migrants, as well as Lebanese Shiite farmers from the south, the Palestinians constituted a competing source for cheap and expendable labor for local Beirut industries. A comprehensive survey conducted in a Beirut camp on the eve of the civil war confirms this fact. The camp Tel Za'tar, which was destroyed when many of its inhabitants were massacred by Phalangist forces in 1976, was not unlike other urban refugee camps, such as those situated in Amman, Damascus, Zarqa, and Irbid. It did, however, have certain features that set it apart from those camps. It contained a substantial proportion (23 percent) of non-Palestinian refugees, for example, and it had a considerable number of Palestinian refugees from pastoral nomadic backgrounds, mainly from the Huleh region. The camp, located in eastern Beirut in a district containing 29 percent of all Lebanese manufacturing industries, employed 22 percent of the total labor force, and absorbed 23 percent of the industrial capital investments in Lebanon.

It was this de-peasantization and economic marginality that established the camp refugees as the political base of the movement calling for the right of return to Palestine as the core of their ideology, and it was from their ranks that the fighting cadres of the various contingents of the Palestine Liberation Movement were recruited. The "cult of return" and the organizational independence of Palestinian movements that it entailed, however, were not always forms of self-imposed political restrictions. I am not suggesting here a necessary determination of ideology and organizational structure dictated by refugee declassment. In both Jordan and Lebanon the Palestinians entered into various alliances with the local forces in order to combat the repression of the national authorities, but the conditions under which the Palestinian refugees lived and worked rendered these alliances much weaker than they would have been if the Palestinians had been fully integrated into their host countries. In Lebanon, where these alliances were more effective, the capacity of their combined force was severely limited by the historic predicament of the Lebanese, whose politics were now embedded in the confessional system. The civil war finally caused a dramatic convulsion in this system, and it pushed the Palestinians into becoming advocates not only for their own cause, but also for the cause of secularism and anticonfessionalism for the Lebanese themselves.

Although the effective social base of the PLO existed among the refugee camps and rootless intelligentsia of Jordan (1967–71) and Lebanon (1971–82), the group's political constituency was dispersed among several social groups throughout the Arab world and the state of Israel. As the quest for nationhood altered the movement's ideological direction, from the "cult of return" to the quest for sovereignty, from total liberation to limited statehood, the PLO's political center of gravity began to shift from its declassed diaspora to those segments of Palestine that remained "intact": the West Bank and Gaza.

THE LOGIC OF OLD HIERARCHIES

The image of declassment and de-peasantization that is often projected based on the conditions of dispersed refugees in urban Lebanon, Syria, and

Jordan often obscures the fact that more than half of the Palestinian people still live in (historic) Palestine—now "united" through common Israeli rule—most of them residing in relatively stable communities in or near the place of their birth. If we use the term "declassment" in the manner Sanbar used it, to mean "expulsion from the means of production," then it can primarily be applied to communities living in refugee camps. Only in Gaza do residents of refugee camps constitute a slight majority of the population, in this case around 55 percent. In the West Bank they count for less than 20 percent of the population, and in the Galilee and the Triangle, refugees (not living in camps) constitute less than 15 percent of the total Palestinian population. Furthermore, most of the remaining Palestinians living in other parts of the state of Israel (villages around West Jerusalem, the Naqab, the Lydda-Ramleh area, and Jaffa) have retained their places of residence.

What is crucial for the occupied territories is the manner in which the Palestinian labor force was incorporated into the Israeli economy, and—since 1994—the emergence of the Palestinian national economy under the aegis of the Palestinian National Authority. In the three decades of Israeli rule over the territories, the crucial impact on the Palestinian social structure was the manner in which Israel engineered the economic and social integration of the West Bank into the Israeli economy. Until the Gulf War (1990–91), this process involved the employment of nearly half the Palestinian labor force in Israeli enterprises on a daily basis and the opening up of Gaza and the West Bank as markets for Israeli commodities. Of those workers involved, the overwhelming majority were of peasant origin (73.2 percent were rural residents, as opposed to the remaining 26.8 percent, which were evenly divided between urban and refugee residents), but few of them today are agriculturalists. By the year 2000 this process of labor integration had disappeared as a result of the regime of closure and separation.

Israeli rule did give rise to a stratum of war profiteers, primarily involved with labor contracting, construction, and real estate transactions. This activity, however, did not qualitatively change the character of the local bourgeoisie. Any growth effects it may have had were probably cancelled out by the desertion of the middle classes to Jordan beginning after 1967. Israeli-Palestinian joint enterprises emerged in the form of subcontracting firms in textiles and construction, but their growth rate declined after the late 1970s, probably due to business instability caused by political uncertainty. Employment in Israel, the most crucial variable in this matter, did create a new stratum of workers from urban refugees and surplus rural laborers.

What is certain is that peasant agricultural labor became supplementary to wage labor, and not vice versa, although in Gaza, where refugees (rather than farmers) constitute a majority of the labor force, it is necessary to take into account the absence of a subsistence economy to which the refugees may resort. The differences between Gaza and the West Bank are rooted in part in the different forms of agricultural production (capitalist citriculture dominates in Gaza, small and medium-sized farms in the West Bank), and in part to the massive weight of the refugee population in Gaza. It is also, however, related to the nature of Jordanian and Egyptian rule between 1948 and 1967 in those two regions. The substantial reduction of labor migration from the West Bank to Israel after 2001, and the virtual elimination of any labor entry from Gaza after Israel's unilateral withdrawal in 2005, did not generate a substantial "return to the land" as might be expected, but instead resulted in a severe drop in employment.

The West Bank nevertheless escaped the destruction of its landed commercial elite and underwent a pattern of limited structural mobility in its occupational and class composition. The Jordanian army and bureaucracy, the expansion of the educational system, and a high rate of out-migration (the latter resulting in sizable supplements to household incomes) all combined to modify the direction of social change in a way that was different from that experienced by Palestinians who remained in Israel and by Gazans under Egyptian rule.

On the surface, the difference between the West Bank and the Galilee would seem to be the degree of integration into Jewish society, which is a result of—among other things—the civic enfranchisement of the Israeli Arab population into the state of Israel (as tenuous as it is), and, conversely, of the colonial relationship between the state and the Palestinians of the West Bank and Gaza. This is admittedly a controversial position, for there are those who argue that the difference between the two communities is not a qualitative one but exists only in the degree of colonial domination. What this problem amounts to is how one interprets the nature of mediation in Israeli rule in the two Palestinian communities.

In the Galilee, where 60 percent of Israel's Palestinians are concentrated, this mediation is articulated through civil society: via the agency of political parties, local councils, clan alliances, and a personal nepotistic network of favoritism that permeates these agencies. The structural foundation of this mediation is the occupational integration of the Arab labor force into the Jewish economy. A considerable degree of coercion and intimidation is nevertheless used to supplement these institutions in order to guarantee the acquiescence of Palestinians to Zionist society, whose raison d'être excludes them, as Arabs, from its polity. Since the abolition of the military government in 1966, however, coercion has been a secondary mechanism of political control. In the West Bank and Gaza, by contrast, Israeli rule functions primarily through the machinery of the military government. The use of systematic physical coercion to maintain Israeli hegemony has far exceeded the force that was inflicted upon Israeli Arabs during the formative years of the Jewish state, when the military government ruled supreme in the Galilee (1948–66). Despite similarities in the structural trends of integration at the economic level in the two regions of Israeli control, the difference cannot be attributed simply to the missing factor of citizenship, that is, the enfranchisement of Israeli Arabs, and its absence among Palestinians in the West Bank and Gaza.

One important factor that may explain the different responses to Israeli rule in the two regions is their varying social composition. While the West Bank had maintained its rural and urban hierarchies, albeit in a modified form, Galilean rural society had lost its original landed elites and intelligentsia and therefore has had to fend for itself in the face of overwhelming odds. The continued links between West Bank Palestinians and the Arab world, through Jordan, provided West Bank society with a network of commercial, political, and cultural ties that were denied to Israeli Arabs, and which drastically curtailed their political options.

The centrality of the West Bank and Gaza in the composition of these social hierarchies lies in two features: first, the West Bank is the only segment of historic Palestine in which agriculture constitutes a meaningful component of the region's political economy; and, second, it is the arena in which Palestinian sovereignty is being contested today. Compared to the Palestinians in Israel and neighboring Arab states, West Bankers were less subject to convulsions in the social structure. They alone have retained a semblance of a social order that is continuous with the nation's history. Only there is a Palestinian peasantry, divorced from its coastal landlords and urban elite, still entrenched in the highlands of the West Bank and in the valleys of the Jordan.

TWO REBELLIONS: SOCIAL CONSEQUENCES

The first intifada (1987–93) was a sustained grassroots movement of civil insurrection against Israeli rule. The nationalism of the intifada, and its broadly (and unclearly) defined objective of national independence, initially succeeded in mobilizing hundreds of thousands of people in acts of civil disobedience against Israeli control. As the years progressed, however, and with increased Israeli suppression of the rebellion, the movement began to lose its mass base and was confined to street action against the army by bands of activists.

Of all the social consequences of the rebellion, the most visible was the massive involvement of youth and children in spontaneous acts of resistance against the colonial forces. Tens of thousands of young people, including students, children younger than fifteen years of age, and lumpen elements in refugee camps and urban areas, were mobilized. Many of those youths, although they themselves did not belong to organized political groups, were eventually mobilized by political groups into enraged street bands that had a rather tenuous political relationship to the national or Islamic movements. Although their main target was the Israeli army, border police, and settlers, the main consequence of their activity—as far as social structure is concerned—was to challenge the patriarchal authority prevalent in Palestinian society. This process had already been set in motion in the early 1960s, which had seen the economic independence of young people, including young women, set in motion by the breakup of the traditional household economy as a result of work demands outside the family farm and the family business, and by the massive expansion of primary and secondary schools and universities.

The challenge to the traditional authority of the Palestinian family took several forms during the intifada. Young people, including women, were able to justify spending prolonged periods outside their homes, and therefore away from the controlling authority of their parents, while engaged in political activities or escaping arrest. Parental authority was directly challenged by claims by the youth that they answered to a higher authority, their commitments to their political groups and therefore to the national cause. These claims were furthermore deemed legitimate by society at large, and public pressure often overrode family concerns for the safety of its members, and, in the case of women, for the family's honor. Even in mourning, political groups often took over the tasks of organizing and receiving ritual condolences, tasks that had traditionally been performed by the family.

One of the most intimate domains of family control was the choosing of marriage partners for one's children. Increasingly, this task was influenced by considerations of political expediency, security, and even love born in the "heat of struggle." Although the number of such "political" marriages should not be exaggerated, nor should they be discounted as a social—as opposed to an individual—phenomenon. In political circles they amounted to thousands of unions, and they were no longer confined to radical social groups.

Against this challenge to the authority of the Palestinian patriarchy we witness an opposite trend. In many villages and refugee camps girls were married off earlier in order to preempt their involvement in political activity. Many young men took advantage of the regime of social austerity ushered in by the intifada, which resulted in the lowering of the *maher* (bride price) and the discouraging of expensive wedding ceremonies in order to encourage early marriages. The result, according to *shari'a* court records, was a drop of about two years in the age of young women who married as compared with pre-intifada days. These early marriages have two results: higher fertility (now incorporated into a national cult of procreation) and tighter control over the social life of young women, who have little chance to experience a public life before marriage. The general proclamation of the independence of youth should be seen in this context as primarily a male phenomenon, and one that often resulted in the control of the mobility of women, either through arrangements for early marriage, or through constraints on their dress code and behavior in the public sphere.

As in the aftermath of the 1948 war (and probably during the 1936 revolt, as well), Palestinians fell back on family resources to protect themselves from their loss of control of the world surrounding them. Among peasants this meant the rejuvenation of neglected lands. In the urban context this meant the strengthening of the family firm and the domestication of resources. In both cases an internal division of labor was reasserted, resulting in the weakened extended family regaining many of its functions that had once eroded. During the first intifada we witnessed an enhanced role for the family shop in the cities, and an attempt to revive marginalized family plots used for highland dry farming, plots that were in an advanced state of neglect as a result of the movement of labor from the village to urban construction sites. Many of these changes, however, were reversed during the second intifada (2000–2004). This uprising ushered in significant new developments in Palestinian society following the collapse of the Oslo Accords (1993–2000) and the Camp David negotiations in the winter of 2000, and following the hermetic sealing of the occupied territories from Israel through a vast network of checkpoints and the building of the concrete barrier inside the West Bank.

The main features of these new developments can only be suggested here. They include the formation of new etatist elite in the context of the Palestinian National Authority (PNA), whose legitimacy was based on two cycles of popular parliamentary and presidential elections, in June 1996 and 2005–2006. Initially this elite accumulated substantial privileges from the creation of state monopolies and from the perks of public office, but the ascension of Hamas to power in the second parliamentary election undermined much of this elite's gains.

This brief introductory overview of the major transformations in Palestinian society in the last century is meant to frame the following ten essays on the intersection of biography and social history. It highlights the manner in which the country devolved from a province in the Ottoman Empire, to a colonial mandate, to a segmented society under Israeli control. The profiles of modernist intellectuals that follow illuminate a culture that continued to identify with and interact with currents of thought and culture in neighboring countries—particularly in Egypt, Syria, and Lebanon—while cognizant of the separate fate that was in store for Palestine after World War I. Their preoccupations were similar to those of Arab and Mediterranean writers of the same period, but—in the case of the Palestinians—their social and political milieu was the struggle for survival in an increasingly hostile environment, one that separated many of them from their historic cultural affinities and denied them the normalcy that they had anticipated would come about from the demise of the old Empire.

CHAPTER 2

The Mountain against the Sea?

Cultural Wars of the Eastern Mediterranean

The distinction between coastal culture and the culture of the peasant highlands has been a recurrent theme in studies of the dynamics of modernity in Mediterranean society. During the civil war in Lebanon, the late Albert Hourani suggested that this dichotomy is a key to understanding the metamorphosis of the communal conflict between the Maronite strongholds of Mount Lebanon (home to independent and autonomous Druze and Maronite peasantries) and the coastal cities of Beirut and Tripoli (strongholds of the Sunni and Orthodox mercantile bourgeoisie).[1] The populist politics of the smallholders, articulated in the peasant rebellions of Tanious Shahin in Kisrawan and Yusif Karam in Mount Lebanon in the nineteenth century, expressed antiurban and antifeudal ideologies that glorified the naturalness of peasant existence, a rural society "created by God . . . [set against an urbanity] created by man."[2] But that vision was ultimately defeated by two countervailing trends: the patronage system upheld by the Sunni urban elites and their coastal Christian allies; and the notion of a Mediterranean civilization resting on a network of precarious alliances between the ideologies of the mountain and the ideology of the coastal city.

But this precariousness was peculiar to Lebanon. In Turkey, Morocco, and Egypt, and ultimately in Palestine, economic hegemony was clearly moving in favor of the coast. The Ottoman Tanzimat were triggered in part by the integration of eastern Mediterranean cities into the commercial networks of southern Europe, and by the transformation of coastal cities into dominant urban centers for the Levant as a whole. By the end of the nine-teenth century Alexandria, Port Said, Beirut, Tripoli, Haifa, and Jaffa saw rapid demographic growth, while the cities of the interior declined. What is more striking is that this growth was not primarily the result of rural mi-gration, but instead occurred at the expense of Cairo, Fez, Aleppo, and Damascus.[3] A significant source of this growth was the relocation of Eu-ropean settlers and merchants, as well as Greek, Armenian, and Jewish communities, which contributed to the cities' cosmopolitan and ethnically diverse character. Ibrahim calculated that close to 10 percent of the pop-ulation of these cities was composed of these communities by the turn of the twentieth century.[4] The proportion was even higher in Alexandria, Izmir, Casablanca, Tangier, and Jaffa.

The ethnic diversity of these cities, as well as the tension inherent in the colonial representation of some of these minorities, had immense signifi-cance for the growth and development of the contemporary nationalisms of the Levant. Çaglar Keydar traces the growth of Greek nationalism, constitutional Ottomanism, and greater Syrian nationalism, as well as Macedonianism and Bulgarian nationalism, to the intermediary activities of minority bourgeoisies in port cities like Salonica, Patras, and Izmir.[5]

There is a limit, however, to the interpretative potential of these coastal/mountain dichotomies. In part this is due to the nature of class and political alliances that had already transcended these ecological cat-egories by the end of the nineteenth century, as Hourani has argued for Lebanon, and in part this is because the proper arena for understanding these diversities is the realm of cultural analysis rather than that of po-litical economy. This contestation of the images of national identity and modernity will be examined in more detail below.

Coastal cities continued to evoke both hostility and fascination in the minds of the indigenous population of the interior. The urban culture of Beirut, Akka, Jaffa, and Haifa embodied everything the peasant feared might disrupt the traditional order. The cities represented foreignness (a popular saying claimed that "nothing comes from the West that pleases the heart"), innovation, and political subjugation, as well as what the peasant desires most: freedom, escape from ruthless nature, and material advancement. In the 1930s, Jaffa, Haifa, and Beirut constituted the world of work, education, financial success, and modernity.

In Palestine popular hostility to the sea reached a new plateau during the intifada of 1987–93, when activists in both the nationalist resistance and the Muslim Brotherhood colluded to ensure that unclad bathers of ei-ther sex would not go to the beaches of the Gaza Strip. A typical directive issued by the United National Leadership of the Uprising (UNLU) on September 25, 1990, referred to those "who frolic by the seashore as if we lived in a state of tranquility and normality. . . . Those are the people who are contemptuous of our values and traditions, and piss on the blood of the martyrs."[6]

The city of Gaza—until the war of 1948 an idyllic port of southern Palestine—became the first city in the history of the Mediterranean where swimming was formally banned. A number of flyers were distributed warning people about the moral dangers inherent in indulging in the pleasures of the sea. Toward the third year of the uprising, even an innocent stroll on the seashore—by then the only social outlet for a community confined by periodic curfews imposed by the Israeli military—was viewed as sacrilegious.

This joyless culture of resistance, enforced by a stern religious ethic, is not uncommon in the eastern Mediterranean. It has also been observed in Greece, Yugoslavia, and Anatolia. Palestine is exceptional, however, in that this hostility was explicitly extended to the acts of bathing and strolling. Both acts, when performed on the seashore, evoke nudity, laxity, the mixing of the sexes, and the disruption of the normative ethics of control embedded in urban fundamentalism, in which the delineation of spatial boundaries for men and women is crucial.

The saying *"al-bahar ghaddar"* (the sea is treacherous) was therefore not only a reflection of popular (in this case, peasant) attitudes toward the uncertainties of nature, but also the peasant's hostility toward the unpredictable social forms that were emerging on the coastal plains. In the following analysis I will examine these changing popular attitudes toward the sea, first in the context of a general treatment of the relationship between modernity and the rediscovery of the sea as a source of pleasure in southern Europe, and then in the context of the social dichotomy between mountain and coastal cultures. Finally, I will examine the manner in which ritual attempts to cope with the uncertainties of the sea were subverted by the demise of the coastal villages and the transfer of the population of port cities to the refugee camps of southern Palestine.

THE SEASHORE AS A FRONTIER OF MODERNITY

The taming and discovery of the seashore as a source of pleasure and recreation is a very recent phenomenon in the history of the Mediterranean. Alain Corbin, who has undertaken the most systematic treatment of this theme in *The Lure of the Sea* (1994), describes the enchanting process by which the Mediterranean haunted the peoples of antiquity as the source of the flood, of the abyss, of chaos and repulsion, and their escape toward the mountains from "the repulsive image of the seaside."[7] In the minds of sailors, the diabolical was always seen as the source of madness, in need of exorcism. Charles Sprawson, author of what is probably the only social history of swimming, traces the "great fall" to the triumph of Christian Puritanism in the Mediterranean basin. Both the Greeks and the Romans were obsessed with water exercises, which had a hedonistic dimension in the case of the Romans; both invested heavily in constructing elaborate gymnasiums, spas, fountains, and swimming pools.

With the coming of Christianity, Sprawson tells us, the West began to lose its interest in the sea and the bathing tradition that had gradually spread from Greece and the Aegean. All along the Mediterranean, coastal villages that had once looked out to the sea turned their energies inland. A maritime civilization turned into one devoted to land, and Islam took possession of the Mediterranean. Of the four hundred steam baths built by the Moors among the fountains of Granada, only one survived the first hundred years of Christianity.[8]

It is not clear from the context, but Sprawson seems to be making a distinction between eastern Islam, which adopted the Judeo-biblical tradition of the curse against the sea, and western Islam (that is, North African and Andalusian civilization), which was Iberian in spirit. Sprawson also seems to suggest a conflict between the Christian and the Canaanite-Phoenician ethos toward water, the former involving a Byzantine fatwa against the Syrian cult of Maiouma (derived from the Semitic *mayy*, meaning "water").[9]

> [The cult of Maiouma] involved performances by naked women in open-air pools before audiences in marble seats that rose from the pool in the form of a Greek theatre. Their strange erotic tableaux were condemned by the clerics, as were the spectators "drowned in the abyss of sin." Swimming, like sexual pleasure, came to be associated somehow with the devil, and was almost suppressed during the domination of Europe by Christianity. It was not until the beginning of the nineteenth century that its popularity was revived.[10]

Until the early modern period, this view, which was rooted in ancient Greek and biblical literature, persisted in the popular consciousness:

> The seashore . . . remains haunted by the possibility of a monster bursting forth or of the sudden incursion of foreigners, who are comparable to monsters; as a natural setting for unexpected violence, it is the privileged scene for abductions.[11]

Ships were seen as the source of infection and epidemics. Vaporous sulfuric emanations that came from the seashore were thought of, until recently, as the result of decaying matter that was deposited by the sea on the beaches. Corbin describes the "horrors of seasickness"—especially prevalent among women—as dominating narratives of pilgrims to the Holy Land during the Middle Ages and notes that there was a significant increase of these tales in the eighteenth century.[12]

The beach was invented, both as a source of recreation and as a planned seascape, toward the end of the eighteenth century by the Italian, French, and Spanish aristocracies, more or less simultaneously. The nineteenth century marked the transition in the use of the seashore and inland spas from therapeutic purposes to hedonistic pleasures.[13] By the middle of the nineteenth century, bathing in the sea and the enjoyment of the seashore began to trickle down to the middle and working classes.[14]

COASTAL CITIES AND MOUNTAIN CULTURE

The latter half of the twentieth century saw the integration of the Syrian economy into the global economy. Port cities in the eastern Mediterranean constituted the seam that connected Syria's rural hinterlands with the outside world. At the same time, these cities were being transformed into a new social entity: a world of internal migration, ethnic diversity, and technological innovation. Izmir, Beirut, Jaffa, and Alexandria emerged as the pivotal urban centers of European economic and cultural penetration into the eastern Mediterranean.[15]

Within each of the regional societies the intensification of trade and the rise of the new coastal bourgeoisie reinforced the differences between the coastal culture and the culture of the mountains. The critical factor here was the manner in which the new commoditized crops of the hinterland were processed and, in some cases, manufactured by a series of intermediaries as they made their way to their European destinations through their respective port cities. On the Syrian coast the role of silk and grain redefined the relationship between Beirut and Mount Lebanon, and citrus, cotton, and olive oil were key to the emergence of Jaffa (and later Haifa) as the cosmopolitan city of Palestine. By the turn of the twentieth century, tens of thousands of skilled workers from inland cities and peasant laborers migrated to the coastal region in cyclical waves, thus transforming not only their own lives, but also the social fabric of the coastal cities. Administrative changes, such as the Ottoman reorganization of the Syrian coastal cities under the single district of

Wilayat Beirut, were apparently aimed at controlling secessionist tendencies in the mountains in a period of rising Arab nationalism.

Eyüp Özveren suggests an important way in which these changes highlighted the manner in which eastern Mediterranean cities, and Beirut in particular, became the agents of both modernity and particularistic nationalism.[16] The peculiarity of Beirut was that, for factional and cultural reasons, it played a pivotal role in the modernization of its hinterland despite, and not because of, its economic functions, so that the decline of the silk trade in the twentieth century enhanced the administrative-cultural role of the city.[17] As in Izmir, Alexandria, and Jaffa, the merchant classes of Beirut successfully introduced civic reforms and municipal structures precisely because it lacked urban patricians and artisanal associations that, in the case of Damascus and Jerusalem, for example, provided for traditional civil control.[18] This explains to a large extent the cosmopolitan, "Europeanized" character of these cities, and the degree to which the new intellectual and professional classes were able to introduce lifestyles and consumption patterns that later became the prototypes of behavioral codes for the cities of the interior. One can glean the centrality of the sea in these behavioral patterns in the autobiographies of people like Yusef Haikal (mayor of Jaffa in the 1930s) and Hisham Sharabi (who wrote about the 1940s).[19]

NEBI RUBEEN: THE WEDDING OF SWEET WATER AND SALT WATER

The celebration of the festival of the Prophet Rubeen (Reuven) along the southern shores of Jaffa presents us with an outstanding example of the seashore acting, in ritualized form, as a libidinous outlet for the urban masses. It is also a unique case in which modern recreational adaptations coped with a traditional celebratory culture without subverting it or disrupting it.

This seasonal festival has had a rich political history. Nebi Rubeen was one of two major celebrations (the other one was Nebi Musa) initiated in the twelfth century by Salah edDin al-Ayyubi and his lieutenants to mobilize the urban and rural population of central Palestine during European pilgrimages to Jerusalem. The object was to create a "counter-pilgrimage" during the Easter observance, when it was feared that the European crusaders might use their pilgrimage as a cover for establishing military outposts around Ramleh, Lydda, Jaffa, Jericho, and Jerusalem.[20] Until the end of the nineteenth century, both Nebi Rubeen and Nebi

Figure 1. Nebi Rubeen festival, 1920. © Eric Matson Collection,
American Colony Photographers, Library of Congress.

Musa incorporated both military and cultural activities. Unlike Nebi
Musa, however, Nebi Rubeen was a coastal festival and predominantly
an urban one. From the early literature it seems that the religious component overshadowed the worldly festivities in Rubeen until the turn of
the twentieth century—but it was a popular hybrid ritual rather than a
distinctly Islamic one. One writer identifies it with the Phoenician Feast
of the Betrothal between Sweet Water and Salt Water still celebrated in
Tyre at the end of the nineteenth century, recalling the cult of Baal-
Peor.[21] In those days (1886) the Awqaf of Maqam Rubin used to yield
about 140 pounds sterling annual income, which was used by the man-
ager of the Maqam to slaughter a hundred goats to feed the poor during
the thirty days of the September festivities.[22]

There is a consensus among participants during the Mandate period
that Nebi Rubeen was a massive celebration involving all classes of Jaffites, as well as peasants from neighboring villages and visitors from as
far as Lydda and Ramleh.[23] It seems more probable from the few contemporary accounts that peasants came to sell their wares and services
while the better-off Jaffites treated the site as a summer resort. Abdul
Rahim claimed that the "entire city" relocated to Maqam Rubeen, fifteen

Figure 2. Nebi Musa procession in Haram al Sharif, Jerusalem, 1918. This was the first procession that took place after Ottoman withdrawal from Palestine, at the beginning of the British military administration. © Eric Matson Collection, American Colony Photographers, Library of Congress.

kilometers south of Jaffa. "Jaffa becomes a deserted city during the season," he wrote—a slight exaggeration, perhaps, but one echoed by a number of observers.[24] A more cautious chronicler of the city, Elias Rantisi, estimates that forty to fifty thousand Jaffites made the pilgrimage annually during the 1940s, a number that would constitute well over half the entire population of the city.[25]

The season began with a huge carnival-like procession (Zaffet enNabi Rubeen) on the first day of July, launched by musical bands and people holding banners near the Great Mosque. The music, dress, and paraphernalia of the procession recall a wedding ceremony, as suggested by the language used to describe the event (*zaffeh* means "betrothal ceremony"), as well as the use of the camel *hawdaj* (cloth compartment) to carry the entourage of women. The parade would tour the commercial district of Jaffa and then proceed on camels and horses to the southern shores of the Rubeen tributary, fourteen kilometers from Jaffa. Jaffites continued to use horses and camels to travel to Rubeen even when buses and cars became available.[26]

Most families would spend two to three weeks at Rubeen, in elaborate tents that were specially constructed for the occasion by the municipality of Jaffa. Ringing the residential tents were makeshift markets, cafés, restaurants, bands of entertainers, theaters, and outdoor cinemas. During the day, horse and camel races, which constituted an important part of the festival, took place on the outer ring. At night, live entertainment competed with radios and phonographs, which were hooked up to electric generators provided by the city council. A daily repertoire of plays, musical concerts, and motion pictures was presented.[27] Performers were local musicians and singers, but their ranks also included singers and players from Egypt and Lebanon. In the 1930s and '40s these included the theatrical troupe of Yusif Wahbe—famous throughout the Arab world; the actress Fatmah Rushdi; Ali Kassar and his musical company; and the well-known singers Fathiyya Ahmad and Muhammad Abdul Mutallib. The latter was extremely popular in Rubeen and was hired every July for a Jaffa performance.[28]

Both Rantisi (a Christian) and Dajani (a Muslim) describe a social milieu that was relaxed and uninhibited. "Old and young, rich and poor, would take off their formal wear and stroll around in white *galabiyyat* and *rosa qanabeez*. . . . Most people wore sandals or simply walked barefoot. . . . Men and women moved around until way past midnight listening to music or attending theatrical performances."[29] Even if one makes allowances for nostalgic license here, there seems to be agreement among contemporary observers that Rubeen was exceptional in that the normative controls of daily life were somehow suspended in a manner that was unique for Palestine, even for an "open" city like Jaffa.

Three features of the Rubeen festival stand out. The first is that although the event was launched as a religious festival, and was presided over by sheikhs and *ulama*—the main white banner of Rubeen, which preceded the others in the procession, was inscribed with *"La ilaha illa allah, wa Rubeen Nabiyya allah,"* ("No god but God, and Rubeen is His prophet")—it was nevertheless an extremely "secular" celebration, if one is allowed to use that word in this context. Religious sheikhs not only participated in the festival's licentious activities, but they also blessed them and gave them public approval. Second, although the Rubeen festivities were held within walking distance from the Mediterranean, the sea itself did not feature in its activities. No swimming contests were organized, and no actual contact with the sea was even hinted at in the vast array of events that took place daily. Third, Rubeen was a family affair. The famous saying attributed to the cunning women of Jaffa was *"Ya Bitrawibni, Ya biTaliqni"* (Either take me to Rubeen, or I will have you divorce me). It was not considered proper for single men to go to Jaffa unaccompanied. And although men and women milled around the public spaces of Rubeen, the organized cultural events, such as the plays, film screenings, and musical concerts, were apparently segregated, although the evidence here is conflicting. Both Yusef Haikal, the last mayor of Jaffa, and Ahmad Abdul Rahim suggest that some events were mixed.[30]

Rubeen was an exceptional case of synchrony: the popular traditional festival creatively adapted to the diktat of modernity, without either tradition or modernity prevailing over the other. It was last celebrated in the summer of 1946, on the eve of the partition of Palestine. By sheer coincidence it was attended by the late historian Elias Rantisi, who took a series of vivid photographs of the event that immortalized the joie de vivre and innocence of a city that was lost forever.[31]

COASTAL VILLAGES FACING INWARD

But the situation in Jaffa, as in Beirut, was exceptional. Both the physical organization and the cultural outlook of coastal towns and villages remained introverted. In Palestine, most coastal towns did not look out toward the sea, but instead faced inland. Furthermore, these towns were built at a considerable distance from the sea, averaging five to eight kilometers from the shoreline. This is particularly true of the towns and villages south of Jaffa: Yubna, Isdud, Arab Iskir, Hammama, and Majdal. Only al-Jura, a fishing village in whose vicinity the festival of Arba'at Ayyub was celebrated, was built right on the sea. All village houses, including those of al-Jura, were built facing east, with their backs toward the sea.[32] The ostensible reason for this was the protection it afforded from the western winds and their humidity, but the social consequences of this orientation cannot be underestimated. In addition, these coastal towns were almost exclusively agricultural villages, where fishing was only a peripheral industry. Few villages had ancillary crafts related to agricultural production, and only Majdal had a number of families engaged in the making and sale of pottery, which, according to one informant, earned them the contempt of the neighboring farmers of Isdud.[33]

In all these coastal villages, swimming was frowned upon and discouraged. Even in al-Jura, whose chief industry was fishing—an occupation

that was passed on to successive generations until 1948—children did not
learn or practice swimming.

THE CLEANSING SEA: FEAR AND LOATHING OF THE SEA
AMONG PEASANTS TURNED URBANITES

I suggest that there is a difference between the fear of the sea embedded
in the life of coastal villagers and the attitude of loathing and contempt
that emerged among mountain peasants. In the Palestinian context, contempt of the sea and the idea that it has the potential to subvert the "purity of culture" are primarily urban phenomena. They reached their
height in the form of mass hysteria about swimming in the sea in the
early 1990s and began to recede with the normalization of daily life after
Palestinian authority was established in Gaza in 1994. In contrast to this
contempt we encounter fear expressed by the coastal villagers.[34] This fear
is at the heart of the folk wisdom expressed in notions of "the treacherous sea" (al-bahar ghaddar), and the claim that "the sea only gives us
death" (il-bahar ma byiqthif illa al-Mayyit). Fear of the sea is contained
in periodic invasions of the seashore by villagers on the quasi-religious
mawasim of Nebi Rubeen and Arba'at Ayyub (Job's Wednesday), during
which villagers celebrate the cleansing and therapeutic powers of the uncontrollable waters, which they use to cure their diseases and purify their
bodies.

Arba'at Ayyub, which comes immediately before Khamis al-Amwat
(Thursday of the Dead) and four days before Easter Sunday, probably
constitutes the Muslim peasant alternative to Christian Easter and to
ancient spring fertility cults, particularly that of Sham enNasim.
Mubayyid lists three rituals associated with Arba'at Ayyub: the ex-
punging of evil spirits; the solicitation of husbands by women approaching their twentieth year (and hence in danger of becoming spin-
sters), and, finally, the ritual of childless women seeking conception.[35]
It was this last ritual of Arba'at Ayyub, in which women engaged in
simulated copulation with the sea, chanting "laqqih, laqqih ya Ayyub"
(implant your seeds, O Job), that provoked such hostility from fundamentalist groups when the practice was transplanted from its pre-1948
village context to an urban environment in the 1960s and '70s.[36]

The Palestinians' relationship with the sea was completely transformed by the dislocation of coastal culture that resulted from the war
of 1948 and the relocation of refugees from southern Palestine to Gaza
City and its environs. Rema Hammami has treated this transformation

in a pioneering essay on the reconstruction of peasant religiosity over the span of three generations.[37] Ritual celebrations surrounding shrines of saints, relating to both the agricultural cycle and seasons as well as life events such as marriages, births, and deaths, were a primary activity though which collective village identities were constructed throughout Palestine. Since each region's collective identity was connected to a specific saint, such ritual practices tended to be nontransferable.[38] In other words, the loss of access to a particular shrine in pre-1948 Palestine was not transferable to another saint's shrine in the area in which the displaced villagers found refuge. However, ritual celebrations focused on the fecundity of the sea itself—such as Arba'at Ayyub—were the exception rather than the rule. In this festival the southernmost part of the Mediterranean Sea witnessed the reenactment and continuation of the same ceremonials of northern villages, and the celebration reasserted the villages' communal identity, which had been disrupted by the war:

> In April 1949, on Job's Wednesday (Arba'at Ayyoub), refugees living in Nusseirat, Shati, and Rafah camps spontaneously went down to the seashore en masse to celebrate the festival. The refugees were from coastal plains villages that had previously celebrated Job's Wednesday in the village of Jura. In the new context, though they were not an organized procession down to the sea, the general festivities of singing troupes, dabke, dancing, games, picnics on the shore and finally the dip in the sea at the end of the day remained the same.[39]

Although sea rituals represented a continuity with former practices, coastal peasants refused to identify with the saints of the host communities in Gaza itself, thus asserting the distinctiveness of their identity as refugees from those of local (nonrefugee) saints.[40]

With the rise of Nasserist nationalist ideology in the 1960s, the state (or, rather, the Egyptian military administration of Gaza) began to foster secular alternatives to what was seen as the archaic religious practices of folk rituals. The result was open hostility toward religious adherence, as well as the intentional marginalization of saint worship. Job's Wednesday (seen as a "celebration of older peasant women . . . related to fertility")[41] was now replaced by the secular festivities of Sham enNasim—the spring fertility of the Nile replaced by the Mediterranean.

Job's Wednesday survived the decline of Nasserism, but it continued to be attacked by the Muslim Brotherhood, whose members saw it as not only a pagan ritual, but also an offense to the modesty of women, since it involved the public exposure of women's bodies to the sea.[42] With the

Israeli invasion of Lebanon, the Muslim Brotherhood succeeded in generating enough public pressure to abolish the celebration altogether.

CONCLUSION

This chapter has pointed out the limitations inherent in a model of conflict between the culture of urban coastal communities in the Levant and the culture of the mountains. Part of the problem lies in the transcendence of these divides by the creation of a national society in which class alliances and interurban migrations, not to speak of rural-urban migrations, have modified the perspectives of two diverse cultures. Nevertheless, the culture of the sea—as opposed to coastal society in general—continues to elicit much hostility from a large segment of society, both rural and urban. In Palestine this hostility was compounded by the wholesale physical dismemberment of coastal society and its urban and rural populations. The result was a combination of a romanticized nostalgia and a reenactment of folk rituals that were divorced from their social context. Elsewhere in the eastern Mediterranean these rituals were also disrupted by modernity and "natural migration" (as opposed to war displacement), but there—unlike in Palestine—they were supplanted by a "modern" and essentially bourgeois view of the sea as a place for frolicking and a venue for emancipating the body from social restraints, such as the dress code, divorced from ritual considerations.

I have also discussed two popular relationships with the sea that are not instrumental, as is the case with fishing and seafaring. The first is the persistence of the ritual celebration of the sea (by a fertility cult), as peasants were transplanted from their agricultural environment to the seaside during the continued observance of Arba'at Ayyub among southern refugees in Gaza. The second is the modernist appropriation of the seashore by the urban masses—beginning with the middle classes—for recreational purposes. Both relationships have provoked the wrath of retrogressive traditional forces attempting to maintain the regime of the virtuous. In the first instance—the struggle against folk religious expression—the ritual was condemned because it provided a form of mass psychotherapy outside the realm of formal, and therefore acceptable, religion. In the second case, the practice of using the seashore for recreation was considered to undermine the code of female modesty. Both cases suggest the existence of a fear of the exhilarating and hedonistic effects of the sea, which began to challenge the strict division of gender roles and the maintenance of social control through a dress code. In a wider context, the treachery of the sea—which in peasant communities reflected the fear of uncontrollable nature—is now reconstituted to evoke anxiety about the uncontrollable and unanticipated impact of emancipated modernity, and of the presumably untamed and untamable sensuality of women.

CHAPTER 3

From Emma Bovary to Hasan al-Banna

Small Towns and Social Control

Small towns invariably evoke an aura of cultural mediocrity and social control. The two attributes go together. When Flaubert published *Madame Bovary* in 1857, Rouen—the site of Bovary's escapades—was a major regional center of about 100,000, at the time twice the size of Strasbourg and three times the size of Grenoble (but one-tenth the size of Paris).[1] But even in a city that large, conditions were not quite ideal for an amorous liaison, and Bovary's second lover—the legal clerk Léon Dupuis—had to hire a cabbie to consummate his relationship with Bovary.[2]

Emma Bovary was escaping to Rouen from Yonville, the market town in which she and the tedious Dr. Bovary settled in an atmosphere permeated with provincial drudgery. Her undoing was the housewives of Yonville, whose gossip about her "vaporish airs" drove her to near insanity.[3] That atmosphere is immortalized in a famous scene set at an agricultural show, in which the protagonist becomes intensely aware—through the overtures of the debonair Monsieur Rudolphe—of the possibilities inherent in flouting tradition and rebelling against the stifling petty bourgeois mores of Yonville. Thus just as Yonville symbolizes social repression and mediocrity, Rouen signals freedom from confinement: it represents the world of the opera, of velvet draperies and Paris fashions, and of illicit love.

The character that best exemplifies the Bovarian condition in the modern Levant is the heroine of Hanan al-Shaykh's extraordinary novel *Hikayat Zahra*. Oppressed by her marriage, which was arranged by her family, Zahra escapes from her West African market town to Beirut, where, in the midst of the Lebanese civil war, she discovers an alienated fulfillment in the form of a mindless sexual relationship with an alley sniper.[4]

The search for anonymity—an anonymity that can only be achieved in the concealed, and concealing, terrain of urban existence—is the common goal of Zahra and Bovary. Raymond Williams discusses the nature of this anonymity in one of the last essays he wrote, in which he names five aspects of urbanity that are conducive to the emergence of modernity from traditional culture: the collapse of "normal relationships" associated with the provincial lifestyle; the self-realization of the individual under conditions of isolation; the "impenetrability of the city"; the emergence of the idea of "the masses" as a replacement for the earlier idea of the "urban mob" and associated notions of social solidarities; and, finally, the "vitality, variety, the liberating diversity and mobility of the city."[5] In a similar vein, Jonathan Raban talks about the fluidity of behavioral patterns as they are unshackled from traditional norms in the "magical" atmosphere of modern urbanity.[6]

One can view these conditions as negative illuminators of small-town culture; in other words, they highlight what is absent in the small-town milieu. We can collapse Williams's five conditions into two broad cultural categories: 1) the dislocating impact of metropolitan consciousness (including normlessness/anomie, social and individual alienation, and atomization of urban consciousness); and 2) the creation of new, emancipated possibilities for intellectual and social behavior (for example, mass revolutionary action, artistic creativity, dissent, tolerance of eccentricity, and plain nonconformity—à la Bovary). Only one of these possibilities can be observed in the popular culture of the modern Levantine town—namely, the emergence of mass culture and mass movements, which are propelled by the penetration of the mass media and consumerism.[7]

By contrast, the social fabric of daily life in the eastern Mediterranean is permeated by an intense awareness of locality, by a strong sense of the community, and by the continued dominance of kinship networks. One might add that these communal solidarities, and their associated modes of social control, are also strongly felt in big-city neighborhoods throughout the third world. In a Europeanized city like Tel Aviv, for example, Shlomo Deshen notes how in the Iraqi neighborhood of Hatikva, "shady activities . . . are thwarted to a considerable extent by reason of the high visibility of people in the neighborhood. Strangers are under the constant and manifold surveillance of housewives staring out of their doorways, of storekeepers from behind their sidewalk stalls, of cafe patrons at their drinks, and of numerous curious and insistent children."[8] Here, exactly as in provincial towns, a combination of social surveillance and gossip achieves the twin objectives of enhancing communal solidarity against outsiders and checking deviations from the prevalent morality. Illicit activities such as petty crime, gangsterism, and drug dealing, though rampant in the area, are kept in check and directed to other parts of the city through these mechanisms.[9]

In the following discussion I will examine the cultural dynamics of small-town society in an eastern Mediterranean region, in the context of the debate about "urban ruralism" and the emergence of the urban peasant. The region on which I will focus, the central highlands of Palestine, has displayed since the loss of its coastal cities in the war of 1948 many social features that are common to Mediterranean basin regions that do not have a primate city (e.g., Cyprus, Malta, and Crete) and regions in which the urban population is dispersed in a number of medium-sized townships (e.g., Syria, Lebanon, Bosnia, Montenegro, and Tunis). The region has several features, however, that are unique. Chief among them are the overwhelming presence of a de-peasantized population in the periphery of towns, the persistence of agricultural production within towns, and the balanced growth of the urban and rural populations, without any significant mobility from country to town, despite the marginalization of agriculture. In effect, it is a society without a metropolitan center.

URBAN RURALISM

"Urban ruralism" can best be understood though an expression referring to the Moroccan town of Sefrou: "The city used to eat the countryside . . . but now the countryside eats the city."[10] Sefrou's predicament is being replicated today throughout the eastern Mediterranean. The historically exploitative relation between town and country, based on the appropriation of the rural surplus by merchant capital and parasitic absentee landlords, is everywhere being reversed with vengeance. District centers are being flooded with peasant migrants seeking jobs and a new future for their children. Urban ruralization is not only an expression of the demographic explosion and a new cultural definition of urbanity. It is also the political expression of the demise of the old segregated political hierarchies, and their concomitant class rigidities. It marks the entry of the rural masses into the world of the city.

There are three aspects of this issue that concern us here. At the elementary level is the question of size. Does the size of small towns determine the nature of economic functions and modes of normative behavior? Do kinship groups, for example, exercise social control more effectively in small communities by virtue of the limited possibilities of physical mobility and the enhanced visibility of the individual?

The second aspect is the nature of the relationship between town and country. To what extent do urban terms of trade, credit, and investment perpetuate exploitative patterns between cities and "their" villages? And, with the demise of agriculture as a mainstay of rural income, have new forms of urban investment replaced earlier ones as forms of new (cultural) domination? Since small towns tend to be market and administrative centers for their rural hinterlands, their metropolitan, urbane character tends to be undermined by the daily influx of rural migrants. On the other hand, one can also view these townships as centers for the diffusion of modern technology and international consumption patterns and behavioral norms into village society.

The third question is whether, in the eastern Mediterranean, we can talk about the absence of urbanity, or what a leading Egyptian sociologist has called "underurbanism." The debate here is focused on cultural continuities buttressed by a lack of internal economic division of functions within city neighborhoods. A Lebanese anthropologist identifies this phenomenon as existing not only in small towns, but also in cities the size of Beirut:

> The city-center is simply an extension of the port and it operates as a terminus for traffic coming from the countryside. . . . [T]he city-center is a suq that serves the whole nation and [is] not simply an organic part of the city structure. . . . [M]any cities in the Middle East like Fez, Aleppo, San'a, Damascus, etc., used to, and many still, have weekly suqs located outside the city limits; literally speaking, they have no "downtowns."[11]

This chapter will attempt to describe how small towns in the Middle East serve as the arena where the cultural definition of urbanity is contested, as they function both as the seat of state power and market exchange (acting as district centers), and as a stepping stone for the discovery of the world by the rural masses.

SMALL TOWNS OR URBAN VILLAGES?

In his survey of small towns in India, R. L. Singh defines "small towns" as those settlements performing a "catalyst role" in the cultural integration of rural communities with metropolitan areas, meaning that they initiate rural migrants into the world (and presumably normative systems) of the big cities.[12] This is a "linkage" concept that does not seem to have autonomous cultural attributes aside from its transitional status. This definition is also congruent with the notion of the "urban village," used by social geographers to identify suburban communities of big cities.[13] Social scientists, in their zeal to quantify, have actually determined the size of a small town. URBAMA has suggested that the term applies to towns with a population of fewer than 50,000.[14] In Belgium, the term is used for settlements that have fewer than 30,000 residents; in the United States, fewer than 10,000; and in India, anywhere from 20,000 to 50,000 inhabitants might be used, depending on the situation.[15]

One person's paradise is another's hell. In a list of the virtues of small towns as compared to big cities, an American survey names the potential for personal contact, accountability, understandability, self-reliance, and "the sheer elegance of things which are small."[16] One might add that these are the very same qualities that drove Emma Bovary away from Yonville in search of sin.

G. H. Blake, who conducted an extensive survey of small towns in the Middle East, indicates that for most of the region it is primarily the administrative status of the town, rather than its original size, that determines its transition to urbanity.[17] However, as the example of the Turkish town of Tutuneli and many similar rural regional centers in the Middle East demonstrate, small towns can experience gradual economic and demographic decline if their service functions (health, education, and transport) are transferred to major metropolitan areas.[18] In his inventory of small and medium-sized towns in the Maghreb, Jean-Francois Troin has suggested a useful topology of functions for small towns, ranging from the administrative, industrial, and commercial to the performance of services. This topology will be useful in an examination of the manner in which cultural dynamics operate within the political economy of those towns.[19]

THE CULTURAL DYNAMICS OF LEVANTINE URBANITY: FEAR OF BEING ALONE

Several years ago Fuad Khuri made a poignant criticism of anthropological assessments of urban research in the Mashriq. Urban studies tend to confuse attributes of the lifestyle of the urban poor, he claimed, with those of rural migrants to the city; that is, they confuse slums with "ruralized neighborhoods." Second, they ascribe to the Middle East cultural traits that are features of social life in many third world countries.[20] Although Khuri's criticism was generally directed against those who succumb to the pitfall of applying Chicago School notions of stratified residential belts to third world conditions, his immediate target was the claims made by John Gulick about continuities of urban-rural trait complexes.[21]

Chief among those traits are farming, segmentary kinship structures, sexual alienation (by which he means segregation), domestic family structures, and commercial networks.[22] In all of these spheres Gulick notes significant commonalities between rural and urban areas, a fact that challenges ideas about modernization and the contrast between rural and urban lifestyles in the Middle East. We might add here that Gulick's arguments have been buttressed—although from a different perspective— by scholars such as Peter Worsley and Bryan Roberts in their contributions on urban ruralization in the third world, and in their discussion of the informal sector in industrial metropolitan areas.[23] Khuri recasts Gulick's propositions to suggest a "syndrome of endogamous formulations" that constitute what he calls "ideological constants" that characterize the processes of group formation in Arab culture.[24] He then proceeds to show the manifestations of this syndrome as they appeared in Beirut during the Lebanese civil war. Beirut is a segmented city that is composed not of ethnic ghettos, but of autonomous cohesive neighborhoods based on kinship and confessional solidarities. Furthermore, the suburbs of the city—like its internal neighborhoods—are socially and economically independent units that, "unlike Western suburbia . . . lack specialization and tend to develop multifunctional services in the sense that jobs, services, recreational centres, schools, clubs, welfare societies, places of worship, cultural activities, banks, hospitals, . . . [are] all centered in individual suburbs."[25] The city center, on the other hand, is not the *suq* of the city, but of the nation, which happens to be located in the city.

In a later work, *Tents and Pyramids* (1990), Khuri advances his theory on the nature of endogamous behavior in urban settings in eastern Mediterranean societies. The idiom of kinship, he claims, thoroughly permeates social interaction in Arab society through constantly imposing familiar, familial, and egalitarian modes of expression and exchange on differentiated and stratified encounters. This is expressed through forms of address (such as *akh, ukht,* and *'amm*) used when speaking to total strangers, and particularly to those of a higher rank than the speaker, and through terms of visitations and exchange, where high-status individuals dilute the privilege of their rank by assuming the mantle of equality with their inferiors.[26]

The organizational principle that epitomizes endogamous behavior is cousin marriage, whose primary consequence for national communities is social atomization.[27] But endogamous behavior is also crucial for creating "social enclosures," and therefore "internal solidarities."[28] Arab cities, it follows, are constituted along these lines as "a series of 'tents' or urban nuclei, each corresponding to a particular social solidarity and having the very facilities and services enjoyed by the others."[29] The control of those solidarities becomes the arena for the contestation of power, and the unstructured egalitarian spirit that permeates the social fabric becomes fertile ground for autocratic rule. At the heart of Khuri's analysis lies the distinction between notions of "private" *(khassa)* and "public" *('amma* and *ummumi)*, a distinction that also happens to demarcate the boundary between the privileged elites and the masses.[30] The totalitarian character of endogamous behavior also renders the realm of the "public," whether in terms of the use of public space or public social interaction, to be infinitely inferior to the private world. (The two paramount examples of the public domain suggested by Khuri are the shared taxi, *taxi 'mumui,* and the whorehouse, *suq 'mumui.* "What matters is the 'private' domain, especially women and the family; everything else—space, streets, traffic, parking, garbage, gardens, schools, state, laws—is of secondary importance," Khuri writes.[31]

Khuri's intriguing analysis of Arab normative behavior is original, but it is also excessively static and essentialist. Its major flaws lie in making too much of Beirut's exceptionalism during the civil war and its attempt to extrapolate some of those features of "endogamous group formation" and its ideological constants to Arab urbanity in general.[32] He underestimates the significant inroads of vertical (class) stratification in primate cities in the Arab world, and, as Gulick does, he underplays the significant dynamics that typify urban formations and set them apart from their rural hinterland. Even with the ascendancy of sectarian strife in Beirut during the civil war, it remains a city quite distinct—in terms of its cultural possibilities—from the large townships of Mount Lebanon, or even Sidon or Tripoli. Similarly, Damascus is not Hama or Homs, and Amman is not Irbid. These differences are a question not only of scale, but also of the texture of cultural life, as reflected in the presence of theaters, a musically diverse nightlife, publishing companies, and daily newspapers—and socially in a considerable range of social and physical mobility, which create conditions of anonymity.

In contrast to Khuri and Gulick, Sami Zubaida, in his examination of the changing urban cultural scene in Iran, Egypt, and Tunisia, concludes—

correctly, I believe—that the model of contained communal solidarities within city neighborhoods is being radically transformed through state intervention and class mobility: "The old quarters were vertical segments of society, with horizontal stratification within. Urban growth," he concludes, "and the changing sources of wealth and state power, the development of new styles of life based on European models . . . led the rich, the educated and, in general, the diffuse strata called the 'middle classes' to move out of the old quarters. Where [those old quarters] still survive, [they] become lower-class area[s], often slums, heavily overpopulated with waves of rural migrants, and maintaining a mix of residence and small-scale commerce and craft."[33] Unlike Khuri, Zubaida regards the distinction between private and public space as fluid and shifting, and thus believes that the context of traditional ceremonies is being reformulated: "the lines of exclusion are not those of socio-economic class but of neighborhood and quarter. Indeed, weddings are the occasions for giving and receiving between constituents of patronage networks which span the different classes of the quarter. The social and spatial transformations of modern cities have altered the nature of these ceremonies, although some of their forms may be maintained."[34] As a result of these changes, we note the emergence in big cities of "class-homogeneous neighborhoods." Ritual celebrations continue to bond kinship groups, but the solidarity of the kin is now largely undermined by class and status networks whose membership is enhanced by social clubs and professional associations that exclude their poorer relatives.[35]

Despite its shortcomings, Khuri's discussion of the power of endogamous behavior and its associated stifling solidarities is nevertheless an apt model for understanding the cultural dynamics of Levantine small towns where normative behavior, hierarchy, and social control are subject to the ideological presumptions of formal equality, but where everyone—men and women, old and young, rich and poor—know their place, or are made to know their place. The constant visibility and recognition of people lends these towns an atmosphere of solidarity, normality, and blissful familiarity. Anonymity is not only absent but impossible. In this context the antithesis of anonymity is not social recognition, as one might expect, but what Khuri calls the fear of being alone.[36] Such fear is expressed in the constant need for sociability, with the concomitant censure of individually unacceptable behavior.

In what follows I will address the extent to which these issues of rural urbanism, social control, and hierarchy manifest themselves in small towns in the highlands of Palestine.

THE LOSS OF URBANITY

The case of Palestine illustrates the dynamics of social control discussed above, because it presents us with a society that at once experienced (in war) the loss of its urban-metropolitan formations and the ascendancy of a small-town culture within the same generation. As in many eastern Mediterranean societies, there existed in Palestine a certain dynamic that pitted a coastal, cosmopolitan, mercantile spirit against an inland, agrarian, conservative highland culture. Historically this dynamic was exemplified by the predominance of an autonomous smallholding highland peasantry that viewed the "alien" culture intruding from the coastal cities with suspicion. This suspicion reflected the peasants' distrust of not only the exploitative urban creditors and the class of absentee landlords and former tax farmers that had relocated to the city, but also the secular culture of the decadent metropole. The coastal cities contrasted with the highland villages much more than did the inland district centers, which were basically market towns, and where the landed elites were involved in relationships of patronage and protection with the peasants, even though those relationships were exploitative.

Since the turn of the twentieth century, the coastal cities have been the home of the commercial classes, of the citrus plantations and their rootless, dispossessed workers, of sailors and fishermen, of real estate speculators, of burgeoning—though still nascent—industrial enterprises, of railroads, and of a working class characterized by increasing militancy and secular notions of democracy and socialism. These cities have also generated recyclable wealth that has been invested in productive enterprises and in conspicuous consumption, in the form of grand mansions, automobiles, theaters, cafés, cinemas, printing presses, daily newspapers, and social clubs. Political life reflects the conflicts embedded in those towns, resulting in a multiplicity of nationalist and socialist parties, trade unions, and ideological and ethnic diversity.

One of the central consequences of the war of 1948 has been the loss of the coastal cities in Palestine—experienced both demographically and culturally—to its Arab population. Not only did major cities like Haifa, Akka, and Jaffa, as well as smaller cities like Ramleh, Lydda, Majdal, and Isdud, experience a displacement of their population, but Palestinian society as a whole experienced the demise of an urbane metropolitan culture that was developing in these cities, and the relocation of its intelligentsia and dominant classes, not to the highlands of Palestine, but to the Arab diaspora. There a new, extraterritorial nationalist movement emerged from the remnants of Palestinian society. The result was a process of de-urbanization within what remained of Arab Palestinian society.

I use the term *de-urbanization* here cautiously to refer to the dual process by which Palestinian society was physically stripped from its coastal cities and culturally removed from a cosmopolitan, urbane tradition that transmitted its influence to the rest of Palestinian society through its press, political parties, trade unions, and secular culture. Of the seven coastal cities listed above, the first five retained a small Arab minority underclass community that was rendered illiterate by the enforcement of a hegemonic Hebrew culture. The last two cities had their population evicted in its entirety.[37]

In the highlands we witness the ascendancy of the mountain towns, crowned by two important urban centers: the feudal-artisanal city of Nablus; and the segmented, ghettoized, and quartered city of Jerusalem, insulated from its rural hinterland, where the main industry (as it had been for four thousand years) was the administration of religious ritual and the production of religious paraphernalia for pilgrims and visitors. The city of Jerusalem acted as the administrative and service center for the entire central highland region. But, despite its size (it had about 80,000 Arabs in the 1960s, and about 150,000 in 1994), Jerusalem historically had a tenuous link with its rural hinterland. The main commercial and artisanal centers of the region were (and continue to be) Nablus and Hebron. The result of this transformation was a society in which a dozen small towns, ranging in size from 10,000 to 90,000 inhabitants, were engulfed by a network of four hundred villages and refugee camps.

Although most Palestinians living in the West Bank today still reside in rural districts, they cannot be characterized as living in a peasant society, that is, a society deriving its livelihood from agriculture and organized around the family farm. The impact of this change, from a peasant society to a merely rural one, however, has been different for urban and rural areas. Two parallel processes relating to this change can be sketched here: the urbanization of rural areas and the ruralization of towns.

The urbanization of villages is associated with a decline in the importance of unirrigated land as a source of village wealth, and the emergence of new, nonagricultural sources of income external to the village. These sources are primarily wage labor and remittances from relatives abroad. Another feature of this urbanization is the gradual suburbanization of many villages in the periphery of large towns and district centers, rendering them residential extensions of those cities. One consequence of this process is the tendency toward class leveling within rural society. As villages have moved from subsistence-based economies to a cash economy, the landowner's privileged position has been undermined, and the income of poor peasants has been enhanced as a result of increased wage labor opportunities.

The urbanization of the countryside is taking place in tandem with the ruralization of urban centers. Palestinian townships, dominated by retail trade and small workshops and home to minor manufacturing sectors, act as regional markets and administrative and service centers for their rural hinterlands. Urban-rural interdependence is thus a dominant characteristic of the regional economy, as is clearly demonstrated by the similar growth rates of towns and villages. As a consequence of the physical proximity of outlying villages to their district centers and an accessible transportation network, urban centers have evolved as both work and service centers for their rural population, as well as the site of commercial investments and real estate transactions for village entrepreneurs.[38]

A third "ruralization effect" can also be described. As a direct consequence of war relocations, former peasants from destroyed villages have piled up in the cities. Today this is most clearly observed in Gaza City. With a population of more than half a million, about three-quarters of whom are refugees, and a small territory covering only 370 square kilometers, Gaza has become the most densely populated area in Palestine. Originally rural in character, today it is 85 percent urban.[39]

TOWN AND COUNTRY IN THE ABSENCE
OF A METROPOLITAN CENTER

Excluding the district of Gaza, which is not the focus of our analysis here, the urban sector of the Palestinian occupied territories (47 percent of the total population) is distributed among eleven townships, the average size of which is 43,000 inhabitants (1987 data).[40] The economies of these townships are dominated by small-scale trade and small workshops. The manufacturing sector is minuscule, with the average employment per establishment amounting to 4.28 persons.[41] In a typical township like Ramallah, the ratio of commercial establishments (that is, retail shops) to workshops and artisanal enterprises is 84:16, with an average of 38.6 retail shops for each one thousand inhabitants.[42] Virtually all of the eleven Palestinian cities constitute regional markets and administrative and service centers for their rural hinterlands, in the manner described by Blake in his topology of Levantine small towns.[43]

Two features distinguish these townships from other urban centers in neighboring Middle Eastern states: the absence of a single dominant urban center in the country, and—more significantly—the almost even growth rates of the rural and urban populations.[44] The first feature can be attributed to the absence of a state (and a bureaucratic state apparatus); to the absence of any substantial manufacturing sector; and to the Israeli military government's willful policy of reinforcing regional dependency in various district centers in the West Bank and Gaza on employment in Israel's metropolitan areas.[45] This was the situation that prevailed until the year 2000.

The second feature, the even demographic growth rates in urban and rural areas, can be explained by the trend toward minimal internal migration, which was caused by the physical proximity of outlying villages to their district centers and the relatively good transport system that connects these villages to their townships. The result has been that these centers evolved not only as work and service centers for a rural population that continued to reside in their villages of birth, but also as locations of commercial investment and real estate transactions by rural entrepreneurs and potentates. Although there is scant empirical data on this subject, we know from chamber of commerce records for towns like Nablus, Ramallah, Bethlehem, and Hebron that between 20 and 25 percent of all commercial establishments are owned by villagers from the district, and that the population that commutes daily to use the facilities of these townships exceeds the size of the urban populations in each town.[46]

The proletarianization of Palestinian peasants was a protracted historical process that began to gain momentum after World War I. Rosenfeld has convincingly argued that, during the Mandate, this process culminated in the de-peasantization of rural society without any significant urbanization taking place. In other words, only a very small segment of the peasantry actually moved to the city.[47] Elsewhere I suggested that under Israeli rule this process of rural proletarianization contributed to the marginalization of the agricultural sector without eliminating it because residual agriculture, and the preservation of the rural abode of the commuting worker, was pivotal in absorbing the periodic recession in the demand for rural and refugee wage labor.[48] Within Palestinian towns, however, the descendants of the 1948 refugees became the core of the urban working class.

But the non-urbanization of the peasant worker did not mean, under conditions of Israeli occupation, that the city itself was not transformed by the new linkages with rural society. Here I shall argue that there emerged a new symbiotic relationship in which the culture of rural society invaded the city, while "urban" commoditization and monetization permeated rural society.

Already in the 1950s, but to a greater extent today, it had become evident that a sizable proportion of urban shopkeepers and artisans did not live in the urban communities where they worked, and that in some townships, like Ramallah, Tulkarem, Jericho, and Gaza City, the majority of local merchants did not originate from the town itself, but were war refugees from the coastal cities, whose populations had been expelled during the war of 1948.[49] Nevertheless, the persistent divisions in each township within the middle classes according to their origins (that is, whether they were refugees or "indigenous" citizens) continued to plague local political alliances. These were particularly evident in municipal and chamber of commerce elections, in which refugee and "native" candidates had to be delicately balanced on each slate. The divisions were (and are) reinforced by the strategy of marriage between members of extended families, and the fact that refugee status continues to be as important as class background in the search for eligible spouses. Despite significant integration (and intermarriage) since the war of 1967, those divisions continue to be a primary obstacle in the social homogeneity of the middle strata in Palestinian urban society, and they contributed significantly to the relative withdrawal of town merchants from active participation in the national movement until the eruption of the uprising in December 1987. One outstanding achievement of the uprising has been a noticeable decline in the social impact of these divisions, as evidenced by new intermarriage patterns and the willingness to waive "family rights" in the event of local feuds.[50]

Finally, a distinction should be made here between shopkeepers and peddlers. Although retail trade expanded considerably as a result of rural business ventures in the district centers, shopkeepers continue in the main to come from urban roots, both refugee and local. Peddlers, on the other hand, are overwhelmingly of peasant origin. They predominate as street vendors of vegetable produce (mostly rural women who bypass kiosk rentals in the vegetable markets) and sidewalk trinket salesmen. During the uprising the number of street peddlers increased severalfold as unemployed workers, pauperized refugee camp dwellers, and tax-evading shopkeepers joined the ranks of the peasant street vendors to eke out a living. This tendency was reinforced during Israel's closure of its borders to workers from the occupied territories in the aftermath of the Autonomy Accords in 1994.

A PEASANTIZED URBANITY

The rural-urban nexus described here has produced in cities a normative system that is essentially a peasantized culture functioning in an urban context. The first feature of this culture is the actual agrarian base of many Palestinian cities. The towns of Jenin, Jericho, Tulkarem, Qalqileh, Hebron, Beit Jala, and Beit Sahour contain vast garden estates devoted to agricultural production. Citrus and banana plantations, vineyards, and olive groves constitute a substantial source of income for these cities. We are not talking about marginal subsistence income in this case, but about marketable cash crops, which all members of the household are involved in producing. These agricultural activities involve a considerable number of refugee laborers from the vicinity of these towns during harvest time.

The presence of refugee camps around these townships has created marked social and cultural distinctions in the urban social fabric. The majority of these refugees come from the ranks of the former peasant population that was transplanted during the war of 1948 to the outskirts of central highland towns, where they have become involved in urban wage labor and retail trade. In the 1970s these communities became a source of cheap commuting labor for the Israeli economy. Socially mobile refugees constantly moved out of camps and became integrated into the lives of the urban middle classes. With time, refugee camps became permanent working-class districts in the major urban centers of the West Bank and Gaza (Am'ari in Ramallah, Dheisheh in Bethlehem, Ballatah and Askar in Nablus, Nur Shams in Tulkarem, and so on).

At the level of social organization, however, refugee families reconstituted their old village kinship structures in the houses inside the camps. Patterns of social interaction, business partnership, and marriage continued to cement communal bonds that existed in the pre-1948 village communities.[51] The persistence of these organizational forms in the city allowed an economically dispossessed strata of refugees to overcome their agrarian skills becoming irrelevant and to adapt to the new urban environment through family, clan, and putative solidarity based on refugee status.

The twin demographic features of refugee habitation in the outskirts of the highland towns and the daily commute by many from the rural districts into town for work and services also marked the culture of urban life in general. Rural (or, in the case of refugees, formerly rural) norms of behavior were reflected in the transplantation of old peasant dialects and women's traditional dress codes to the new urban environment. At the level of daily social interaction, an assumed egalitarianism mitigated against formal ranking. This is reflected in the use of kinship terms, such as *abu-, akh, ukht, ʿamm,* and *khal* (father, brother, sister, and paternal and maternal uncle), to address those outside one's family.[52] Terms of rank *(sayyid, ustadh, hadrat)* were used either sarcastically or as terms of endearment. Very rarely were they used instrumentally. Terms expressing aristocratic privilege *(bey, agha, pasha)* have been completely expunged from the Palestinian urban dialect, unlike in neighboring Jordan or Egypt, where they still carry some social significance.

But the urban adoption of this rural hostility toward urban ranking was not entirely an ideological stance, as it functioned to mystify real social differences. It actually reflected a trend in Palestinian society toward substantial class mobility in the second half of the twentieth century. This trend was basically generated by free access to higher education and opportunities that became available because of out-migration.[53] What reinforced this structural change in the class composition of both rural and urban communities was the loss of privileges by the landed elites in the course of the war of 1948, and the out-migration from the country of the upper and professional classes since then. In the final analysis, the two countervailing trends of urban peasantization and rural suburbanization have narrowed the disparities in the habitat conditions over the last quarter of a century, both in terms of class diversity and in terms of the cultural distinctions that separate villages from townships.

Such conclusions do not suggest, however, that Palestinian society is being leveled. A survey of Palestinian households conducted in 1993 indicated that widespread social cleavages continued, particularly within urban areas.[54] The study focuses on the main mechanisms for social mobility, education, work, and migration. It suggests two main hypotheses: first, that given the limited work opportunities, the saturation of the labor market with high school and university graduates has rendered higher education a weaker mechanism of social mobility; and, second, that the income gap between white collar (professional and semiprofessional) employment and wage labor employment is decreasing. This suggests a partial leveling of income differentiation between those social-occupational groups, but not in society as a whole.[55]

Such a narrowing in the income gap need not be interpreted as a decline in the social status of professional and semiprofessional employment. The household data, however, did not conclusively establish any significant correlation between one's habitat and one's educational or occupational status, suggesting that access to mobility is similar for village, camp, and urban residents.[56]

SMALL TOWNS: POLITICAL EGALITARIANISM, SOCIAL AUTHORITARIANISM

The emergence of homogenizing tendencies in Palestinian urban society has produced a society of formal egalitarianism that is common to mountain peasant cultures in the eastern Mediterranean (Syria, Lebanon, and Anatolia). But while this tradition expresses hostility to rank and privilege (while preserving elements of both), it is also very authoritarian and socially repressive.[57]

In this chapter I have suggested that egalitarian ideological stances in Palestine have been reinforced by a number of structural and ideational trends. Chief among these are patterns of social mobility leading to the professionalization of rural migrants; the leveling consequences of migration and wage labor; the emigration of upper-class and landed families; the persistence of wider kinship bonds that act as a network for the employment and welfare of extended family members; and sentiments of communal solidarity during the years of collective resistance against Israeli rule.

The culture of collective resistance and Palestinians' feeling of encirclement by the Israeli military regime buttressed among the urban population a consensual ideology that acted to reduce the perception of internal conflict.[58] Intraurban class conflict and other social disparities were publicly deferred in the interests of national unity. Intergenerational strain, on the other hand, was intensified during the uprising of 1987–93 because of the widespread involvement of younger family members in street action against the wishes of their elders.

At the social level, the ideology of communal solidarity generated a culture of authoritarian control by the forces of tradition. While political dissidence was tolerated because it took the form of rebellion against the national enemy, social dissidence was proscribed because it undermined the vision of a common destiny.

Two such constructs of a common destiny have evolved in the last few decades. One revolves around the struggle for the preservation of an idyllic traditional culture rooted in rural virtues and expressed as the essence of the Palestinian soul. Urban intellectuals and academics, active in folk-lore societies and intent upon protecting Palestinian national culture from erosion as a result of the forces of colonial settlement and moder-nity, contributed to the emergence of this intellectual tradition in the 1970s and '80s.[59] The second construct, which has become very power-ful since the early 1990s, and especially during the intifada, was the mil-lennial Islamic revivalism adopted by Hamas and Islamic Jihad.

Although both ideological tendencies evoked communitarian solidar-ity and thrived in small-town settings such as Jenin, Hebron, and Beth-lehem, they had considerably different effects on the social reconstruc-tion of public morality. The first tendency was secular, intensely nationalist, and minimally interventionist in the issues of gender roles and dress codes. The Islamic tendency, by contrast, was antinationalist and made a priority of eradicating the degenerate impact of secularism, co-education, the mixing of genders in public places, and Western (read: modern) modes of behavior and dress in urban Palestine. With great ef-fectiveness it used mosques, youth clubs, student unions, and profes-sional syndicates to mobilize young people around its agenda.

Both intellectual tendencies—the secular defense of the virtues of rural culture and Islamic revivalism—were united in their attempt to revive from the distant past a community that was marked by serenity and con-cord. Both defended an endangered (and imagined) community of tradi-tion that was challenged by an imported modernity. Both used the idiom of kinship as a mechanism of establishing communal solidarity. But this is where the similarities end.

While the nationalist defenders of tradition were content to propose an abstract and nonactivist vision of the future, the revivalist tendency placed at the top of its agenda an interventionist program of remolding society in the image of this perceived glorious past. The institutional mechanisms for this intervention were a number of societies, funds, and networks that acted to serve the welfare of disadvantaged groups in most Palestinian townships. These services included the operation of kinder-gartens, clinics, *zakat* committees for the poor, vocational training for women, "marriage committees" *(firaq afrah),* and youth clubs.[60] The ser-vices were invariably dispensed with substantial ideological packaging.[61]

During the intifada, however, the interventionist program of religious fundamentalism and the nationalist "secular" defense of traditionalism began to converge. The crucible of this convergence was the small-town ideology of preserving tradition from the ravages of modernity. This unity of purpose between the new nationalism and religion is particularly relevant to our discussion on three fronts: the issue of women's dress codes and gender segregation; the question of social deviance; and the family's control over its children.

Perhaps the most potent and effective campaign launched by fundamentalist forces was its successful bid to segregate the sexes in public places and to diffuse (and impose) an "Islamic" dress code for women in the place of Western dress codes. This campaign was overwhelmingly successful in the townships of the Gaza district (Rafah, Khan Yunis, Deir al-Balah, and the camps), and very effective in the northern and southern districts of the West Bank. Only in the central districts, and to a lesser extent in the city of Nablus, was it challenged and in part reversed.

With the exception of women's groups, the nationalist movement made only feeble attempts at resisting these impositions.[62] In the end, the movement succumbed to these measures, as attempts to challenge them were seen by the local nationalist leadership as leading to national divisiveness.[63] There is no doubt, however, that one factor that contributed to the lack of confrontation between the two groups was the voluntary nature of the dress code. Women experienced primarily social coercion, in the form of public sentiment supporting the dress code. That public sentiment, which was contestable, represented only a minor current at the beginning of the intifada, but later the dress code became a prototype of correct behavior. Women who decided to make individual statements rejecting the new code of ethics were penalized, mostly by public ostracism.[64]

The question of social deviance was raised during the intifada in the context of dealing with collaborators. Both the Islamists and a number of nationalist forces believed (not without foundation) that drug dealing and sexual services were used by the Israeli security forces as a means of entrapment (isqat) of young militants. According to the claims of Hamas, those who did so were "nonpolitical" agents of the Israeli security apparatus.[65] "They are moral collaborators whose function is social sabotage [takhrib akhlaqi] through the spreading of vices and moral corruption exemplified in prostitution, drug dealing, alcohol [consumption], the diffusion of pornographic films and publications, immodest dress, and [mixed] trips."[66]

Secular intellectuals were seen as critical in creating the fertile ground for the diffusion of moral corruption. These intellectuals included the adherents of Marxism, atheism, Darwinism, and Freudian psychology. They even included advocates of the sexes mixing in public places.[67] Since these claims resonated with nationalist calls for the defense of tradition and the conception of "moral corruption" as a prelude to the entrapment of activists, many nationalist and even leftist groups (like the Popular Front) actually adopted this Islamist position on "objective collaboration" and encouraged the phenomenon of liquidating "moral deviants."[68] This is a paradoxical position, since the main source of diffusion of these deviations, according to the Islamists, are the secular ideological tenants of the secularists. One of only a few Palestinian researchers who did a systematic examination of this phenomenon, Saleh ʿAbdel-Jawad, estimates that about 30 percent of cases involving the elimination of collaborators during the intifada targeted "moral deviants."[69]

CONCLUSION

I have suggested here that small-town authoritarianism is a product of social control mechanisms rooted in the size of the urban community, which allows for monitoring deviant behavior, and in the persistence of kinship organization in providing for the employment and investment needs of family members. Authoritarian tendencies also gained strength as a response to a loss of control over the activities of younger family members during the intifada. This took the form of the reassertion of traditional family control over the marriage strategies of its daughters and sons, and, in a wider sense, it took the form of reviving "rural virtues" in urban areas and the tightening of control over various forms of "social deviance." The struggle against political collaboration in the guise of "deviant behavioral patterns" during the intifada no doubt contributed to the emergence of new conservative and restorative ethics. Pivotal in this regard was the convergence of Islamic revivalism and provincial nationalism in fighting moral corruption.

It is often assumed—falsely, I believe—that the emergence of religious fundamentalism in Palestinian society constitutes a reassertion of traditionalism. What feeds this attitude is the observation that fundamentalist demands that women act modestly in their daily behavior and their attack on Western norms of conduct among middle-class Palestinians resonate with traditional virtues. This equation, however, is patently false, for religious fundamentalism is primarily an urban phenomenon that has as much contempt for aspects of modernity as for traditional adherence to clan solidarity and nominalist religion. Many traditional norms are as unacceptable to them as Western behavior. If fundamentalists consider secular individualism as the embodiment of evil, it is because their immediate milieu is urban nationalist political life.

During the intifada, this conflation of religious fundamentalism with traditionalism gained momentum for intertwined political and behavioral reasons. Politically, the nationalist and leftist movements failed to provide practical solutions to the daily misery of occupation. More importantly, however, the left failed to forge a cultural milieu to help the masses cope with the loss of the traditional support system: the declining role of the rural family, the threatening and unknown nature of life in the big city, thwarted employment expectations for tens of thousands of young people on the threshold of adulthood, and the general inability of established role models to cope with the demands of a changing social order. It was this failure of traditionalism and of the agencies of change to grasp the nature of the period that created fertile ground for the emergence of the Islamic solution.

In Palestine, the loss of metropolitan centers through war also meant the loss of urbanism as a cultural product of big cities. Small towns became the arena for the formulation of the ethics of political resistance, but also for the restructuring of normative behavior. In this sense the values of small towns became the values of society in general.

CHAPTER 4

Bourgeois Nostalgia and the Abandoned City

Testimonies commemorating the fiftieth anniversary of the Nakba in the spring of 1998 confounded both narrators and listeners. The former were perplexed about why they had kept silent for what seemed like an eternity before relating their untold stories. The listeners (most of them belonging to the younger, third generation) were also confounded by the silence of their elders. Was it because their catastrophe was an expression of divine retribution? Or was it because their elders demonstrated a collective inability to face a superior enemy?

In addition to the testimonies, which constituted a collective biography of the war generation, commemorative activities included a "march of the million" organized by a number of political parties, poetry recitals, documentary films, posters, and endless lectures and essays analyzing the past and reinterpreting it in the light of the present.

The most poignant Nakba oral testimonies were those that were primarily contemporary eyewitness accounts of the war of 1948. In the main these were unembellished stories of events lived by the narrators, mediated only by the problematic prism of their memories, and by the presence of a younger audience and their recording machines. Most of those narratives were distinguished from intellectual discourses by their spontaneity and simplicity and because they kept a distance from the world of the intelligentsia and politicians.[1] Most of the narrators were average people—mainly drivers, fighters, *mukhtars* (notables), sheikhs, peddlers, and the like—who were involved in the events while being on the margin of society. Many of them were, and still are, illiterate.

The dominant characteristic of the narratives was an emphasis on the dramatic nature of the incident, as if the war itself and the displacement that followed it were not dramatic enough. Siege, confrontations with the enemy, fighting, massacres, martyrdom, and expulsion were at the core of the stories. The following is a typical example:

> When the training period in Syria was over, we entered the country via the Allenby Bridge. We then headed to Jaffa via Ramleh and then to Yazour. Two hundred and forty of us fighters gathered in Al-Ajami in four detachments. We witnessed several skirmishes in Tel Al-Reesh, from where we moved to Manshiyyeh, where the situation started to deteriorate. I recall a Yugoslav group that included three Christians who committed suicide at Hasan Bey Mosque, each of them allowing himself to be shot by his colleague. After that, I left Manshiyyeh for Ajami for the second time with Musa Al-Qattan, who was an explosives expert, and from there we went to the Salamah Duwwar [a traffic circle]. When we tried to withdraw, the car drivers refused to take us with our weapons, and we refused to withdraw without our weapons. This continued until the British secured our exit in a caravan that included twenty-one fighters. I then returned to Silwad, where I joined the fighters. The last scene I witnessed was the departure of most Jaffa inhabitants in motorboats and light barges to the steamers waiting at sea.[2]

What is absent in this story—and many other similar stories of the war—is information about the fabric of daily life, which could have provided the framework for these incidents and helped to explain them. What the narrator perceives as normal, it seems, is taken for granted and considered not worth recalling. The event moderators, mostly academics, tried in vain to provide the social and political background for these testimonies, and to provide the necessary context, but they invariably collided against a barrier of astonishment, denial, or forgetfulness.

Above all, however, the stories reveal an overriding sense of localism. What happened during the Nakba is seen as having happened to a particular town or village, isolated from the onslaught that affected Palestine as a whole. Although the narrators recognize that the collective tragedy of the Nakba happened to the country as a whole, this realization is not reflected in the protocols of narration, nor in the pattern of the stories told. There is an astounding absence of the overall picture, and of the networks that affected the lives and behavior of the combatants and onlookers alike. Thus the siege of Jaffa and Lydda, the massacres of Deir Yasin and Dawaiymeh, and the exodus from Safad and Haifa are all described in these narratives as disparate incidents unconnected to the general saga of the war.

THE VISION TRANSFORMED

Today, equipped with hindsight, we can explore the transformations that eventually differentiated the consciousness of exiled Palestinians from those who remained in Palestine. In doing so, we can examine the shifting concepts of what "the homeland" meant to these two groups, and how they understood the notion of a return to the homeland.

The concept of a categorical return to Palestine, which was linked to an abstract vision of liberating the land, came into being in the era of the first dispersion (1948–67). This vision was embodied in the paintings of Tamam and Ismail Shammout, which focus on the image of a Paradise Lost and idyllic peasant landscapes. In the Shammouts' paintings all internal conflicts in Palestinian society were obliterated in favor of a pastoral picture based on the collective memory of Palestinian refugees in Arab host countries. The most salient traits of this vision are found in the tortured relationship between the exiled refugees, who are continually seeking to return to their homes, and their usurped homeland. In this sense their homeland was their home, in the extremely localized sense of the village community or the town neighborhood. The nation was reduced to the village. The people who steadfastly remained on their land, on the other hand, were excluded from this vision in a magical act, as if their staying in Palestine was no more than a coincidence unworthy of consideration.

In the period of the second conquest (after the war of 1967), the relationship between the Palestinians in exile and those who remained in the West Bank and the Gaza Strip, as well as in the Arab communities of the Galilee, was reformulated. The Palestinians who had remained in the Galilee and other Israeli territories were looked upon as heroes, albeit ineffective ones. This opinion prevailed until the Land Day incidents broke out in the Galilee and the Negev, when the status of these steadfast Palestinians was upgraded. Now their epitaphs described them as "heroes of return" *(abtal al-ʿawda)*, a term that previously had been reserved for Palestinian refugees living in exile.

This relationship changed yet again into a new form after the establishment of the Palestinian National Authority and the signing of the Oslo Accords. The return to the occupied territories of tens of thousands of exiles signified a shift in the weight of Palestinian decision making and identity in the direction of a new territorial base inside the homeland. As a result, the diaspora Palestinians—especially those in refugee camps—now found themselves marginalized.

With this political and demographic transformation, the concept of a return to Palestine has acquired different nuances. The abstract vision of liberation has collided with a "realistic" political vision of limited and qualified repatriation. Tension emerged immediately after the signing of the interim accords since these agreements allowed a return to Palestine only through individual visitation rights, with Israeli permission, and denied the possibility of returning collectively to refugees from the 1948 war.[3]

This qualified return to the homeland was mediated by two new developments. The first involves the rediscovery—or, actually, the discovery—of the material presence of the forsaken Palestinians in their homeland: the presence of living communities that have retained their own social fabric, their specific cultural traditions, and their literature and art. This presence engendered a new problematic in relation to Palestinian society in exile, which in the past had hardly acknowledged its existence. The second phenomenon involves what may be referred to as "visiting encounters" by the third generation of Nakba victims. This generation lived the Nakba through the imaginations of their parents and grandparents. The members of this third generation only lived in a truncated Palestinian society, which was either under colonialism (in the West Bank and Gaza Strip), or subjected to a military invasion (Lebanon), or lacked a normal daily life (exile in the Arab countries).

A VINDICTIVE RETURN

In the summer of 1994, a number of activist intellectuals who returned to Palestine with the PLO cadres following the Oslo Accords began publishing a series of essays on the experience of return from exile.[4] These pieces collectively constitute a rich body of discourse on journeys toward the reformulation of self-identity. If there is one theme that unites them, it is the theme of shock at the rediscovery of their homeland. They all seem to have landed after a prolonged flight, but it was not clear in whose homeland they have landed.

The poet Ghassan Zaqtan portrays the homeland as the new site of exile. He returns to his village, Zakariyya, now the Hebraized Kfar Zakariyya, and tries to recall the stories of his forefathers:

> Zakariyya did not look as it was described at all. The hill was not astonishing, as in the description, and the Jews who were wandering along the roads did not relate to the place; rather, there was a distance separating

them from it. . . . It seemed to me that they were totally removed from what was happening. . . . I said something I no longer remember. I did not abandon it. I have no right to do that; I have no right to abandon it. This is a knowledge that is more sublime than the vehicle of yearning that brought me here, or rather the exile that brought me to my father's place.[5]

Zaqtan compares the situation to the Arab exodus from Andalusia:

We have become the new Andalusians. It all seemed very appropriate. Our rendition of exile appropriated the same vocabulary of the Andalusian exodus. All of a sudden our "return to the homeland" appeared as a betrayal of all those allusions—to the idea of exile and to the Andalusian paradigm.

Zaqtan refers to the disintegration of the concept of holiness when imagining the sacred land as he confronts the Israeli Other:

Sacredness here presents another problem when facing the holiness of the other who cannot be expunged from the scene. The ability of the other to propagate his own sacredness and make it part of the contemporary universal scene cannot be negated. I was never convinced that the sacred . . . stands on our side. The Other had already established his mythology, reformulated it as a racial doctrine, and descended on our villages, towns, and roads like a huge silver bird coming from a neighboring unseen mythology. This was at a time when our own myth was collapsing and disintegrating on the ground with the elapse of time, forgetfulness, and a fading conviction.[6]

This fetishism of the homeland dominates the imagery of poet Zakariyya Mohammed. Unlike his colleagues, however, he decided not to philosophize. Instead he chose literary metaphors to treat the dilemma of the returnees. He equates the aridity of the Palestinian return to the arid soil left to the remaining part of Palestine after the Israelis appropriated the coastal regions:

I thought I would double my idols and mirrors in the homeland. What is this homeland? It is no more than a piece of land that is left for us. It is a piece of stone. It is a land of mountains and hills . . . a land of stone and rock. They took the coast and left rocky hills for us. No, in fact, they did not leave it; we try to make them leave it. What can we do with stone? We can at least bear our agony.[7]

Hasan Khader, by contrast, attacks Palestinian narcissism and its accompanying self-pity. This narcissism, he claims, lifts the idea of return to the level of a cult, which needs to be transcended in favor of normalizing daily life through a new praxis.

What we lived through in the past was the time of a transitional culture of contingencies [thaqafat tawari'], the culture of transforming refugees into a people. The problem now is how to transform those people into a new normalcy away from the domain of the "miraculous children."[8]

This search for "normalcy" is viewed as the problem of a culture that has finally shifted from focusing on an "exemplary homeland" to coming to grips with a "flesh-and-blood" homeland—that is to say, a culture that has shifted from ideology to reality. "This is a shift that requires the writer to depart from the illusions of a 'stolen homeland,'" Khader writes.

> There is no possibility of reproducing the homeland as a paradise lost. The homeland is at hand, disfigured and distorted and waiting for salvation. We have an identity that is still in the formulation stage. This identity will become larger with every meter we are able to extract from the occupier, with every road we construct, every book we print, every woman we free, every window we open in our life, which is so burdened with stagnant air, and every decision we take in the fields of social and political organization and human rights.[9]

Of all the returnees, Khader is the one most obsessed with the process of the return to normalcy in Palestinian daily life—an internal normalcy that he regards as a precondition for creating notions of reciprocity with the Israeli protagonists.

Murid Barghouti arguably demonstrates the greatest inner peace of all the returnees. He is probably the only one among them who is not a refugee, or whose family did not leave coastal Palestine to become a refugee family. He is also the most relentlessly self-critical when viewing his own past. "How can we explain today," Barghouti says in *I Saw Ramallah,* "after we have grown and become mature, how we in the towns and villages of the West Bank treated our people who were expelled by Israel from their coastal cities and villages . . . and came to stay in our mountainous towns and villages. We called them refugees, we called them immigrants!"[10]

Barghouti's return to Palestine involved a temporary sojourn to his village of Deir Ghassaneh (a formerly feudal estate in the Ramallah district). It was Jerusalem, however, that became the focus of his nostalgic recollection of the sensuous experiences of his adolescence. He describes

> that vague enjoyment we felt when our adolescent bodies touched the bodies of European tourist women on the Saturday of Fire [Sabt enNour, the Orthodox celebrations on the day before Easter Sunday], when we shared with them the darkness of the Church of the Holy Sepulcher and carried the white candles that illuminate the darkness, just like them. This is mundane Jerusalem, the city of our petty concerns that we had forgotten too quickly. Because such is life, just as water is water and lightning is lightning, and just as our hands were lost, it has now emerged as an abstraction.[11]

For the poet who grew up in the socially repressive milieu of the high-land villages, the Holy City evokes a keen sense of eroticism. Thus the tragedy for Barghouti is not the Nakba itself, but rather the loss of the city that resulted from it. "The occupation has left the Palestinian villages as they were and reduced our cities to villages," he writes.[12] At the end, the writer preserves his Palestinianism in the imagination and returns to *his* promised land in Cairo.

THE ABANDONED CITY

In the current debate concerning the significance of the Nakba and Awdah, the political and the emotive are intertwined. So long as the lines separating exile from the homeland are clear, the Palestinian discourse pertaining to notions of return remains abstract and categorical. The main price for this clarity and purity, however, was—until recently—the exclusion of the people who remained rooted in their homeland from the discourse of liberation. But as exiles begin to return, as they did after the establishment of the new Palestinian entities the West Bank and Gaza Strip, the issues have become problematic, and the imagined constructs of the homeland had to be reformulated.

I will review here the nature of this debate through an analysis of the heated polemics about the meaning of the Nakba and Awdah that have been taking place among exiled intellectuals and natives of the city of Jaffa, who have pondered the meaning of the city's iconography over the last decade. This contested dialogue is significant, first, because of the centrality of Jaffa in the culture of Palestine before dispersion, and, sec-ond, because it sums up the nature of the new relationship between exile and the homeland.[13]

The concept of return and the incidents of 1948 discussed in the testi-monies on this subject often produced a contradictory picture of the Pales-tinian experience. The discussion also dealt with the experience of internal estrangement by those Palestinians who remained in Jaffa, including those who moved into the abandoned city after the war. In addition, it dealt with the experience of those who returned to Jaffa on personal visits after the 1967 war, but refused to accept what had happened. Finally, the discussion explored the experience of Palestinian intellectuals who, in hindsight, tried to reconstruct what happened to the city. Why did the social elite abandon the city before it fell militarily, and could this fate have been avoided?

In these narratives we find the following overlapping themes: an al-most hostile attitude expressed by the city's remaining residents toward the returnees for ignoring the realities of the present city and elevating it to the level of an abstract memory; the vision of the Other (the Israeli Jew) and attempts to come to terms with their displacement; and the attempt by refugees to restore the past through modification of the new reality, or through a protracted attempt to coexist with this new reality.[14] Altogether, by examining these narratives we can distinguish three different groups from Jaffa, all of which lived through the experience of the Nakba, but in different places and at different times.

The experience of the first group is communicated through the writings of the first generation that lived through the war and expulsion and which tried to restore through their memoirs their vision of the city before it fell to Israeli control. This restorative memory expunged contradictions and tried hard to enable a mental return to the lost paradise. The issues that occupy this group revolve around three themes:

- An obsessive nostalgia. This group attempts to recapture Jaffa through the reinvention of its dramatic aspects, such as the festival of Nebi Rubeen, and the invocation of idyllic vignettes from the prewar city.[15]

- The reconstruction of the social fabric of daily life in Mandate Palestine in a pastoral and static manner. Much of this reconstruction is genealogical and based on documentary records of the "original" families within the city. Invariably this genre is "frozen" in the sense that it fails to take into account any changes in the city structure since it fell. It also neglects to seek a connection between the city's social fabric and its national networks.[16]

- An attempt to understand what happened. We can locate a number of memoirs and monographs whose objective is to interpret the factors behind the fall of Jaffa to Israeli forces within the larger epic, namely, the fall of Palestine. Those who provide these explanations and justifications focus on the atmosphere that prevailed in the city during the Rebellion of 1936, the British suppression of Jaffa's rebellion by 1939, and the heroism of Jaffa's defenders in the 1947–48 period, in spite of the "defeatism" of the Arab leadership.[17]

The second group consists of second-generation post-Nakba Palestinians, who have experienced life in Jaffa through their parents' memories, have carried the burden of exile, and have tried to comprehend the experience of the Nakba while living through Israeli occupation and the war of

1967. This generation differs from the Nakba generation because it visited the city later and saw its transition from the "bride of Palestine" to the "hashish den of Israel." The dominant attitude of this generation tends to be a critical nostalgia that borders on cynicism. Although many of the works by this group are somewhat sarcastic, they are nevertheless affectionate as well.[18] Recalling her relationship with her family, Samira says:

> I was fourteen when my uncle, who lived in Greece, visited us. For a certain reason that I learned later, my mother, who was a non-Jaffite, was quarreling silently with my father one day. When she said something about the many orange orchards that the family had lost in Jaffa, my uncle, who did not know how much family history my father had told my mother, intervened and said to me, "Your grandfather did not have any orchards in Jaffa. He was a merchant in the wholesale market, not the owner of an orchard." My mother lived for twenty years of her marriage recalling stories about the family's glory and its orchards in Jaffa. As for my father, he never had the courage to tell her the truth.[19]

In another narrative, which is set at the Clock Center in Jaffa, Shaker, who was born in Jaffa in 1945, visits the shop of Shlomo the Moroccan, who sells Oriental records and cassettes. When Shlomo asks Shaker where he was born, he replies, "In Ajami" (a neighborhood in Jaffa). "Strange, I came to Jaffa from Morocco and started my new life there the same year [of your birth]. Isn't that a coincidence!" "No," says Shaker, adding politely, "You could say that it was an exchange operation." Shlomo opens his mouth in astonishment and keeps on repeating the word, "Exchange . . . exchange," until all of a sudden he is able to comprehend the meaning of the word, and loudly shouts "Exchange!" first smiling and then shaking his head sadly.[20]

The third group consists of Jaffa residents who remained entrenched in the city after the majority were expelled or had departed, and those who came to the city from the northern areas looking for work. The voice of this group is rarely heard outside Palestine, despite the impressive record of resistance by the various associations of Jaffa Arabs. It is intriguing that the Nakba generation opted to ignore the present reality of Jaffa and the conditions of its resident Palestinians, despite their frequent encounters with these residents while visiting the city.

One can venture several explanations for this myopia. First, it allows the returnee to ignore the present squalor of Jaffa—its poverty and the physical dilapidation of its buildings—which contrasts sharply with the "glorious past" the first generation remembers. But there is another reason the Nakba generation dissociates itself from present-day Jaffa: the

majority of the Arabs currently residing in Jaffa are not descendants of
the original Jaffites who left the city in 1948, which means that the returnees do not see a direct line of descent between the city their families
were compelled to abandon and the current residents, except perhaps
in a tenuous, symbolic manner. This whole phenomenon underlines an
essential localism in the way the 1948 war is experienced, which is enhanced by an obsession common among both urban and rural Palestinians of distinguishing between indigenous members of their towns
and latecomers (*ghuraba* or *wafidun*).[21] Moreover, as was mentioned
above, the majority of Arab Jaffa residents whose families have lived
there since the prewar era belong to marginalized social groups that
took little part in the city's past glories in the eyes of the returning
middle-class families.

The exiled Jaffites' idyllic (and highly selective) view of the present situation in Jaffa is precisely what provokes the anger of the current Arab
residents of Jaffa and many of the city's intellectuals and professionals
toward the Nakba generation. This reaction is clearly articulated by
Andre Mazzawi, who took it upon himself to deal with what he deemed
the "poverty" of the nostalgic writings of the Jaffa residents in exile.[22]

In his criticisms of the returnee Nakba generation, Mazzawi is struck
by how their writings paint a romanticized, pastoral picture of the city,
a picture "that ignores social differentiation or conflict." Their reconstructed image of the city is confined to the lives lived by the mercantile
elites, orchard owners, and the professional strata, while the texture of
daily life as experienced by the majority of city dwellers, including sailors
and port workers, is ignored, except as it appears in vignettes of seasonal
festivals such as Nebi Rubeen. Mazzawi cites Ahmad Zaki Dajani's assessment of the social makeup of the city in support of his claim about
this blindness to class:

> The majority of Jaffa residents belonged to well-known indigenous families.
> These were families that occupied a prominent position in the economic life
> of the city, such as in commerce, ownership of agricultural land, and in the
> higher echelons of the civil service and the judicial apparatus. One does not
> find a poor class in Jaffa, except those seasonal workers who came to the
> city from Syria and Egypt to work in agriculture or in municipal services
> such as paving streets and the like.[23]

We find a similar streak, albeit in a more sophisticated style, in a well-
known collection of memoirs of Jaffa before the war, which dwells on
the exoticism of life in exclusive social clubs, private schools, and the
nightclubs of the city's middle classes.[24]

Mazzawi also criticizes the writings of the Nakba generation for their unmitigated and deliberate failure to recognize the current realities of the city. He cites *Yafa: Itr Madina* (Jaffa: The perfume of a city), the well-known compendium edited by Hisham Sharabi and Imtiaz Diab, as an example of this failure. The volume includes fifty-three interviews with former residents of Jaffa now living in exile in Amman, Cairo, and Beirut, but not a single interview with a current resident of Jaffa. Readers will find no view of the contemporary conditions of the city. It is as if the city died when its original inhabitants left during the war of 1948.[25]

Mazzawi tackles the diaries of several members of the Nakba generation and their justifications for leaving the city. Reviewing the memoirs of Dr. Yusef Haikal, the last Arab mayor of the city, he points out that Haikal left the city and took refuge in Amman in May 1948, when Jaffa was under siege by Jewish forces, claiming that he wanted to get military support from Jordan. Haikal authorized his administrative staff in the city council to handle the affairs of the city, but he never returned to Jaffa. His failure to do so paved the way for the Zionist conquest and subordination of the city. Had he remained in the city, according to the writer, he would have been able to negotiate with the Israeli forces officially, as an elected leader, or at least ensure that the city remained open, thereby preventing it from being plundered and ransacked.[26] In this regard the writer poses the question:

> Why did Mayor Haikal obstinately insist on leaving the city for Amman after May 3, 1948? Why wouldn't he remain and negotiate with the Jewish side from a more powerful stand than a delegated commission of second-rank politicians and in his capacity as the city's mayor? Had he stayed, wouldn't he have been able to protest, ex officio, the Jewish takeover of the city and the subsequent transgressions of the Jewish-Arab agreement, especially the annexation of Jaffa to Tel-Aviv?[27]

It seems to me that Mazzawi's criticism of Haikal is in fact an indirect indictment of the behavior of the social class that deserted the city and left it to its inevitable destiny in the spring of 1948. That social class did not understand the extent of the consequences of their evacuation. When recalling their joyful past in the city, the members of this group do not link their frivolous lifestyle before the Nakba to the collapse of the city after they left. Finally, they subsequently behaved, in retrospect, as if their departure from the city was synonymous with the eradication of the city from history. The rejuvenated contemporary city and its residents in the memoirs of many people of this class thus exist today as background for their tragic nostalgia.

This critical approach by several intellectuals of the post-Nakba generation aims at the deconstruction of the nostalgic discourse of antebellum Palestine and focuses on countervailing tendencies that are inherent in a new reading of that past. A number of historians are already working in this revisionist vein.[28] Romantic pastoral histories of Palestine, however, are bound to continue to be written by exiled writers side by side with these critical assessments, in large part because no satisfactory political solution is likely to address the aspirations of the exiles in the foreseeable future. The current debate between those exiles and current residents is likely to create a historic rapprochement between exiled Palestinians and those who remained in their towns. A second discourse, but far from a rapprochement, is also emerging between the Arab residents of mixed towns in Israel (Jaffa, Haifa, and Akka, for example) and their Jewish neighbors.

Although I agree with much of Mazzawi's critique of Jaffan nostalgia, or "Jaffamania," as Musa Budeiri calls it, I believe that he is sometimes inclined to direct his criticism at the wrong target. In his attempt to highlight the conditions in Jaffa and the lives of the people who are now confronting Israeli rule, his writings seem to delegitimize the collective memories of the exiled Jaffa elite. His depiction of the nostalgic collective memory as a class memory, however, is not convincing. In the Arab world, the memoirs and diaries of political activists and other intellectuals often reflect the bourgeois (and sometimes aristocratic) social background of their authors. One can easily claim that the Nakba devastated the lives of "ordinary" Palestinians, such as farmers, laborers, and craftsmen, much more than the lives of the bourgeoisie of Jaffa and Palestine—after all, it was much easier for middle-class refugees to rebuild their lives than it was for plebeians—but very few of the latter left us with a written record of their tribulations and yearnings.

Nevertheless, the absence of the voice of average people from these private histories and biographies is indeed an astounding void. It is the task of the new researchers to provide these people with a forum and the appropriate tools (including oral histories) so that they are able to articulate their own experience. It is a mistake, however, to exclude or downplay the suffering of the bourgeois intelligentsia or works by historians of the middle class *because* the other voices are absent.

In the case illustrated, as in other current writings about the Nakba, not only is there a sustained critique of the lifestyle of the prewar Jaffa elite and other Palestinian urban elites, but the collapse of the national will in the face of the military onslaught of the Jewish forces is attributed to them and the political class that articulated their interests. There is a tendency here to underestimate how superior the enemy's forces were. Suppose we accept the allegation that this elite or some part of it could have remained in the city to defend it and to negotiate on behalf of its residents. What guarantee is there, then, that its destiny would have been different from its actual fate? What could have guaranteed that the result would have been any different than that experienced in other cities in Palestine (such as Nazareth), in which a large proportion of local elites opted to stay?

The point that I am suggesting here is that the romantic reimagining of pre-1948 Palestine is not necessarily a bourgeois vision. Rather, it is an escapist vision that is found as much in the writings of the radical intelligentsia as in the images of the citrus plantation owners. It is also the essence of nostalgic writings and paintings. We find it in the Shammouts' canvases and in an enormous number of autobiographies and works of fiction dealing with Palestinian rural life in the 1930s and '40s. Examples include *Ghorbat Al-Ra'i* (The shepherd's exile), by Ihasn Abbas, and *The Plums of April*, by Ghassan Kanafani. A sharp illustration of this vision is found, moreover, in the series of monographs on destroyed villages that aimed at systematically reconstructing the social history of these places before they were expunged from the map. In these studies, a pastoral and harmonious world, free from any conflict or contradictions, is presented. It is indeed Paradise Lost. Almost all of these studies are far removed from being an elite fantasia or a discourse by an upper-class intelligentsia.[29] Obviously, this critique should in fact target the discourse itself, not the social background of the people who created it.

In the early 1990s, after the entry of PLO forces into Palestine (but not necessarily because of it), Nakba narratives began to become more balanced but also more problematic accounts of Palestinian history. This trend began with the initial serious efforts of the first generation, the members of which tried to record their bitter experiences as accurately and as honestly as possible. This start, however, faltered at the time, as the writers were able to imagine their experience only through the lens of nostalgia.[30] However, there are important exceptions. In his autobiographical works, for example, Jabra Ibrahim Jabra was not only able to transcend a nostalgic streak in his treatment of his early years in Bethlehem and Jerusalem, but he also asserted an Arabist nationalist identity that went beyond the confining atmosphere of Palestine.[31] From a revolutionary humanist perspective, Ghassan Kanafani also transcended a nostalgic vision by examining the enemy through the lens of psychological empathy.[32]

The second generation, on the other hand, had suffered from both the heavy burden of the Nakba experience and from the estrangement of exile. Tackling the memories of their fathers' generation, they acutely criticized the patrimony of defeat and defeatism they had inherited. The third generation has been liberated, or so it seems, from the conditions of exile, but not from self-exile. They returned to explore the past with the spirit of an avid investigator who is dedicated to finding out the truth despite the consequences, even if the price is to undermine the received narrative.

Current Palestinian political realities have destined that a large proportion of Palestinians remain in perpetual exile. Those who have ended their exile, either by coming back to their homeland or by adapting themselves to their adopted homes, have managed to come to terms with their predicament. But, for most exiles, only a political solution to their refugee status will create the desired conditions of normalcy, a solution that is unlikely to be implemented in the current political environment. As for the intelligentsia, whose writings we discussed in this chapter, one can say that their self-estrangement is a perennial state of the intellectual condition, a state that is nevertheless compounded by physical exile. For them, an end to their territorial exile may indeed be the beginning of a new and profound internal exile. And it is this condition that many of the returnees have expressed in their antireturn narratives.

CONCLUSION

This chapter has attempted to bring together several experiences of exile and the reconstruction of the homeland in the imagination of Palestinian writers. The most striking feature of this reconstruction is the delayed reaction to the experience of war and uprootedness, and the accompanying repression of those memories. When the waves of disclosure did emerge, as happened during the commemorative ceremonies of the Nakba half a century after the event, the ravages of war appeared as a localized event disconnected from the larger tragedy that engulfed the refugees.

I have identified several different trends in the works of the exiled writers. Among the earlier generation of exiles there is a tendency to freeze the homeland in a frame depicting a pastoral, idyllic lost paradise. This is especially true of the works of artists and poets, but it also naturally flows from the nationalist historiography of the period. A more radical current appears in works by the second and third generation of exiles, who questioned the conventional experience of exile and the causes of the exodus. Of particular interest here is the manner in which these critics interrogated the pre-1948 society that allowed itself to be defeated and dismantled. The bourgeois nostalgia of that society was seen as a blindness that joined its prewar fragility to its impotent behavior in the war itself.

The turning point in this nostalgic narrative was the return of the PLO and its intelligentsia to Palestine in the mid-1990s. Here we encounter the shock of return to what seems to be a marginal part of the homeland under conditions of political compromise and physical confinement. The main impact of this truncated return was to demystify the whole ideological discourse on the right of return under the rubric of political realism, and to initiate a new discourse that centered around notions of normalcy and the normalization of daily life. Here normalcy is related to the question of carrying on with a dual (and conflicting) intellectual agenda; on the one hand, the consolidation of a new social formation based on building the institution of statehood; on the other hand, the conceptualization and practice of a mundane, normal society out of the "heroic" images of Palestine, whose intellectuals have become addicted to their exiled status. The main victims of this process have been those Palestinians who were not exiled, those who steadfastly remained as an Arab minority in Israeli society. Originally portrayed in the literature of exile as the forgotten lot, they were later granted an abstract heroic status. If effect, however, their conditions, as well as their struggles, remained left out of mainstream political discourse. The turning point referred to above is therefore both a conceptual and a historic benchmark. It refers to the beginning of a Palestinian narrative that attempts to synthesize these different experiences of exiles, experienced by three generations under three different geographical conditions. In doing so it will have to deal with exile as a permanent condition: for those who returned and experienced an internal exile, and for those who did not return and established their lives in their diasporas.

CHAPTER 5

A Musician's Lot

The Jawhariyyeh Memoirs as a Key
to Jerusalem's Early Modernity

The great singer Sheikh Salameh Hijazi was already half para-
lyzed when he was invited by Mayor Hashim al Husseini to
come from Cairo to Jerusalem to celebrate the Constitutional
Revolution of 1908. His orchestra was led by George Abyad,
and a huge tent *(surdaq)* was set up for him on the terrace
facing Jaffa Gate on the road to the train station. Sheikh
Salameh performed sketches from several of his musicals, including *Salah ed Din al Ayyubi* and *Romeo and Juliet*. At the
time I was eleven and was lucky enough to attend (with my
father) several of his performances. Salameh was dragging
himself onstage, yet despite his handicap, the audience was
ecstatic with delight. People were moved to tears as he sang
"Hata li khamarata al-Shifa" [Pour me the wine of deliver-
ance]. Even the Greeks in the audience, who did not understand a word, were crying. At night, after some begging, I
was admitted to meet the sheikh, where I kissed his hands.
Admission to Sheikh Salameh's concerts was half a French
pound, a fortune in those days.

Memoirs of Wasif Jawhariyyeh

Conventional narratives about the modernity of Jerusalem regard the
city in the late nineteenth century as a provincial capital city in the Ottoman hinterland whose social fabric was basically communitarian and
confessional. Ethnicity and sectarian identities were identical, as confessional consciousness was defined in ethnic-religious terms, and the
boundaries of these identities were physically delineated by habitat in the
confines of the Old City quarters.[1] The quartered city corresponded, in

these narratives, to the ethno-confessional divisions of the four communities: Muslim, Christian, Armenian, and Jewish. In these quarters social nodes were more or less exclusive, physically defined, and reinforced by mechanisms of mutual aid, craft specialization, ritual celebrations, internal school systems, and, above all, the rules of confessional endogamy. Although there was a substantial degree of interconfessional interaction in the city, it was confined mainly to the marketplace and ritual social visitations. The modernity of the city is seen as the product of the breakup of the Ottoman system under the triple impact of European penetration, Zionist emigration, and the modernizing schemes of the British Mandate.

Although on the eve of the First World War Jerusalem had a strong communitarian makeup and religious identity was very pronounced, the communal boundaries were nevertheless not defined primarily by confession or ethnicity, but by the *mahallat*, the neighborhood unit. (An exception is the case of the Armenians, who congregated around the Armenian Patriarchate.) This neighborhood unit was dropped from usage as an administrative unit under the British Mandate in favor of the quarter system *(hay* or *harat)*, which was based on distinctly religious sectarian identity. The communal bonds of confessional affiliation were superseded and supplemented by bonds of patronage and clientelism.

In this chapter I will use my reading of the memoirs of a Jerusalem musician, Wasif Jawhariyyeh, to point to substantial weaknesses in this conventional narrative. I suggest that Jerusalem's modernity was a feature of the internal dynamics within the Ottoman city, and propose that the social structure of the walled city was much more fluid than is generally believed. Furthermore, I will argue that the quarter system dividing the Old City into bounded confessional domains was introduced and retroactively imposed on the city by British colonial regulations.

Jawhariyyeh, who was a musician and an interpreter of popular Arabic music, left behind memoirs and his unpublished "Musical Notebook," which can be gainfully read as a record of the formation of a regional tradition of Mashriqi music. This transformation transcended the regional boundaries of greater Syria and Egypt through the interaction between a new technology—the gramophone and the vinyl record, which created a novel tool for the diffusion of a new music—and new musical tastes, which were enhanced by the increased mobility of performers between Egypt and Bilad ash-Sham. In this chapter, however, I focus on Jawhariyyeh's description of quotidian life in late Ottoman Jerusalem. His vignettes of daily life allow us to (re)discover a community that is no longer with us, and they shed significant light on the modernity of Palestinian urban life, both in the confines of the apparently ghettoized Old City, and in the emancipated environment of Jerusalem outside the Old City. His memoirs tell the tale of a late Ottoman and early Mandate Jerusalem with a thriving nightlife and a considerable degree of intercommunal interaction and cultural hybridity.

I am aware of the conceptual problems inherent in using the term *hybridity* to describe the city's cultural scene in the period around the time of the First World War. The term as it is currently used generally refers to the proliferation of multiethnic identities sharing the same space, and the creation of creolized cultural forms—lifestyles, dress codes, cuisine, and even language—as a result of their interaction.[2] The main arena of this hybridity is the postindustrial metropolitan city, which in recent decades has witnessed large-scale third-world migrations, creating multiple ethnic forms of habitation and categories of dual or more citizenship for the same ethnic identity.[3] In the case of prewar Ottoman Jerusalem, by contrast, the city fostered a communitarian identity, a prenationalist confessional consciousness that competed with emergent but vigorous Arab nationalist and localized (Syrian-Palestinian) nationalist sentiments, as well as an embryonic Jewish-Zionist movement vying for the allegiance of native Jewish communities. A local narrative like that of Wasif Jawhariyyeh compels us to rethink these categories of analysis and ultimately to reimagine the city's social history.

Jawhariyyeh's memoirs are mostly written in the anecdotal style of the street *hakawati*, which mesmerized the author as a child. Jawhariyyeh describes in vivid detail the stories told in Turkish and Arabic by the traveling performers of *sanduq al ʿajab* (magic lantern shows) and *qara qoz* (shadow plays) in the alleys of Mahallat as-Saʾdiyyeh and at the Damascus Gate of Jerusalem before the Great War. The simplicity and apparent frivolity of Jawhariyyeh's style tends to camouflage the narrative's profundity. One can comprehend its depth only after delving into the web of social and personal networks that the author weaves. The reader is reminded of F. W. Dupee's remarks about Flaubert's *Sentimental Education:* "It was [his] feat, and one that followed from his comic aims, to have made an epic novel out of the accumulation of anecdotes. The novel is epic because of the fates of numerous characters and a major revolution are embraced in the action; it is anecdotal because each episode recounts, as I think anecdotes do by nature, the momentary defeat or the equivocal victory of someone in a particular situation."[4] In Jawhariyyeh's case, the revolution was the Great War, and the fictional characters are the contemporary Jerusalem people he encountered in his neighborhood, in the new city outside the walls, and during his convoluted career as a musician.

THE ʿOUD PLAYER AND HIS FAMILY

> I was born on Wednesday morning, the 14th of January 1897, according to the Western calendar, which happened to be the eve of the Orthodox New Year.[5] At the moment my father was preparing a tray of *knafeh,* as was customary then in Eastern Orthodox households. I was named Wasif after the Damascene Wasif bey al-ʿAdhem, who was then my father's close friend and the sitting judge in Jerusalem's Criminal Court.[6]

Thus opens the memoirs of Wasif Jawhariyyeh, one of Jerusalem's most illustrious citizens: composer, ʿoud player, poet, and chronicler. They cover a period of forty-four years of Jerusalem's turbulent modern history (1904–48), spanning four regimes and five wars. More significantly, they mark the transition of Palestinian society into modernity and the breaking out of its Arab population beyond the ghettoized confines of the walled city.

Wasif's father, Jiryis (Girgis), was the *mukhtar* of the Eastern Orthodox Christian community in the Old City (1884) and a member of Jerusalem's municipal council under the mayoralty of Salim al-Husseini and Faidy al-Alami. Trained as a lawyer, he was well versed in Muslim *shariʿa* law and spoke several languages, including Greek, Turkish, and Arabic. He worked briefly as a government tax assessor, but later turned to private business as a silk farmer and café proprietor. He was also a skilled icon maker and amateur musician, and he encouraged his son's musical talents. Wasif's mother, Hilaneh Barakat, was descended from a leading Orthodox family from what later became known as the Christian Quarter.

Wasif's father and grandfather both occupied important public positions, but the men of the family also held a number of more modest occupations. Wasif's elder brother Khalil was a carpenter's apprentice before being conscripted into the Ottoman army, and Wasif himself held a number of odd jobs before he became an itinerant ʿoud player and began singing at wedding parties. The family's fortunes improved significantly when Jiryis became a prominent lawyer and bailiff, Khalil opened a successful café near Jaffa Gate, and Wasif entered government service. We can say with some certainty that the family members inhabited that precarious space between artisanal work and the middle ranks of the civil

Figure 3. Wasif Jawhariyyeh at age four with his father, Jiryis Jawhariyyeh, in Jerusalem, circa 1900. Photo by an unknown studio photographer. © IPS Beirut.

service. However, it is impossible to understand the Jawhariyyehs' social position in pre-Mandate Palestine without relating it to their critical bonds as protégés of the Husseini family, feudal landlords and patricians in Jerusalem's inner circle of *a'yan* (notables). Jiryis spent part of his early career looking after the Husseini estates in Jerusalem's western villages, and after his death Wasif was "adopted" by Hussein Effendi, who later became mayor of Jerusalem. Hussein Effendi arranged for Wasif a number of jobs in the city and ensured that he was treated well in the Ottoman army.[7] The family was on such intimate terms with their patrons that Wasif was entrusted with the welfare of Hussein Effendi's mistress, Persephone, when she became ill.

Wasif's musical career occupies a substantial part of his memoirs. We are fortunate to have his unpublished "Musical Notebook," which he began just prior to the war.[8] They reflect the progression of Wasif's interests from classical *andalusiat* and Aleppo *muwashshahat* to choral music (which he performed at weddings and family celebrations), love songs, melodies based on classical poetry, and finally *taqatiq* and erotic songs.[9] Untrained in musical notation, Wasif invented his own system. He also wrote a chapter on the adaptation of the Western notation system for the 'oud.[10]

Using a method of marking time that is typical in semiliterate cultures, Wasif traces the beginning of his musical career to the "year of the seven snowstorms," which he later figures was either 1906 or 1907, when he was nine years old. During the festival of Saint Dimitri that year the Jawhariyyeh household was celebrating the saint's birthday when their neighbor and friend, Mitri Abdallah Khalil, then an apprentice carpenter, constructed for Wasif his first tambourine.

> Qustandi al-Sus was one of the most famous singers in the Mahallat. He sang for Sheikh Salameh Hijazi on his renowned 'oud most of the evening, and then they allowed me to perform. I danced the *dabkeh,* then I sang a piece of "Romeo and Juliet" to the melodies composed by Sheik Salameh and the accompaniment of Qustandi's 'oud. When the latter heard me he was so pleased that he handed me his precious 'oud—which drove me into a frenzy—and I began to play it and sing to the tune of "Zeina . . . Zeina." The next day my father took a barber's blade and forged me a beautiful handle for my tambourine. . . . Thus began my musical career at the age of nine.[11]

The Jawhariyyeh house was the perfect location for developing his musical talents. All the family members—with the exception of Tawfiq, who was tone deaf—either played instruments or sang, or at least enjoyed good music. Jiryis was one of the few Jerusalemites who owned a Master's Voice phonograph (as he called it), and he had a number of early recordings by leading Egyptian singers, such as Sheikh Minyalawi and Salameh Hijazi. He encouraged his children to lip-synch along with these records, and was particularly severe with Wasif when he made mistakes. Jiryis was also keen to host prominent singers and musicians visiting Jerusalem. One of those, the Egyptian 'oud player Qaftanji, spent a week with the Jawhariyyehs, and from him Wasif learned a number of melodies that he used to sing on summer nights on the roof or in the outhouse.[12]

Jiryis was sufficiently moved by his son's desire that he allowed him to accompany a number of well-known performers in Mahallat as-Sa'diyyeh to learn their art. They included Hanna Fasheh, who crafted his own instruments, and Sabri Abed Rabbo, who sold Wasif his first 'oud[13] when he was eleven years old.[14] Jiryis was so impressed with Wasif's persistence that he even hired one of Jerusalem's best-known 'oud tutors, Abdul Hamid Quttaineh, to give him lessons twice a week.

Contrary to the impression conveyed by Wasif's comments about his truancy and rebelliousness, he had a substantial amount of formal schooling in addition to his musical training. This education is reflected in his polished language, rich poetic imagination, and elegant handwriting. References abound in his diaries to classical poetry and contemporary literature by figures such as Khalil Sakakini, Ahmad Shawqi, and Khalil Jibran. Wasif and Tawfiq first attended the Dabbaghah School, which was governed by the Lutheran Church next to the Holy Sepulcher. At school Wasif was taught basic Arabic grammar, dictation, reading, and arithmetic. He also studied German and Bible recitation. His school uniform was the *qumbaz* and the Damascene red leather shoes known as *balaghat*.[15] In 1909, when Wasif was twelve years old, the brothers were taken out of the Dabbaghah School after being savagely beaten by the mathematics teacher for mocking him. For several years thereafter, Wasif accompanied his father while he worked as overseer of the Husseini estates, while occasionally performing as a singer (and later as 'oud player) in the neighborhood.

When Khalil Sakakini established his progressive Dusturiyyeh National School in Musrara, Jiryis intervened with the mayor to have Wasif admitted as a day student. Sakakini had acquired a reputation for using radical methods of pedagogy in his school and for strictly banning physical punishment and written exams. In addition to advanced grammar, literature, and mathematics, the curriculum included English, French, and Turkish. Sakakini was a pioneer in introducing two disciplines unique to his school at the time: physical education and Qur'anic studies for Christians. Wasif was strongly influenced by his study of the Qur'an. He writes:

I received my copy of the Qur'an from al-Hajjeh Um Musa Kadhem Pasha al-Husseini . . . who taught me how to treat it with respect and maintain its cleanliness. My Qur'anic teacher was Sheikh Amin Al-Ansari, a well-known *faqih* in Jerusalem. Sakakini's idea was that the essence of learning Arabic lies in mastering the Qur'an, both reading and incantation. My Muslim classmates and I would start with Surat al-Baqara and continue. . . . I can say in all frankness today that my mastery of Arabic music and singing is attributed to these lessons—especially my ability to render classical poetry and *muwashshahat* in musical form.[16]

Sakakini was a music lover who had a special fondness for the ʿoud and the violin. Some of the Dusturiyyeh students had seen Wasif performing in local weddings and taunted him for being a "paid street singer" *(ajeer)*, but Sakakini defended him and taught the students to enjoy Wasif's music. Eventually, despite his love for the Dusturiyyeh National School's liberal environment, Wasif was compelled by his patron, Hussein al-Husseini, to enroll in al-Mutran School (St. George's) in Sheikh Jarrah "in order to gain knowledge of the English language and build a solid base for [his] future."[17] At al-Mutran Wasif excelled in acting in school plays, in which he was also able to develop his musical talents. He remained there for two years (1912–14), until the school was closed at the beginning of the war. Wasif finished the fourth secondary class (his tenth year of studies), and ended his formal schooling without a secondary school certificate.

After the termination of his formal schooling, Wasif continued his musical education in the company of Jerusalem's foremost ʿoud players and composers, including his first tutor, Abdul Hamid Quttaineh; Muhammad al-Sibasi; and Hamadeh al-Afifi, who taught him the art of *muwashshahat* in the Turkish tradition. But Wasif's most important mentor was the master ʿoud player Omar al-Batsh. In the spring of 1915, after his father's death, Wasif accompanied Hussein Effendi and several Turkish officers to a party at which a division of the army military band known as the Izmir Group was performing Andalusian *muwashshahat*. Wasif was mesmerized by the playing of a young ʿoud player wearing a military uniform, who was introduced to him as Omar al-Batsh. Omar became Wasif's constant companion for the duration of the war. Wasif prevailed upon Hussein Effendi, now his official patron, to hire Omar to give him four ʿoud lessons a week at the headquarters of the army orchestra in Mascobiyyeh.

From Omar, Wasif learned how to read musical notation and considerably expanded his repertoire of classical Arabic music. Omar began to bring Wasif to his performances to sing and accompany him on the ʿoud, but above all he taught him to be a discriminating listener and instructed him in the performance of the classical *muwashshahat*.[18] Throughout his diaries Wasif refers to Omar as "my teacher" and "my master."

Throughout his adult years, Wasif saw himself as a musician and ʿoud player above all else. Nevertheless, he held a number of different jobs during his adolescence and afterward. These jobs ranged from apprenticeships held in his youth to government positions arranged by his patrons. When Wasif sought employment in various government and municipal agencies, it was only to provide the resources he needed to dedicate himself to his passionate obsession: the 'oud and the company of men and women who shared his vision.

As was customary in the Old City, Wasif held a number of apprenticeships during his boyhood. These assignments supplemented his formal schooling and often furthered his evolving musical career. In the summer of 1907, at the age of nine, Wasif became an apprentice in the barbershop of Mattia al-Hallaq (Abu 'Abdallah). A barber in Ottoman Jerusalem was much more than a hairstylist: he was also an herbalist, was trained to apply leeches for bloodletting and suction cups for the relief of congestion, and in general performed the function of a local doctor. It is possible that Jiryis wanted one of his sons to follow such a vocation, but Wasif had other ambitions:

> I would hold the customer by the neck while Abu 'Abdallah was washing his hair so that the water would not drip down his shirt. Water was poured from a brass pot and would flow directly from his head to another brass container that was clasped around the customer's neck. [Initially] I was delighted with this first job. In the evening my brother Khalil would pass by in the company of Muhammad al-Maddah, a *qabadayy* [tough guy] and grocer from Mahallat Bab al Amud. Muhammad was initiating Khalil into the arts of manhood, and both of them would take me to their *odah* (garçonnière), where we would play the tambourine and sing.[19]

Wasif learned creative truancy during this period. He would escape his master's shop to listen to the 'oud played by Hussein Nashashibi at another barbershop—that of a certain Abu Manuel, whose shop was owned by the Nashashibi family. It was during this period that Wasif's obsession with 'oud performance began and he started to seek out musical instruction.

Wasif's first paid job, as a clerk in the municipality of Jerusalem in charge of recording contributions for the Ottoman war effort, was arranged by his patron, Hussein Effendi. After a short bout of service in the Ottoman navy, Wasif resumed his career in the municipality at the end of the war, when he was promoted to the position of court clerk in the Ministry of Justice, serving under Judge Ali bey Jarallah in Mascobiyyeh. After the death of Hussein Effendi (whom Wasif called "my second father"), Wasif resigned from his job at the court in order to help Hussein's widow, Um Salim, with the administration of the Husseini estates in Deir Amr.

Hussein Effendi, who had served as mayor from 1920 to 1934, was succeeded by Ragheb Bey al-Nashashibi, after the position was briefly filled by Isma'il al-Hussaini and Musa Kazim al Husseini. Ragheb was an amateur 'oud player and socialite who hired Wasif to give 'oud and singing lessons to him and his mistress, Um Mansour. As compensation, Wasif was added to the payroll of the Tax Bureau with a monthly salary of twenty Egyptian pounds. At the end of each month, Wasif would go to the Regie (tobacco state monopoly) Department and collect his salary, without being required to perform any further duties. Wasif's relationship with the Husseini family, and later with the Nashashibis (who became ascendant under British rule), helped him to pursue his career as a musician while maintaining a steady income from public coffers. Here is how he describes one of those many jobs:

> Musa Kazim Pasha, then mayor of Jerusalem, sent for me through Sergeant Aref al-Nammari. I went to meet him in city hall, then located at Jaffa Gate. He rebuked me for staying out of touch since the death of the late Hussein Effendi and asked about my family, especially about the health of my mother. Then he appointed me as assistant inspector [mufatish baj] with a temporary income of twenty-four Egyptian pounds per month, until the position was institutionalized. I kissed his hands and signed for the new position working under the late Abdel Qader al Afifi Effendi. My job consisted of the following: I had to inspect all animals sold in Jerusalem at the animal market [suq al-Jum'a] every Friday near the Sultan's Pool area. I was to work under the supervision of the late Mustafa al-Kurd, known as Abu Darwish, a top expert in this fine art. Abu Darwish would say to me, "Do not burden yourself! Sit there, drink your coffee, and smoke the arghileh. I will do all the inspection and will hand you the receipts on a daily basis." This suited me very well. I would start my day at the Ma'aref Café with friends smoking the arghileh until ten or eleven in the morning, when Abu Darwish would arrive and order his first smoke, then his second, and then his third. Then he would pull five pounds from his 'ajami belt: "Here, Wasif Effendi, this is your spending money for the day," he would say, and then he would pay me another sum against a signed receipt, which I would hand over to the municipality.[20]

Wasif was entering adulthood, but he had not quite reached the age of reason. He was overwhelmed by what he called this "period of total anarchy in my life." He lived like a vagabond, sleeping all day and partying all night. "I only went home to change my clothes, sleeping in a different house every day. My body was totally exhausted from drinking and merrymaking. One moment I am in Mahallat Bab Hatta . . . in the morning I am picnicking with members of Jerusalem's 'ayan families, the next day I am holding an orgy with thugs and gangsters in the alleys of the Old City. My only source of livelihood was my salary from the Regie

Department arranged by Ragheb Bey." When his mother complained
that he came home late at night, if at all, he retorted with the famous line
"He who seeks glory must toil the nights" (Man talaba al-ʿula sahar al-
Layali).[21] Wasif thus became involved in a libertine popular culture and
café scene, an aspect of Jerusalem life hidden in previous accounts of the
city's modernity. His account of his childhood and adult life in the city
tell us about the advent of modernity in this urban context and hint at
the complex nature of the interactions between Jerusalem's communities.

URBAN LIFE AND COMMUNAL BOUNDARIES

Wasif's vivid depiction of daily life in Mahallat as-Saʾdiyyeh (situated between Bab es-Sahira and the Via Dolorosa) during the first decades of
last century is one of the most valuable records of Palestinian urban life
that exists anywhere. Wasif periodizes and describes in detail, for example, the bourgeoisification of domestic living arrangements:

> During the summer months [of 1904] we would sit around the lowered
> table for the main meal. Food was served in enameled zinc plates. That year
> we stopped eating with wooden spoons imported from Anatolia and Greece
> and replaced them with brass ones that were oxidized periodically. We re-
> placed the common drinking taseh tied to the pottery jar with individual
> crystal glasses. In 1906 my father acquired single iron beds for each of my
> siblings, thus ending the habit of sleeping on the floor. What a delight it
> was to be relieved of the burden of having to place our mattresses into the
> wall alcoves every night.

For the social historian, Wasif Jawhariyyeh's diaries also provide a
contemporary record of the growth of the city outside the city walls.
Although Sheikh Jarrah, Yemin Moshe, and Waʾriyyeh were established
before his time, Wasif describes the growth of Musrara and the Mascobiyyeh neighborhoods along Jaffa Road during his boyhood, followed
by Talbieh and Katamon in the 1930s. These expansions—and the similar one that preceded them in Baqʾa—saw hundreds of families move to
modern tiled buildings built of mortar fortified by iron railings. It was in
these neighborhoods that the implements of modernity were introduced:
electricity, first in the Notre Dame compound just opposite the new gate;
the automobile on Jaffa Road; the motion picture projector; and, above
all, the phonograph, which introduced Jawhariyyeh to the world of
Salameh Hijazi and Sayyid Darwish.

Jawhariyyeh's cognitive map of Jerusalem's neighborhoods and his
identification of communal boundaries prevalent in his youth clearly

suggest that the division of the city into four confessional quarters was a late development. The British demarcated the new boundaries in order to preserve an equilibrium between the city's four ancient communities. The basis of this balance was the preservation of the status quo in the administration of Jerusalem's holy sites, which was carefully negotiated during the late Ottoman period and elaborated and codified during early Mandate rule.

The diaries implicitly challenge this notion of regulating relations between Jerusalemites by dividing them into four different religious and ethnic habitats. Wasif's recollection of daily life in the alleys of the Old City shows the weakness of this concept in two respects. First, it suggests that there was no clear correspondence between neighborhood and religion, and instead that there was a substantial intermixing of religious groups in each quarter. Second, the primary unit of habitation was the *mahallat*, the basic unit of social demarcation, within which a substantial amount of communal solidarity was exhibited. Such cohesiveness was clearly articulated in periodic social visitations and by the sharing of ceremonies, including weddings and funerals, but also by active participation in religious festivities. These solidarities undermined the fixity of the confessional system with a premodern (perhaps even primordial) network of affinities.

But the confessional boundaries were also being undermined by the rise of the nationalist movement in Palestine, initially in the context of the constitutional Ottoman movement at the turn of the century, and then after the 1908 coup, which received a lot of support among intellectual circles in Jerusalem, and later by the anti-Turkish trends within greater Syrian nationalism. Such shifts are depicted in Wasif's memoirs in a haphazard and selective manner. Jawhariyyeh—who was not involved in any political party but was an Ottoman patriot and later a Palestinian nationalist—clearly believed that the move toward modernity (and presumably post-Ottoman nationalism) was linked to the rising middle classes' migration to the outskirts of the city.[22] Already by mid-nineteenth century members of the notable clans had established bases in Sheikh Jarrah to the north and in Wa'riyyeh to the south.[23] Within the Jewish population, there was a similar move originating with the construction of the new neighborhoods of Mia Shi'arim and Yemin Moshe—signaling a separation of ways between modern Palestinian Arab nationalism and Jewish communal consciousness, even before the entrenchment of Zionism among the city's Jewish population.[24]

Jawhariyyeh's relationship with the Jewish community of Jerusalem is complex. His narrative is no doubt colored by memories of clashes

between Palestinian Arabs and the Zionist movement during the 1920s
and 1936–39, and his perspective is mediated by the events of the 1948
war. But he also recalls a different era, when as a teenager he participated
in the events of Purim (which he describes in great detail, including the
costumes he used to wear with his brother Khalil) and took part in family picnics in the spring to the shrine of Shimon as-Siddiq in Wadi al-Joz.
He also mentions a number of Sephardic families with whom his family
was on intimate terms, including the Eliashar, Hazzan, Anteibi, Mani
(from Hebron), and Navon families.

Deeply involved in the affairs of the Arab Orthodox community,
Jawhariyyeh nevertheless exhibits a unique affinity for the Muslim culture
of his city. His narrative compels us to rethink the received wisdom about
Jerusalem's communal and confessional structure in Ottoman times. For
example, endless stories—many scandalous and satirical—draw a picture
of the profound coexistence of Christian and Jewish families in the heart
of what came to be known as the Muslim Quarter. This was not merely
the tolerant cohabitation of protected *dhimmi* minorities, but rather a
positive engagement in the affairs of neighbors whose religion was coin-
cidental to their wider urban heritage. There is no doubt that the
Jawhariyyeh family, though deeply conscious of its Orthodox heritage,
was immersed in Muslim culture. Jiryis made his sons read and memorize
the Qur'an at an early age. When he died, in September of 1914, he was
eulogized by Khalil Sakakini ("with the death of Jawhariyyeh, the era of
wit has come to an end") and by Sheikh Ali Rimawi, who lamented, "I
cannot believe that Jawhariyyeh's soul will remain in Zion [Cemetery] . . .
for tonight surely it will move to Mamillah [the Muslim cemetery]." This
attitude clearly transcended the normative rules of coexistence at the time.

Many of Jawhariyyeh's anecdotes challenge social and religious
taboos and would seem unthinkable in today's puritanical atmosphere.[25]
An example is the anecdote titled "A Dog's Religion":

> My father was strolling with his intimate companion Salih al-Jamal, who
> died a bachelor. They passed several elderly gentlemen who were sitting by
> the wooden niche built by the municipality opposite the special opening
> constructed at Jaffa Gate to receive the German emperor. After they saluted
> the men, a dog happened to pass by. One of the notables asked my father,
> "Ya Abu Khalil, would you say this dog is Muslim or Christian?" This
> question was an obvious provocation since the enquirer was a well-known
> Muslim, and my father was clearly a Christian. But his quick wit saved him
> from aggravating the situation further: "It should be easy to find out, my
> dear sir. Today, Friday, is our [i.e., the Orthodox] fasting day. You can
> throw him a bone. If he picks it up, then he is definitely not a Christian."[26]

CULTURAL HYBRIDITY: A CHRISTIAN RAMADAN
AND A MUSLIM PURIM

The Jawhariyyeh diaries invite the reader to share a world of religious syncretism and cultural hybridity that is difficult to imagine in today's atmosphere of ethnic exclusivity and religious fundamentalism. It was a prenationalist era in which religious groups incorporated the Other in their festivals and rituals. Jawhariyyeh describes the feast of Easter/Pessah as an occasion for joint Muslim, Christian, and Jewish celebrations. He details the Muslim processions of Palm Sunday (which proceeded from the Abrahamic Mosque in Hebron toward Jerusalem). The festival of Nebi Musa is recalled as a Muslim popular celebration that merged with the Christian Orthodox Easter. The fantasia of Sabt enNour (Fire Saturday, commemorating the resurrection of Christ) was the greatest popular Christian celebration in Palestine, and was closely coordinated with Muslim folk festivals. Purim was celebrated by Christian and Muslim youth in Jewish neighborhoods, and Wasif describes in detail the costumes they wore on this occasion. Twice a year Muslim and Christian families—including the Jawhariyyeh family—joined the Jewish celebrations at the shrine of Simon the Just in Sheikh Jarrah (an event known as ʿshatʾhat al-Yahudiyyaʾ, or "The Jewish Outing"), where "Haim the ʿoud player and Zaki the tambourine player would sing to the accompaniment of Andalusian melodies."

But the greatest celebrations of all happened during Ramadan. Wasif devotes a substantial section of his diaries to the street festivals, the foods, and the dramatic displays of *qara qoz* (shadow plays) and *sanduq al ʿajab* (magic lantern shows). Many of the shadow plays were performed in a mixture of Ottoman Turkish and Aleppo dialects, and some included daring social satire and veiled political criticism of the regime, although Wasif does not explicitly mention these displays of dissent. Several manufacturers of goods and sweets shops (such as Zalatimo) used the performances to introduce commercial presentations sung by the shadow players, in order to enhance their sales.

The city also celebrated seasonal events that were not tied to religious feasts. Wasif identifies two such "secular" occasions: the summer outings *(shatʾhat)* of Saʾed wa Saʾeed, and the spring visits to Biʾr Ayyub. In the pre–World War I era, Saʾed wa Saʾeed became the choice location for the Old City's Christian and Muslim families to picnic on hot summer afternoons. These excursions were especially encouraged by the growth of new mansions around Musrara and the American Colony area. The

picnickers consumed large quantities of 'araq and food during these outings, which usually lasted until late in the evening, when revelers had to
return before the city gates were closed. In the spring, similar parties
were held at Bi'r Ayyub, at the springs of Lower Silwan, where Jerusalem
families found a reprieve from the severe winters of the Old City.

With the implementation of the terms of the Balfour Declaration during the British Mandate, this era of religious syncretism came to a close.
Palestinian nationalism—previously a secular movement—started to become infused with religious fervor. The new colonial authority interpreted
the protocols regarding religious control and access in terms of confessional exclusivity. Christians were banned by military edict from entering
Islamic holy places, and Muslims were excluded from Christian churches
and monasteries. It had been customary for young Jerusalemites of all religions to picnic in the green meadows in the Haram area, but now the
area was off-limits. Wasif describes an adventure on an April day in 1919,
during the early days of the British military government, when he passed
as a "Musilman" to the Indian Guards of the Haram area, while his blue-
eyed companion Muhammad Marzuqa was barred because Wasif explained to them that he was Jewish.

The complexity of Jerusalem's Ottoman identity is also shown in
Wasif's account of his involvement with the Red Crescent Society, which
was founded in 1915, ostensibly to garner support in Palestine for the
Ottoman armed forces against the Allies.[27] Through public musical
events and direct solicitations, the Red Crescent Society was able to raise
substantial funds for the war effort. Jawhariyyeh also believed that the
group could create a bridge between the interests of the Jewish community in Palestine and the Ottoman government before the appearance of
Zionism as an active force. Both Ibrahim Entaibi, the director of the Alliance Israelite school system in Jerusalem, and a Miss Landau—
described as "the liaison between the Jewish community in Jerusalem
and the Ottoman military leadership"—were pivotal in cementing those
ties. With this objective, they mobilized a large number of young
Jerusalem women, who wore ceremonial Ottoman military uniforms
with a red crescent insignia, to solicit contributions for the army. Wasif
describes several of them as "attractive ladies" who developed intimate
relations with high-ranking Ottoman officials: Miss Tenanbaum ("one
of the most beautiful Jewish women in Palestine")[28] became the mistress
of Jamal Pasha, commander of the Fourth Army (after the war she married Michael Abcarius, the famous Jerusalem attorney); Miss Sima al-
Maghribiyyah became the mistress of Sa'd Allah Bey, the commander of

the Jerusalem garrison; and Miss Cobb became the mistress of Majid Bey, the *mutasarrif* (governor) of the city. During the war years, personal as well as political links thus played a part in the complex interaction of Jerusalem's communities. Through his literary and enormously entertaining narrative of the events, Wasif reveals the radical transformations that were encompassing Palestinian and Syrian society in that period: the emergence of secular Arab nationalism, the separation of Palestinian national identity from its Syrian context, and the enhancement of Jerusalem as a capital city.

MUSIC AND MODERNITY

The memoirs devote an extended section to musical and artistic life in Jerusalem during the Ottoman period. Wasif provides a long list of 'oud makers, 'oud players, dancers, and singers. Many of these musicians performed as a family at local weddings, and later—during the Mandate—in cafés and cabarets outside the walled city. In combination with his special compendium on the typology of musical traditions that prevailed in Palestine at the turn of the century, Jawhariyyeh's observations provide us with an original and unique source on the modernization of Arabic music in Bilad ash-Sham and the influence of such great innovators as Sheikh Yusif al-Minyalawi and Sayyid Darwish on provincial capitals like Jerusalem.[29]

The members of Wasif's household were amateur musicians, 'oud players, and sophisticated listeners who did not restrict their musical interests to any particular religious community. Jiryis treated Qur'anic incantations as a form of music and taught his children to distinguish a good *adhan* (call to prayer) from a bad one. Once Jiryis led a delegation from Haret as-Sa'diyyeh to the Awqaf Department to request the replacement of a local imam whose voice he could not stand. When the official in charge questioned Abu Khalil's credentials as a Christian to request the removal of the *mu'adhen,* he responded in verse that was replete with double entendre:

> I hear the call to player in a voice, which keeps buzzing in my ears . . .
> I wondered as my ears were humming,
> Is this a sacred prayer, or did he mean to damage my ears [adhana]?[30]

When it was pointed out to him that the *mu'adhen* was a poor orphan who had a large family to support, the elder Jawhariyyeh suggested that they relocate him to the mosque by the American Colony (Sa'ed wa

Sa'eed), where there were fewer people living to suffer from his voice.[31] The people of the Awqaf Department were so amused by this outrageous attitude that they obliged Jawhariyyeh and replaced the sheikh.

Wasif also performed or associated with a number of Jewish musicians (p. 64), including Shihadeh, Badi'a Masabni's 'oud player. He also mentions the prominent role played by groups of Aleppo Jews, known as Dallatiyyeh, who resided in Jerusalem and were choral musicians who performed Andalusian music in weddings of Jerusalem Arabs (p. 155). Before the onset of the Mandate, Wasif used to play in a number of Jewish communities surrounding Jerusalem (pp. 327 ff.). In one such episode, he accompanied an Ashkenazi choral group at the house of Khawaja Salmon, the tailor from Montefiore (a neighborhood also known as Yemin Moshe), performing what appears to be Oriental music. The group's Arabic rendition of a well-known skit at the time ("Na'im Na'im hal-Rihan") was so convoluted that Wasif assumed it was "a new Ashkenazi ballad." His mock Ashkenazi version of this song became a popular and often-performed item in his own comical repertoire. "This," he adds sadly, "was before the onset of the cursed Balfour Declaration" (p. 328).

A self-taught chronicler, Wasif had a photographic memory that enabled him to recall not only the dramatic (the entries of Jamal Pasha and Lord Allenby to Jerusalem, for example), but also the quotidian thrill of the seemingly mundane. As Wasif forged for himself a local reputation as one of the city's foremost 'oud players and composer-musicians, he immersed himself in Jerusalem's musical and artistic scenes. Playing in the mansions of urban notables, he recorded—with great wit and satire—the musings and tribulations of the city's patricians and paupers.

What emerges from Wasif's writings is an intimate portrait of Jerusalem's Ottoman modernity at the very moment when Zionism was about to clash with an emerging Palestinian nationalism. Wasif's memoirs often view this modernity through the lens of his musical interests. He recounts the introduction of the phonograph and motion picture projector to the city's cafés in 1910, and the wonderment he experienced as he saw moving images for the first time in the Russian compound. In 1912 he saw for the first time a horseless car (a Ford) driven by Mr. Vester of the American Colony at the Municipal Park by Jaffa Street. In the summer of 1914 he rode a donkey with his father to Baq'a, in Jerusalem's southern suburbs, to watch the landing of an Ottoman military airplane. Unfortunately, the plane crashed in Samakh (Tiberius), and its two Turkish pilots were killed. Wasif composed a special eulogy in their honor, which, he claims, was sung throughout the country.

Jawhariyyeh's writings introduce us to the rich social milieu of Jerusalem in the postwar period and the early 1920s, which can only be described as hedonistic. Nightly episodes of drinking, dancing, and sometimes hashish smoking repeatedly occurred throughout the era. Wasif's family made a significant contribution to this milieu with the 1918 opening of Café Jawhariyyeh, near the Russian compound at the southern entrance of Jaffa Road. Wasif's brother Khalil brought to this café-bar the skills he had acquired in Beirut while serving in the Turkish army. These included serving a special *mezze* menu that included ʿaraq and ice water, the latter a new innovation for Jerusalem, made possible by the introduction of electric power. Within months after its opening, the café became a major attraction for pleasure seekers all over the city and was renowned for hiring the best singers in the country, including Sheikh Ahmad Tarifi, Muhammad al-ʿAsheq, Zaki Effandi Murad, and Badiʿa Masabni. Wasif's association with the Syrian Lebanese cabaret dancer Badiʿa Masabni and her husband Najib al-Rihani dates to this period.[32] Masabni used to visit Jaffa periodically in the summer en route from Cairo to Beirut, and she occasionally came to Jerusalem. Wasif initially met her in the summer of 1920 (p. 361), when she performed at the al-Maʾaref theater-café just outside Jaffa Gate. He describes several of her risqué song and dance sketches, performed in what he terms "transparent costume." She also sang several Sayyid Darwish songs, which were very popular—especially her social satire of the rich, "Il Haq ʿal Aghniya." One stanza often moved her audience to ask for encores:

Eimta baqa nshuf qirsh al-sharqi
Yifdal bi baladuh u-mayitlaʾshi

When will we ever see the piastre of the Eastern man
remain in his homeland and not depart [to Europe]

Wasif, Badiʿa, and others often met at intimate parties, either in the mansions of Jerusalem notables such as Fakhri Nashishibi and Mustafa al-Jabsheh,[33] or in the Hotel St. John. Heavy drinking and cannabis enhanced the atmosphere of these evenings, and both Masabni and Rihani habitually used cocaine. On one occasion Wasif himself accompanied Badiʿa on his ʿoud during an all-night party that started at the Jawhariyyeh Café and continued at his father's house—a night that he fondly documented with photographs. Badiʿa was one of several Egyptian and Lebanese performers with whom Wasif associated, a group that also included Salameh Hijazi, Daʾud Husni, and Sheikh Yusif al-Minyalawi.[34]

Many of these singers became popular in Palestine with the importation of the new music machines: first the cylindrical wax record machine, and then the hand-cranked gramophone using 78-rpm vinyl records that Wasif calls "Edison phonographs." At the beginning of the First World War there were only ten such gadgets in Jerusalem, and each cost about twenty-five French pounds—a small fortune—which made them accessible to only a small number of owners.[35] During the war several Jerusalem cafés began to attract customers by purchasing phonographs and playing selected pieces on demand:

> I would take a *matleek* [the smallest Ottoman coin] from my father and go to Ali Izhiman's café near Damascus Gate. A blind man by the name of Ibrahim al-Beiruti operated a phonograph in Izhiman's café. The machine was raised on a wooden cabinet full of 78-rpm records and covered by red velvet to protect it from the evil eye. I used to throw my *matleek* in a brass plate and cry to the blind man, "Uncle, let us hear 'Ballahi Marhamatan wa-Sabran lil-Ghad,'" by Salameh Hijazi. The blind man would immediately pull the requested record from the cabinet—only God knows how—and would play it on the phonograph. Later, my music teacher Kamil al-Qal'i used to say, "Listening to this music is like eating with false teeth!"

This postwar libertinism of the early Mandate era was not a novelty; Wasif's memoirs also recount his involvement in similar cultural spheres during and before the war. Wasif was blessed with an exquisite voice that placed him in high demand for performances at weddings, even when he was a teenager. His eternal love, however, was the 'oud, which by 1918 Wasif claims he had mastered enough to make him one of the most sought-after players in Palestine. He played primarily for members of the city's elite, usually in special homes kept by and for their mistresses. Several members of Jerusalem's patrician families—including the Husseinis and the Nashashibis—kept special apartments for their mistresses (many of them Greeks, Armenians, and Jews) in suburban areas of the new city. The most famous of these concubines was Persephone, a Greek-Albanian seamstress who in 1895 became the mistress of Hussein Effendi al-Husseini. She lived in a special apartment on Jaffa Road and used her clout with Hussein Effendi to trade in cattle in Beit Suseen and Deir Amr—both Husseini estates. Wasif became her musical companion and helped her market *za'tar* (thyme) oil. When Hussein Effendi became mayor of Jerusalem in 1909, he distanced himself from Persephone and gave her permission to marry Khawaja Yenni, a Greek confectioner. During the war Persephone became sick, and after her husband deserted her she was brought to the Jawhariyyeh household, where Wasif took care of her until her death. The Jawhariyyeh diaries relate numerous episodes of festive events spent in the company of members of the social elites and their concubines. Muslim, Christian, and Jewish entertainers all performed at these events.

Another feature of cultural life in Ottoman Jerusalem recounted in the diaries is the *odah,* a bachelor's apartment equivalent to the French garçonnière. It was customary for single middle-class men from the Old City to rent a furnished one-room apartment where they would spend their evenings playing cards, smoking, drinking, and—during the long winter nights—participating in 'oud sessions. The apartments were also used to conduct love affairs, or to bring in the occasional prostitute. The *odah* did not necessarily have a negative reputation, although it is clear from Wasif's narrative that older family members, and especially female ones, were not privy to what took place in them. Jawhariyyeh lists a number of well-known *odahs* in the Old City and in Sheikh Jarrah, where he used to perform. For several years he had a key to Hussein Hashem's *odah* behind Mamillah Cemetery, where he used to entertain "Russian and Greek ladies" in the company of Ragheb al-Nashashibi (later the mayor of Jerusalem) and Isma'il al-Hussaini.

These episodes compel us to rethink the image of Jerusalem at the turn of the century. It is often (falsely) characterized—by visitors and natives alike—as a grim, conservative, and joyless city. ("The only thing he ever said about it [Jerusalem] was that it reminded him of death," says Edward Said about his father's recollections of the city.)[36] How do we account for this incongruity? We have to remember that Jerusalem was a city of religion, but not an excessively religious city. In other words, its religious status generated a large number of industries and services that catered to a visiting population of pilgrims, but its native population was not necessarily more religious than those of other urban centers in the hill country. Nablus, Hebron, and Nazareth, for example, all had decidedly more religious reputations than Jerusalem.

Jawhariyyeh's narrative comes from an era of the city's history when class boundaries and seignorial privilege created an atmosphere in which the upper crust felt relatively insulated from the moral judgments of the public. In many cases they even flaunted their behavior without fear of retribution, as with their public drinking and their keeping of mistresses. Another source of protection was that Jerusalem was still a reasonably closed city, exhibiting limited influx from the surrounding villages or from Mount Hebron. Peasant migrants who arrived later exercised a conservative influence on the city's norms, for which it became renowned.

During the late Ottoman and early Mandate period, however, the thriving cultural scene of *odahs*, cafés, and cabarets described by Jawhariyyeh was an integral part of Jerusalem's popular culture.

CONCLUSION: SYNCRETIC RELIGION AND SECULAR CULTURE

Jawhariyyeh's memoirs contest the conventional picture of Jerusalem as a grim and conservative city dominated by religious organizations and institutions of pilgrimage. They illustrate the syncretic character of popular religion in the city, in which popular celebrations and processionals were manifested as shared popular celebrations by members of the three religious communities. This sharing occurred both at the level of popular involvement in the activities of the Other, as well as in the presence of deities and saints such as Saint George (al-Khader) and Saint Elijah (Nabi Elias), whose veneration was common to all three communities. For example, Jawhariyyeh describes how biblical prophets such as Moses and Reuben became both popularized and Islamicized in these ceremonials.

The life of Wasif Jawhariyyeh underscores the significance of aristocratic patronage in the late Ottoman period for the survival and success of musicians and other performers. In this case, patronage involved the securing of employment possibilities (municipal jobs, often on paper) and the provision of entertainment venues (the mansions of the upper classes and wedding ceremonies), as well as intercession with the central authorities in order to secure periodic leaves from army service and promotions. The memoirs demonstrate the extent to which the patricians of Jerusalem and other regional capitals were integrated into the Ottoman system, and the amount of clout they had in influencing the securing of administrative jobs and seeking the intercession of military officers during the war period to secure favors.

The diaries also bear witness to the emergence of a new and *secular* middle-class celebratory culture. This popular culture was enhanced by the spread of secular education (both missionary and state-supported) and the movement of the new professional and salaried classes to the new city outside the city walls just before the First World War. A new cultural space was opened through the proliferation of cafés and institutions of public performance involving musicians and singers visiting Palestine from Egypt and Syria. Local vocal and instrumental performers acquired a multiplicity of new audiences, in part because of the diffusion of forms of musical entertainment and technology, including the availability of the phonograph and vinyl musical records. Of the new cultural spaces, the public café-cabaret was the most significant, but they also included performances by Ottoman army military bands, wedding and betrothal ceremonies, and private functions at the bachelor apartments of the upper classes. Traditional celebrations of popular holidays, such as Nebi Musa festivals and Sabt enNour rituals in Jerusalem, were now enhanced by the spread of modern transport routes and vehicles. The contrast between these two features of modernity is striking: religious syncretism and hybridity gave way to new forms of ethnic nationalism in which the clash between the emergent territorial Zionism and Palestinian nationalism became more pronounced during the early Mandate period. On the other hand, the secular popular culture persisted well into the 1940s and beyond as Jerusalem became the capital of the country and attracted thousands of newcomers: job seekers, entertainers, entrepreneurs, civil servants, and villagers coming to the city in search of a new life.

CHAPTER 6

Lepers, Lunatics, and Saints

The Nativist Ethnography of Tawfiq Canaan
and His Circle

The separation of Arab and Jewish lepers in the Talbieh Leprosarium during the war of 1948 marked a defining moment in the annals of Jerusalem and the Arab-Israeli conflict. In its absurdity, the event encapsulated the depths to which the process of ethnic exclusion and demonization had sunk after decades of conflict between Jews and Arabs, settlers and natives. It also signaled the turning point at which the intellectual debate and popular sentiment about the future of the country and its nationhood began to crystallize around two separate and exclusive narratives of origin.

In the early 1940s Tawfiq Canaan, a Jerusalem doctor and noted authority on leprosy, ethnographer of Palestinian peasants, head of the Palestine Medical Association, and (briefly) president of the Palestine Oriental Society, became the director of the leprosarium, the only home in the Holy Land for those diagnosed with this dreaded affliction. By that time Dr. G. H. Armauer Hansen, of Bergen, Norway, had discovered the complex genealogy of the disease, and Canaan had studied it both as a medical condition and in its cultural context and had contributed to its eradication in Palestine. Leprosy had for generations been associated with the Holy Land and evoked in the popular imagination not only parables of healing, but also a rich and textured tradition of isolation, confinement, and exclusion that stretched back two millennia. It was therefore with a great deal of historical irony that the war of 1948 in Jerusalem brought about the expulsion of all Arab lepers—together with

Figure 4. Tawfiq Canaan's wedding photograph, Jerusalem, 1912. Canaan married
Margot Eilender, the daughter of a German
importer living in Ottoman Jerusalem.
© Canaan Collection, Birzeit University.

about 800,000 Palestinian non-lepers—to the eastern front. Jewish lepers remained in West Jerusalem, while Arab patients were taken from
Talbieh and marched first to a new location in Silwan, and then several
years later to Surda Mountain, north of Ramallah, where Dr. Canaan
was invited again to become the caretaker.[1]

Today this incident is hardly remembered, an unnoticed detail buried
in the saga of the 1948 war. Canaan's contribution to the eradication
of leprosy is also barely noted. In small scholarly circles he is known for
his contributions to the study of Palestinian peasants and ethnography.
But between the two World Wars, when most of his research was published, he and his circle of Palestinian ethnographers produced some important original work on popular culture in Palestine and the Arab
world in general.

This chapter will address features of this corpus that constitute a nativist ethnography of Palestine during the Mandate period. I use the term "nativist ethnography" (and "nativism" as an accompanying ideology) to refer to the attempt to establish sources of legitimation for Palestinian cultural patrimony (and implicitly for a Palestinian national identity that began to distance itself from greater Syrian and Arab frameworks). In this case these affinities were sought in primordial sources of identity. Interpretation of Palestinian history has always been amenable to selective borrowing from a versatile package of accumulated cultures in its ancient past. The Bible was a useful index to these "other" ethnicities—with the Canaanites and the Philistines (or their construction by their Israelite protagonists) heading the list.[2]

The term *nativism* has been used widely in the literature to identify movements and ideologies that are broadly advocative. For example, it has been defined as referring to "social movements that proclaim the return to power of the natives of colonized areas and the resurgence of native culture, along with the decline of the colonizers."[3] Frantz Fanon dwelled at length on the concept of return to native roots and the need to overturn the internalized colonial consciousness that is exemplified in emulating European culture.[4] The term later found more substantial elaboration in the literature on Négritude, which celebrated African popular cultural roots. In a recent study on Iranian intellectual reactions to the West, Mehrzad Boroujerdi addresses the "tormented triumph of nativism." Following Raymond Williams and Henry Christman, he defines nativism as the doctrine that calls for "the resurgence, reinstatement or continuance of native or indigenous cultural customs, beliefs and values. Nativism is grounded on such deeply held beliefs as resisting acculturation, privileging one's own 'authentic' ethnic identity, and longing for a return to 'an unsullied indigenous cultural tradition.'"[5] He periodizes the height of this movement in the third world to the post–World War II era of decolonization during which intellectuals from Southeast Asia and the Caribbean were attempting to assert their own identity and end "their condition of mental servitude [and] perceived inferiority complex vis-à-vis the West."[6]

Boroujerdi attributes the triumph of nativist ideologies to two developments: first, to the challenges posed by a globalized culture to the "life worlds" of traditional intellectual elites; and, second, to the entry of new popular classes (e.g., seasonal migrants, city-dwellers of rural origins) into the national political scene, assuring nativism of "a steady stream of new adherents, recruits and instigators."[7] While arming the nativist intellectuals with an arsenal against Eurocentric models of emulation, Boroujerdi castigates the movement for essentializing a presumed local culture that "sees everything in the context of the binary opposition between the authentic and the alien," and for a tendency among its adherents to fetishize local traditions. He refers to Edward Said's identification of the movement as "an infantile stage of cultural nationalism . . . often leading to a compelling but demagogic assertion about a native past, narrative or actuality that stands free from worldly time itself. One sees this in such enterprises as Senghor's negritude, or in the Rastafarian movement, or in . . . the rediscoveries of various unsullied precolonial Muslim essences."[8]

In North America, by radical contrast, *nativism* became the watchword in the 1830s and '40s for movements asserting the rights of early settlers (and very rarely of Native Americans) in favor of those of later immigrants, particularly Catholic immigrants.[9] More recently, Mahmoud Mamdani used the term as a feature of postcolonial citizenship emerging from problems of ethnicity in African tribal formations.[10]

It is obvious from the discussion above that the term *nativism* is used to refer to widely disparate notions of preserving cultural roots and their "authenticity." Some uses—such as that implemented by early English and German settlers in North America and notions of Négritude in West Africa—conflict with one another. I use it here in the sense described by Mehrzad, as a "resurgence and reinstatement of native or indigenous cultural customs . . . privileging one's own 'authentic identity.'" But unlike in the Iranian case, as we shall see, this movement in Palestine was not a reaction to Orientalist discourse, but an attempt to modify that discourse in favor of finding a niche within its confines.

Tawfiq Canaan and his colleagues did not use the term *nativism*, nor did they consciously think of themselves as belonging to an intellectual movement. They emerged as a group only in retrospect. They published most of their intellectual output in one major forum, the *Journal of the Palestine Oriental Society* (JPOS), whose lifespan corresponded to the life of the British Mandate itself (1920–48). Those present at the inaugural meeting of the society, on March 22, 1920, reflected on the future character and interests of the society. According to its first president, Pere Lagrange, the society owed its origin to the American Assyriologist Albert Clay, who conceived it as an instrument for fulfilling "a useful part in the new epoch in the study of the antiquities of the Holy Land."[11] The meeting was held under the auspices of Colonel Ronald Storrs, who was the military governor of Jerusalem and soon to be the founder and head of the Pro-Jerusalem Society, the association that was to bring Muslim, Jewish, and Christian Jerusalemites together to preserve the heritage of the city under the Mandatory government.

The journal reflected the intellectual interests of the membership: the history, philology, archaeology, and ethnography of Palestine—the last two disciplines being the dominant ones, if we consider the number of articles devoted to each. French and German biblical scholars were among the most prominent of the society's contributors, but the group also included a significant number of Palestinian Arabs and Jews. Among the latter we find Eliazar Ben Yehuda, the founder of modern Hebrew, who contributed to the journal an article about the Edumite language,[12] and Yitshak Ben Zvi, Ben Gurion's colleague in the labor Zionist movement. The latter was particularly interested in investigating Jewish residual cultural features in contemporary Palestinian villages.[13]

By far the largest number of ethnographers in the society, however—those whom I will here call Canaan's circle—were Palestinian Arabs.[14] The most prolific and significant figure among them was Tawfiq Canaan himself, but they also included writers with a wide range of talents: Khalil Totah, the pedagogue and historian who coauthored with Barghouti *The History of Palestine* (1922); Omar Saleh al-Barghouti, the lawyer and nationalist activist who contributed several studies on Bedouin lore and common law to the JPOS; Stephan Hanna Stephan, who made significant contributions on peasant notions of time and the periodization of the agricultural cycle; and Elias Haddad, who made contributions on blood revenge, peasant factions, peasant notions of hospitality, and peasant pedagogy. With the exception of Totah, who came from Ramallah, every one of these ethnographers was a Jerusalemite, by residence if not by birth. In a manner that replicated a similar tradition that emerged in central Europe (Poland, Hungary, and Austria) and Scandinavia (especially Finland) half a century earlier, Jerusalem became the arena for an intellectual circle that regarded the peasantry as the soul of the nation—the salt of the earth, uncontaminated by radical intrusions of technology and a Westernizing culture.[15]

Canaan and his circle were driven by one overriding preoccupation: that the native culture of Palestine and that of peasant society in particular, was being undermined by the forces of modernity.[16] They saw it as their task to document, classify, describe, and interpret this threatened culture. Implicit in their scholarship was another theme, which was made more or less explicit by Canaan himself: namely, that the peasants of

Palestine represent—through their folk norms and material artifacts—
the living heritage of all the accumulated ancient cultures that appeared
in Palestine (principally the Canaanite, Philistine, Hebraic, Nabatean,
Syrio-Aramaic, and Arab). Their conceptual assumptions were basically
essentialist and reductionist.[17] They postulated that peasant behavior
and norms, as manifested in their songs, sayings, norms, and practices,
reflect an earlier mode of existence whose language and time may have
been different, but whose content is essentially the same.[18] Most of them,
including the Muslims among them, in this regard held a notion that
might be called *biblical parallelism*—that is, they believed that many
Palestinian Arab popular traditions are modern and *residual* manifestations of daily life as it was described in the biblical narratives.

These essentialist assumptions did not prevent Canaan and his circle
from producing an ethnographic corpus that was rich in empirical detail
and textured in the manner it examined regional variations in peasant lore
all over Palestine. Tawfiq Canaan in particular managed to combine his
professional medical career with field trips to rural areas throughout
Palestine, where he gathered much of his folkloric material while recording his observations about disease patterns and their treatment. In this
sense the group differed substantially from travel writers who in their contemporary ethnographies attempted to show the "living Bible" in the
peasant traditions of colonial Palestine.[19] Among these foreign writers,
only the works of Gustav Dalman and Hilma Granqvist, both contemporaries of Canaan and the Palestine Oriental Society, show a similar sensitivity to the complexities of peasant society at the turn of the century.[20]
Canaan's work on the architecture of the peasant house, for example, is
a masterwork on the evolution of building styles, and their response to
both environmental factors and the peasant cosmology of the habitat.[21]

This search for nativist ethnography stands in stark contrast to the
post-Nakba folklorist revivalism among Palestinian intellectuals such as
Nimr Sirhan, Musa Allush, Salim Mubayyid, and the Palestinian Folklore Society of the 1970s.[22] Among the latter writers we witness a keen
attempt to establish pre-Islamic (and pre-Hebraic) cultural roots for a reconstructed Palestinian national identity. The two contending putative
roots in this patrimony are Canaanite and Jebusite cultures.[23] The former was clearly symbolized by the celebration of the Qabatiya Canaanite Festival by the Palestinian Ministry of Culture, the latter by the annual Musical Festival of Yabus.[24] Writing against what he termed
"Canaanite ideology," the critic Zakariyya Mohammad suggests that it
is an intellectual fad, divorced from the concerns of ordinary people:

We are witnessing today [at the end of the twentieth century] the height of Canaanism. Its metaphors have dominated our poetry, graphic arts, journalism, and festivals. The Palestine International Festival, for example, has adopted the phoenix as its emblem, assuming that it is a Canaanite bird. The Sebastiya Festival in Nablus concocted a procession of Canaanite cities in its opening celebration. Even Iz Ed Din al Manasra, the poet, has recently launched a "Canaanite initiative" to reconcile the Association of Jordanian Writers to the Union of Palestinian Writers. It looks like a holistic ideology. Its heroes are Baal, El, and Anat—imported from our antiquity to energize the symbolism of this new movement. . . .

I have to say that this ideology is based on an illusion. While it might be useful as paraphernalia to artistic creativity, it is a losing ideology when used to manage our conflict with the Zionist movement. For "Canaanism" concedes a priori the central thesis of Zionism. Namely that we are engaged in a perennial conflict with Zionism—and hence with the Jewish presence in Palestine—since the Kingdom of Solomon and before. Those who adopt Canaanism are actually seeking a Palestinian presence that precedes the claims of [Jewish nationalism] for itself. If Israel goes back one thousand years before Christ, then we go back much earlier than the ancient Hebrews. . . . Thus in one stroke Canaanism cancels the assumption that Zionism is a European movement, propelled by modern European contingencies.[25]

Much of Palestinian nationalist revivalist writings of this period was a reaction to Zionist attempts at establishing their own putative claims to the Israelite and biblical heritage. In doing so, the Jebusite-Canaanite revivalism of the 1970s and '80s had given up any attempt to relocate (or even relate) modern Palestinian cultural affinities to biblical roots. They seem to have abandoned this patrimony of biblical representation to Jewish nationalist discourse, in a paradoxical manner that reinforced the claims of their protagonists. Canaan and his group, by contrast, were not Canaanites.[26] They contested Zionist claims to biblical patrimonies by stressing present-day continuities between the biblical heritage (and occasionally prebiblical roots) and Palestinian popular beliefs and practices.[27]

It is paradoxical that earlier debates among Jewish nationalists reflected a heated search for nativist roots among the various groups of the Hebrew Yeshuv—both among the Zionists and the so-called Can'aanite (anti-Zionist) followers of Yonatan Ratosh. For example, the chief ideologue of the Zionists, Ber Borochov, claimed that Palestinian Arabs had no crystallized national consciousness of their own and were likely to be assimilated into the new Hebraic nationalism, precisely because, in his view, "the fellahin are considered in this context as the descendants of the ancient Hebrew and Canaanite residents 'together with a small admixture of Arab blood.'"[28] Similarly Ahad Ha'am wrote that "the Moslems [of Palestine] are the ancient residents of the land . . . who became Christians on the rise of Christianity and became Moslems on the arrival of Islam."[29] In 1918, David Ben Gurion and Yitshak Ben Zvi, writing in Yiddish, tried to establish that Palestinian peasants and their mode of life constitute the living historical testimony to Israelite practices in the biblical period. But the ideological implications of this claim became very problematic, and these writings were soon withdrawn from circulation.[30]

In turn, Canaan, writing at virtually the same time but from a Palestinian nationalist perspective, stressed the notion of Palestinian ethnography as a manifestation of a *Semitic* culture. In one of his earlier essays (1920), Canaan describes the belief in water demons as a "widespread belief in all Semitic countries. . . . [It holds that] springs, cisterns, and all running waters are inhabited."[31] When discussing the demoted status of women among peasants, he refers to the "dual function of traditional law affecting women as . . . a legacy from the earliest days of Semitic civilization."[32] He also keenly studied Palestinian popular religion and demonology to demonstrate that magical practices were common to Christian, Muslims, and Sephardic Jews.[33] As the discussion of the binary systems of belief evolve, it becomes clear in Canaan's analysis that the depository of these practices is the contemporary Palestinian peasant. He writes, "This representation of good against evil, white against black, angels against devils, light against darkness . . . and God against Satan is a very old idea in Semitic religions and we could not have it better pictured than as reproduced by the simple imagination of a Palestinian fellah."[34]

Canaan was skilled at framing his observations about peasant practices with copious references from the Old Testament and, less frequently, the Qur'an. The point here was not to show the unity inherent in the monotheistic texts, but to establish a historical continuity between pre-Islamic social and normative systems and the modern Arab rural lifestyle. But ultimately it was his ethnographic field observations that lent solidity and depth to his analysis of the changing mores of his subjects, with the biblical references acting as a historical backdrop.

STEPHAN'S BIBLICAL PARALLELS

Nowhere are these claims for the biblical affinities of modern Palestinian Arab practices as pronounced as in Stephan Stephan's intriguing study "Modern Palestinian Parallels to the Song of Songs."[35] Stephan was an archaeologist, the curator of the Palestine Museum, and a civil servant in the Mandate government. He was perhaps the least acknowledged figure in Canaan's circle. Nevertheless, he made several important contributions to Palestinian ethnography of the period. The first was his study of the Canticles, discussed here; the second was his study of madness among Palestinian peasants.[36]

The first study, on the Song of Songs, is ostensibly a study in literary aesthetics, but it is bold in its assertions and meticulous in its detailed examination of what was essentially an erotic popular repertoire. It attempts to compare the "ancient and modern modes of describing the beauty of men and women" over two and a half millennia.[37] Stephan describes "the striking resemblance between the old and the new, both in the expression of the ideas and in the grouping of words . . . [reflecting] the freshness and vigor of their imagery as well as the gloom of their passions in the nuptial and erotic pieces."[38] To examine this contrast he analyzes seventy-seven wedding, love, and bawdy songs from contemporary Palestinian popular lore—the vast majority of them originating in an urban environment—and systematically compares them with parallel passages in the Song of Songs. In doing so he analyzes the construction of the love song; the description of the physical attributes of the male and female beloved; the metaphoric use of plant lore, aromas, and attributes of nature in each collection; and so on. What makes his selection of ballads particularly interesting is that he lists variations on common melodies that he collected personally from the Jerusalem area, as well as from Jaffa, Nazareth, Nablus, and Tulkarem.[39] His conclusions are astounding. In contrast to love songs that we inherited from the written classical texts (Andalusian melodies and medieval love texts, for example), both the biblical Canticles and modern Palestinian Arab folksongs show uncanny textual resemblance, both in the structure of the language and in the features attributed to the beloved, particularly the female beloved:

> His love for her inspires him to describe her with a variety of pretty appellatives, common to both periods [biblical and Palestinian], such as dove, reed, an enclosed garden, a spring shut up, a fountain sealed, a garden fountain, a well of living water. He is captured by her beauty; first he considers her fair, and then as spotless. . . . [T]o him she is at the same time a rose in a flower garden, and a proud horse.
> . . . [H]er breasts, seemingly the most attractive part of her graceful person, are to the old singer like wine, even far better. We consider them as pomegranates and rarely as clusters of grapes. But in common parlance, "the groom may take one breast for a cushion and the other as quilt."[40]

Stephan then compares these descriptions to those we find in *Alf Leilah wa Leilah* (The Arabian nights), but here his comparison is not as thorough and systematic as his work on the Canticles.

> The face shines like the full moon. The form is slim, yet the body is plump, likened to a silver bar or ivory, as soft as the tail of a sheep. The eyes fascinate and captivate like those of the gazelle, and are painted with kohl . . . [and] the cheeks—rosy apples, with a freckle, which enhances their beauty. The teeth gleam like pearls, the lips are as sweet as honey or sugar. The breasts are budding; they are well rounded, like pomegranates, seductive, as white as ivory. The navel may hold an ounce of oil, and is like the bottom of a tiny coffee cup. The legs are round columns of choice marble, the thighs are cushions stuffed with feathers, and the nates are full and heavy as a heap of sand.[41]

In one area Stephan finds a significant gap between biblical and Palestinian aesthetics. Although the general theme of the two sets of ballads is "the mutual love of the sexes," he finds that the "beauty of the man is a subject almost neglected" in Palestinian popular lore.[42] While "in the Canticles the man is compared to a deer or a hart, in our days it is the wife to whom these attributes are solely applied. The palm tree and the bird are common to both parties."[43] Stephan makes no attempt to explain to the reader this striking divergence.

PEASANT MADNESS

"Lunacy in Palestinian Folklore" was published in 1925, three years after Stephan's study of the Canticles. It basically pursues two chief preoccupations of Stephan's previous essay and the Canaan circle in general: nativist roots and biblical parallels. Stephan also continues to examine love in the popular imagination and elaborates on a significant theme in the Song of Songs: love as a form of madness. He examines thirty-one manifestations of madness among Palestinian peasants, ranging from the condition of *junun* (a "state of madness," equivalent to "being in a fit of passion") to *'mukhtal ash-shu'ur'* (i.e., having a disordered mind). The latter is derived from *shi'r* (poetry), the *sha'ir* (poet) himself being seen as a kind of madman in popular culture. Stephan here makes an important conceptual contribution: in peasant lore, lunacy has divine attributes. God inflicts madness on you as a punishment for evil deeds. On the other hand, a madman is also possessed by the *djinn* (good or bad) and can be healed by exorcism. These countervailing interpretations create a tension (and sometimes a contradiction) in the popular interpretation of madness, since divine punishment and exorcism cannot be reconciled. Thus "lunacy is something divine" *(ahkam rabbaniyah)*, an ambivalent formulation that, according to Stephan, reflects this dilemma in the popular mind about madness.[44]

The most important cause of madness in peasant psychology is possession by *djinn*—a condition that is often brought about by the "transgression of universal moral laws."[45] But it is also caused by other non-normative transgressions, including defiling the dwellings of saints *(maqamat)*; a mother beating her child on the threshold of her house; pouring water out of doors; the use of aphrodisiacs with wine; and the inscribing of amulets to make an enemy mad.[46] Much of peasant lore on lunacy addresses the relationship between love, insanity, and hysteria. This is a theme that Stephan began to treat in his study of the Canticles but elaborates upon here:

> Some hold the opinion that love combined with any other sudden emotion, such as sorrow, grief, or fright, is apt to make a man mad. Paralysis is one of the serious manifestations caused by the irritation of the *djinn* by men. Epilepsy is another illness inflicted by the evil spirits (in this case *djinn tayyar*, flying *djinn*). Hysteria, melancholia, neurasthenia, etc. may also be attributed to the evil spirits. Then there are the non-lunatic symptoms caused by *djinn*, e.g., the nervous impotence of a husband, who temporarily cannot fulfill his marital duties, much against his will. During this period he is considered as being "bound up" by those spirits—*marbut*.[47]

Canaan analyzed the relationship between madness and possession in a different context—that of eccentric behavior exhibited by *darawish*, followers of Sufi cults. The *darwish* belongs to the lowest order of *awlia*' (saints). These are usually drawn to an external source of inspiration that leaves them in a trance. The *darwish* becomes so absorbed in this external calling that he neglects everything in favor of his inner calling. He abandons his outer condition and appears to the ordinary observer as childlike, simple, or even imbecile.[48] The etymology of the word *majdhub* is thus related to madness. It comes from *jadhab* (to be drawn, inspired). Thus a *majdhub* (attracted, drawn by an external calling) is a person who has taken leave of his senses, and hence is crazy or demented.[49]

In following a Sufi order, the member of a *tariqah* is possessed by the spirit of the good *djinn,* and is therefore drawn closer to the presence of God. In this condition the *darwish* acquires superhuman attributes. But the link between being mad and being saintly is also established. "Both the *majdhub* and *majnun* [are] inhabited by the spirits, and sharing many points of resemblances," argues Canaan, so "it is easily explicable that many insane persons are regarded by the people as *awlia*'."[50]

In this condition the *majnun* shares the same status as babies—they are on earth, but "at the same time in heaven." Canaan quotes the popular saying *"haki es-ghir haki weli"* (the talk of a child is the talk of the saint).[51] We might add here that like children and poets in Arab culture, the saint-madman is given leeway that is not afforded to ordinary human beings. The usual ethical rules are suspended and they are allowed to exhibit eccentric behavior and make utterances that would otherwise not be tolerated. They disrupt the routine of everyday life to inspire an extraordinary way of looking at the ordinary and the mundane.

CANAAN'S DEMONS

The ethnography of Tawfiq Canaan, although much wider in scope than that of Haddad, Stephan, and Barghouti, was preoccupied with peasant religiosity and belief patterns. He devoted much of his writings to popular demonology, which he treated "scientifically" as a mode of coping with the stressful aspects of the lives of peasants, who were held hostage to natural and human disasters. In his work we observe a link between a doctor's systematic attention to peasant ailments (disease patterns, modes of treatment, and herbology) and to the ideological aspects of folk medicine (uses of magic and magic potions, talismans, magic bowls, and the worship of saints). His concerns are reflected in his earliest writings on folk medicine, in which he attempted to link his training in dermatology and his study of leprosy with peasant practices throughout Palestine. Early in his medical career, in 1912, he published "Demons as an Etiological Factor in Popular Medicine."[52] Later he began to investigate the relationship between folk religion, magic, madness, and superstition. He collected a huge number of amulets and fear cups *(taset al rajfeh)*—mostly in lieu of payment for his treatment of patients in his frequent tours of rural Palestine.[53] He developed his thesis on peasant Semitic parallelism in five essays on religiosity: "The Child in Palestinian Arab Superstition," "Water and the Water of Life," "Modern Palestinian Beliefs and Practices Relating to God," "Light and Darkness in Palestinian Folklore," and "Arabic Magic Bowls." In 1930 he published a monograph on religion among the Bedouins of Wadi Musa (Petra), a work in which he examined the persistence of phallic worship from Nabatean paganism in contemporary local practices.[54]

The most systematic work on peasant religion by Canaan was his seminal *Mohammedan Saints and Sanctuaries in Palestine* (1927), which he published when he was elected president of the Palestine Oriental Society.[55] One can glean Canaan's "biblical nativism" from the introduction to this work. "The primitive features of Palestine are disappearing so quickly that before long most of them will be forgotten. Thus it has become the duty of every student of Palestine and the Near East, of Archeology and of the Bible, to lose no time in collecting as fully and accurately as possible all available material concerning the folklore, customs, and superstitions of the Holy Land."[56] He then goes on to list the conditions of modernity that are undermining these roots of Palestinian patrimony, juxtaposing an "uncontaminated Palestinian peasant culture" against an "unnatural" European culture:

> This change in local conditions is due to the great influences which the West is exerting upon the East, owing to the introduction of European methods of education, the migration of Europeans to Palestine, of Palestinians to Europe and especially to America, and—above all—to the influence of the Mandatory Power. The simple, crude, but uncontaminated patriarchal Palestinian atmosphere is fading away and European civilization, more sophisticated but more unnatural, is taking its place.[57]

This notion of a pure peasant culture that "remained virtually unchanged for thousands of years"[58] runs throughout Canaan's work and in that of his circle. Yet what one might call here a "nativist Orientalism" is modified considerably in his empirical analysis of peasant mores, which is a highly nuanced examination of local practices, regional variations, and changes in response to urban intrusions.

Canaan is careful to show that Palestinian Christians, Muslims, and Jews display similar attachments to popular saints and often share the same saint and the same shrine, as with al-Khader (Saint George) and Mar Elias (Saint Elijah). They also have similar ritual practices, even when these run counter to those of established religion, as we witness, for example, in rain processions in periods of drought.[59]

Mohammedan Saints and Sanctuaries in Palestine is a massive examination of shrines *(awlia')* and sanctuaries *(maqamat),* and the cults that articulate popular Islam in Palestine. Canaan examines the topography and history of these sites, their relationship to the agricultural cycle, and their healing attributes. Popular religion in Palestine is neither Islamic, nor Christian, nor Jewish, but a local magical adaptation of the sacred texts to the daily needs of peasants. Although local saints are ostensibly rooted in Muslim traditions, they are actually ennobled sheikhs who, after their death, have been elevated to sainthood. Canaan quotes C. R. Conder approvingly: "It is in the worship of these shrines that the religion of peasantry consists. Moslems by profession, they often spend their lives without entering a mosque, and attach more importance to the favour and protection of the village saint, than to Allah himself, or to Mohammad, his prophet."[60] Canaan reminds his readers that these same fellahin "are heirs and to some extent descendents of the heathen inhabitants of prebiblical times, who built the first high places."[61]

From his typology of saints and sanctuaries Canaan proceeds to explain how local *awlia'* and their sanctuaries become the core of peasant religiosity, and why the peasants become distanced from urban religion, which to them seems abstract and formalized:

> All *awlia'* were once human beings, who lived as we live, and experienced in their own flesh all miseries, difficulties, diseases and woes of our life. They also know human falsehoods and intrigues. Thus they feel with us in our afflictions and understand us better than God does. At the same time their anger can be more easily soothed and thus one always hopes, by taking the necessary precaution, to escape or moderate their punishment. This explains partly how they have gradually taken the place of God. More vows are made in their names, more offerings are brought to them and more help is asked from them than is the case with God. In reviewing the formulae used in oaths, vows, etc., this point becomes clear. The first recourse is always to them, while the Almighty is thought of only on especial occasions.[62]

Although this dethronement of God makes religion more accessible and responsive to the needs of the peasants, it is accomplished at the expense of involving the saints in their daily struggles. They reflect the peasants' political factions (known as Qays and Yemen), as well as their binary cosmology of good and evil, black and white, light and darkness, and male and female attributes. These distinctions are crucial in ordering the moral outlook of the peasants and their normative system. A critical distinction is made, for example, between "irritable" saints and those with forbearance *(nizqeen* versus *tawilin er-ruh).*[63] While tolerant saints show a great deal of patience with human frailties and give mortals time to fulfill their obligations toward others and their creator, irritable saints are ruthless about human shortcomings and exact severe punishment on those who trespass, make false oaths, or violate the shrine of the saint. In general, this distinction gives peasants a certain degree of latitude in their appeals for intercession, their search for healing powers, and their requests for the lifting of divine sanctions and the effect of the evil eye. The significance of irritable saints, however, becomes obvious in the dispensation of local justice.

> The irritable saints . . . do not show any pity to transgressors. This group of saints is therefore more feared and respected than the former group. When

a man is suspected of having committed a major crime, the judge may ask
the defendant to take an oath at the shrine of a well-known saint, who is always chosen from this class [the irritable saints]. When a person is maltreated and oppressed by an influential man, from whom he cannot get his
rights, he hurries to such an easily irritated *weli* and asks for his aid. Generally the saint is treated in such a way as to irritate him still further, as . . . in
treating the subject of oaths.[64]

The author shows that this manner of dispensing justice through invoking the judgment of irritable saints is common throughout the highlands
of Palestine and is not an isolated case.

Canaan attributes the extreme variety of saints and their differing
responses to peasants' appeals for intercession to the persistence since
prebiblical times of pagan religiosity in Palestine, with its stress on a hierarchy of demigods in conflict with one another. Since most irritable
gods tend to be *'adjamis* (outsiders), they have a lower degree of sanctity,
and therefore they have "inherited some characteristics of the heathen
local divinities of antiquity."[65] He also notes how evil spirits and demons
(djinn) dwell in the vicinity of holy shrines and must be placated in a
manner similar to that of good spirits. Their impact and intercessions are
even felt in the course of political events. Canaan narrates, for example,
several contemporary legends related to the defeat of the Ottoman army
and the victory of the British, which are attributed by local peasants to
the insensitivity of Turkish soldiers to the needs of Palestinian *djinn*.

LOCAL DEITIES AND MADMEN

Saints originate, as Canaan systematically illustrates from numerous anecdotes, as local leaders who are elevated to divinity after their death
rather than as resurrected biblical figures or residual Canaanite
demigods. They were often village sheikhs with a reputation for sound
judgment and intervening successfully in local disputes. Some were ringleaders who exercised a degree of military power against raiding
Bedouins or the encroachment of the state. Their powers continued to be
invoked after their death. This explains why, with very few exceptions,
such as that of al-Khader (Saint George), saints tend to be local figures,
with limited regional influence. Among those he cites are Mar Niqula
(Saint Nicholas) from Beit Jala, En-Nabi Saleh, from the village of the
same name, and the female saint Sitna el-Ghara, from Beit Nuba.[66] In addition to lifting injustices and treating individual ailments, the main ways
in which saints intercede are tied directly to the agricultural cycle: by

removing natural blights (attacks by locusts, earthquakes, droughts, and disease), invoking rain, and granting good harvests.

Canaan also describes the local nature of saints as a manifestation of ancestor worship. He lists the names of local leaders from all over Palestine who attained the title of *weli* (saint), which, interestingly enough, also means "patron" or "protector." The sons and grandsons of such protectors are also identifiable as sheikhs of great distinction, regardless of their achievement. This makes the *weli*/ancestor a local deity:

> They are not only the owners of the small piece of ground surrounding their tomb and shrine, but are the protectors of the properties of their descendants and [act as] the patrons of the whole village. Palestine has inherited from its heathen ancestors the idea that the whole country is not governed as a whole by any one deity, but that each locality has its own divinity. Although there may be several saints in one and the same village, only one of them is the real patron of the village. The resemblance of this belief with biblical statements is striking.[67]

In Canaan's classification system of saints, the hierarchy of *awlia'* mirrors the peasants' earthly order of patrons and sheikhs. The order begins with the higher divinities—prophets and messengers who are venerated but only barely accessible—and ends with the saintly sheikhs who are the peasant's own ancestors, or at least the village patron saints. And while the higher prophets are revered for their intercessionist powers, it is from lower saints, residing in the village *maqam,* that the common folk find solace and support against the injustices of the world. But it is only with the traveling *darawish*/madmen—followers of *tariqah*—that we see living saints who are personally known to the peasant and whose actions break up the routine and drudgery of daily life. "Whenever a *darwish* gets into ecstasy—while praying, dancing, or beating his drum—it is said that his spirit is absent with the *awlia'* or even with God himself, and his bodily actions become mechanical."[68]

In this context, "mechanical action" is an eminently suitable metaphor. In Canaan's religious ethnology it evokes the conventional mode of the peasant's existence, squeezed, as it were, between his servitude to the agricultural cycle and the relentless demands of his social obligations. The escapism, or rather the spiritual flight, of the *darwish,* his "attraction" *(indjidhab),* by contrast, takes the shape of insanity to the external observer, because he defies the mundane (the "mechanical") while seeming to perform it. In this way he challenges the conventional and discovers a new truth in his madness.

Canaan lived to see the dismantling of this system at the intellectual and physical levels with the dispersal of Palestinian peasants throughout the Arab world and the diaspora. Many of them replaced their patron saints with national martyrs, who were elevated to the level of national sainthood, as in the case of Jamjoum (hanged in Akka), Abdul Qadir al Husseini (killed in Qastal), and Izz ed Din al Qassam (killed in Ya'bad). But throughout the mountain villages of central Palestine, saints' tombs continue to inspire considerable allegiance from local worshipers—more often female than male, and more often elderly than young—vying, as it were, with newly built mosques that challenge their influence.

NATIVIST ETHNOGRAPHY AND PROTONATIONALISM

Virtually all the ethnographic work of Canaan and his colleagues was written in an implicitly functionalist vein. In particular, they saw the prescriptions of the customs and mores of popular culture as contributing to the continuity, stability, and integration of a perennial society—until it was disrupted by the intrusion of external forces: the modernity of the central Ottoman state, the forces of British colonialism and the Zionist movement, and, finally, the emergence of a Palestinian nationalist identity that undermined the sense of localism.

Like their central European and Nordic counterparts, those in Canaan's circle saw the peasantry as the repository of the national soul, and they perceived the city as the conduit of disruptive intrusions that undermined tradition. As in the central European folkloric tradition, a substantial body of Palestinian ethnography in the 1920s and '30s was devoted to the recording of peasant material culture: the agricultural cycle and its implements, the architecture and spatial allocations of the peasant house, saints' shrines and the organization of pilgrimages, and rural crafts and skills.

Canaan's ethnographic work appeared in a particular intellectual milieu that can be described as protonationalist. I use the term *protonationalist* because Palestinian nationalism during the Mandate period was still in its formative stage, emerging as it was from both the defeat of Ottoman decentralization and greater Syrian identity formation. The colonial regime imposed on Palestine two ideational parameters: that of geographic separation from its Shami (greater Syrian) boundaries, and a nascent (colonial) state formation that set it against the Zionist project in Palestine.

Moreover, Canaan and his colleagues were not writing for an Arab intellectual class, nor, certainly, were their comments directed at a nationalist base. Their nativist ideology was rarely articulated in Arabic. Writing primarily in English and German, they targeted a European audience that included the Mandate political elite and Western biblical scholars, archaeologists, and historians. Like George Antonius in the 1930s, they were challenging a colonial policy that questioned the authenticity of Palestinian roots in the land, and which they saw as giving credence to a putative Jewish nationalism on the basis of a Western biblical tradition that coincided with British imperial strategies.

By contrast, most Palestinian nationalist writers of the period, such as Muhammad Izzat Darwazeh, Awni Abdul Hadi, Musa Alami, Ajaj Nweihid, and many others, were rather oblivious to the writings of Canaan's circle and their nativist ideology.[69] For the nationalist writers, Palestinian claims to the land were based on self-evident assumptions of historic patrimony and did not need any nativist justifications. In the postwar period these claims were consolidated within a wider Arab nationalist secular framework. The Palestinian folklorist revival of the 1970s and '80s took these claims as a given, but its adherents had their own nativist ideology. Unlike those in Canaan's circle, they abandoned the search for biblical parallelism and focused their search instead on pre-Israelite, prebiblical roots—Canaanite, Jebusite, and Philistine.

During his lifetime Canaan was well known as a doctor, but his scholarship remained largely unread. The resurrection of his ethnographic work took place in the early 1970s, when the study of folklore became a linchpin of cultural resistance to Israeli occupation and settlement activity. Without exception these works on Canaan were hagiographic and uncritical. In the last two decades alone at least five different Arabic translations of his work have been published, each including appropriate acclaim for his achievements.[70] The writings of the rest of his circle—and particularly the original work of Stephan and Haddad—however, remain virtually unknown and unacknowledged.

The strength of Canaan's nativist ethnography lies in its sensitivity to the details of local practices, to variations over time (despite its claims about perennial peasant traditions), and to the interpretation of these practices in their wider social context. Above all, both Canaan and Stephan— in the best anthropological tradition—combined their intimate observations of peasant and urban popular practices with a textual analysis of the oral narrative. This textured and contextual approach is evident in Canaan's study of saints and sanctuaries discussed above, and in Stephan's treatment of popular erotic songs and his study of peasant madness. By contrast, the current corpus of folkloric ethnography is primarily based on

the codification of a recorded oral tradition that tends to reflect little variation across Palestine and is consciously aimed at preserving the "purity"
of that tradition. It has little or no sociological content. One reason for this
difference has to do with the erosion of village autarky, to the extent that
it existed at all at the turn of the twentieth century.

The context in which the new revival took place is the radical transformation of Palestinian (and Arab) rural society typified by visible in-
dicators: the relative decline of agriculture as a source of rural livelihood,
the massive movement of peasants to urban employment, the suburbanization of rural habitats, and the creation of hybrid lifestyles affected by
mass media, emigration, and formal education. The result has been the
linkage of the nationalist project with the study of folklore and the creation of a homologous and reified ethnographic corpus with little engagement with the dramatic economic changes that have affected contemporary Palestinian society. This is clearly noticeable in Barghouti's
extended lexicon of the peasant vernacular (published in 2001), which
presumes that there is one set of vernacular usages with little or no regional variation, and almost no urban or foreign influences.[71]

It is also a *reactive* nativism that sees itself as an instrument of the nationalist struggle with little concern for historical nuances. A good example of this phenomenon is Yabus, the Palestinian festival organization.
Yabus explains its objectives in choosing its title for the annual international musical festival in Jerusalem in direct ideological terms: "Yabus is
the primordial name of Jerusalem. It is derived from the Jebusites—a
Canaanite tribe that built the first city that evolved into modern
Jerusalem almost five thousand years ago. We have selected the name in
1995 at the founding of the festival in a contentious political atmosphere
that responds to the [Israeli-initiated] campaign of *Jerusalem 3,000*."[72]
The campaign was clearly a jibe at Ihud Olmert's municipal campaign
that publicized Israeli claims for the Hebraic origins of the city and ignored its antecedent pre-Israelite roots. But it also ignored any claims for
historical accuracy about the Jebusites, whose origins are dubious and
whose language and culture is most likely to have been non-Arab and
even non-Semitic.[73]

It is true that both Canaan's circle and current Palestinian nativist
ethnographers aimed at preserving a culture that was threatened with ex-
tinction. But while Canaan's ethnography examined a living tradition, the
more recent writings have created a "frozen" ethnography that aims
at celebrating and glorifying a tradition that no longer exists, or exists
only as part of a nationalist narrative that has little to do with artistic and

literary production in the Arab world today. The fate of Tawfiq Canaan's lepers with whom we started this chapter has made a full circle. Leprosy as a disease has been eliminated in Palestine and most of the world, but leprosy as a metaphor still haunts the nativist ethnography of his successors, and the country that Canaan and his colleagues tried so valiantly to preserve from its demons and saints—both irritable and forbearing.

CHAPTER 7

Sultana and Khalil

The Origins of Romantic Love in Palestine

In my wakefulness during the day, as I go about doing my
daily chores, I walk in the streets of New York listening to the
din of speeding trains, and of trams on the ground and
aboveground, and the sirens of ships, and the deafening
clamour of people piercing my ears, and the bustle of
streetcars and carriages, and the glitter. . . . I only come
around soaring in the skies of Jerusalem, over the school,
over the house that I love, and often over Artas and Kalona,
and Ein Karim, and Beit Jala. And when I go to sleep it is not
because I am sleepy, but because I wait for slumber to
overtake me. Not to sleep, but to get rid of the pains of
wakefulness, hoping to get rid of my heaviness, and hoping to
get rid of my body—to leave it in America, and to fly in
dreams to Jerusalem.

Khalil's Sakakini's letter to Sultana Abdo,
December 13, 1907

The recent release of Khalil Sakakini's diaries by his family is cause for
celebration. Close to 3,400 pages of handwritten memoirs constitute the
author's intimate record of his life from the moment he boarded the ship
in Jaffa to head toward his American exile (October 1907) until his second exile in Cairo, after he was displaced from his Katamon home in
West Jerusalem in the war of 1948.[1] Sakakini's diaries, a daily record
of his thoughts and presumably not intended for publication, are the
only such memoirs of a major modern Palestinian intellectual, and possibly any Arab writer, known to exist. This alone makes these diaries

Figure 5. Khalil Sakakini on the eve of his departure to
America in 1907. This is the picture he left with Sultana.
Photo by Khalil Raad. © Khalil Sakakini Cultural Center,
Ramallah.

of immense literary significance. The entries related to his sojourn to the
United States constitute a small but significant portion of the diaries, for
they were recorded during the formative period of his intellectual development, when he was in his mid-twenties. They cover his encounter with
exiled Syrian (i.e., Shami) intellectuals in New York, and his work with
the important literary journal *al-Jami'ah*, as well as his brief stint working at a paper mill in central Maine. They also relate the period of his

stormy courtship with his future wife, Sultana, and the pangs of separation he experienced when she remained in Jerusalem.

Sakakini is best known as a Jerusalem essayist, a progressive pedagogue, and an anticlerical freethinker. His diaries, according to a leading literary critic, reflect the entry of Palestinian literature into modernity.[2] His teaching method, introduced in his Dusturiyyeh National
School after World War I, was revolutionary. He abolished physical
punishment of students, condemning it as "barbaric and medieval," and
replaced exams with self-evaluation by the students and teachers.
Teachers were instructed not to take a roll call to record students' ab-
sences. Students were free to leave school if they got bored; this proce-
dure, he felt, would force the teacher to be innovative and entertain the
students, to capture their attention.[3] All this he undertook by the early
1920s. Yet despite his radical departure from the prevailing ideas about
education of the time, he was eminently successful as an educational re-
former and administrator, and was appointed by both the Ottomans
and the British as an education inspector in Palestine. Through his innovative method of teaching Arabic, published in the widely distributed
series *al-Jadid*, and his journalistic essays he introduced a crisp, concise,
and novel language, which in 1948 earned him a place in the Academy
of the Arabic Language in Cairo. This is what the scholar and novelist
Ishaq Musa al Husseini, author of *Diary of a Chicken*, wrote about
Sakakini's language:

> Sakakini called for a basic revamping of the teaching of Arabic grammar by
> simplifying its basic general rules and the popularization of teaching
> through usages, opening the door wide open for innovation. He saw lan-
> guage as an endowed skill *[malika]*, not a craft, to be learned through com-
> monsensical training *[saliqa]* rather than acquired through formal rules. He
> replaced rote learning with precedent *[qiyas]*, and imitation with practice.
> He defended this system in two of his books: in *al Jadid*, in which he revo-
> lutionized grammar by transforming male-based sentences into plural ones
> and encouraged the student to internalize the basic rules of the language
> without realizing that he was studying; and in his book *'alihi Qiss*, in which
> he introduced cases and paradigms from which students could deduce the
> principles of grammar without them needing to be explained.[4]

Until his memoirs were released we had limited knowledge of Sakakini's
personal life, except that he was an eccentric scholar and bon vivant. His
Kadha Ana Ya Dunia (1954), published posthumously, included only limited selections from his memoirs, chosen by his daughter, Hala Sakakini,
who died in 2002. The book highlights his career as an essayist with a flair

for Nietzschean philosophy but suppresses his distinct anticlerical tendencies. His skepticism and universalist humanism dissuaded him from joining any political party in his lifetime, but he did take part in the founding of Hizb as Sa'aleek, the "Party of Vagabonds," which formed a circle around the café with the same name in the vicinity of the Old City's Jaffa Gate.[5] His anticlerical and, later, antireligious tendencies were quite provocative for his conservative, provincial community, even by today's standards. These tendencies were muted by his daughter, who selected the parts of his memoirs that appeared in *Kadha Ana Ya Dunia,* but they come out quite clearly in the newly released diaries. For example, his long battle against the Orthodox Church is well known, but it is usually described as a struggle for the Arabization of the church from Greek control. Less known is his openly atheistic attitude, reflected in his call for the replacement of the Lord's Prayer with a pre-Islamic pagan stanza from "Umru' Al-Qays."[6] He found prayers boring and a waste of time. He was probably the only Arab thinker who was openly antinationalist. His *carte de visite* had only two lines: "Khalil Sakakini: *Ta'alu li-nanqarid*" (Let us make ourselves extinct).[7] In 1932 he proposed that his countrymen abandon institutional religion and adopt ritual narcissism as a form of worship, "since this is a form of worship that all of us can undertake without threatening other religions . . . for Christ has said, 'If you cannot love your brother whom you see, how can you love God that you cannot see.' But I [Khalil Sakakini] say to you: 'if you cannot love yourself, then you cannot love God or anybody else.'"[8]

Khalil became infatuated with Sultana Abdo less than a year before his departure to the United States. A distant relative of Khalil, she was born in 1888 in the Old City.[9] Both grew up in the Christian Quarter and came from Arab Orthodox families. Khalil's father was a master carpenter (*mu'alim*), as well as the *mukhtar* (elderman) of the Greek Orthodox community in Jerusalem. Sultana's father, Nicola Salem Abdo (Abu Adeeb), was also a prominent figure in the Old City, having been appointed by the Patriarchate as overseer of Orthodox pilgrims during the Easter and Christmas seasons, with the responsibility of looking after their lodging, food, and welfare. Sultana's father, according to his granddaughter Hala Sakakini, was progressive for his times, and he sent both of his daughters to board at the Friends' School in Ramallah, which was a "three-hour mule ride" to the north.[10] A letter from 1906 that Nicola Abdo wrote to Sultana's sister, Amalia, upon her marriage to a Nablus physician offers some insight into the relationship between this man and his daughters:

I cried all day today as I saw you leaving the house, for now you belong to another person. In one moment you voluntarily dropped my name and chose another. You shared my love with another man. My mind, my beloved, knows that your husband should have priority over me . . . and that I will come second. Let it be, but please keep a corner in your heart for me. And give me some time to adjust to your departure, after twenty years of being your companion.[11]

Nicola Abdo must also have been a very open-minded man by the standards of his time to allow his two daughters (a third died young) to be courted publicly by their male acquaintances without the presence of an escort.

Immediately after graduation from secondary school, in 1903, Sultana took up teaching at the Arab Orthodox School in the Old City, and then in 1905 at St. Mary's School for Girls, an Anglican school. It was there that Khalil came to know her when he was commissioned to train her as a teacher of Arabic language and literature. Khalil himself was a schoolmaster, trained by the renowned teacher of Arabic literature Nakhleh Zureik (1861–1921).

When Khalil began to court Sultana, in 1907, he was twenty-nine and she was twenty-one. In that period both the Abdo and Sakakini families had summerhouses outside the city walls, as did many middle-class families eager to escape the stifling atmosphere of the congested quarters. The Sakakini house was in Musrara, while the Abdos' was near the railroad station and was known as Haririyyeh, "the silk factory," after the workshop that had occupied the space before they moved in. (Almost a century later the residence became the Khan Theater in West Jerusalem.)[12]

Since Khalil and Sultana were both involved in Orthodox community activities, they had ample opportunity to see each other. At that time Sultana had befriended Milia, Khalil's elder sister, and she thus became a frequent visitor to the house. In the evening Khalil would walk Sultana back home, first with Milia and then alone. Later they would take longer walks or donkey rides into the countryside, mostly to Ein Karim or the Mount of Olives. It was during one of these outings that Khalil disclosed his love to Sultana. We are privileged to have this intimate moment recorded for posterity. Khalil's love is expressed here in modern romantic terminology that was virtually unknown in that period—certainly not in local Palestinian literature, and very rarely in Syrian-Lebanese or Egyptian contemporary narratives.

"On Thursday, the third of October [1907], I went with Sultana and my sister [Milia] to Qalona," he confided to his friend Dawood al Saidawi, in a letter written a few days after the event.

There under the lemon trees we spent the day. . . . Near sunset we rode our donkeys and turned back. The atmosphere was loaded with our love. I walked next to her until her donkey almost fell [yata'atharu], so I held tightly to its harness and led it the rest of the way. In the evening she came and spent a few hours at our house. When the night descended, I walked her home and told her that I would be writing her a letter. Early the next morning I poured all my sentiments into this letter. Then I went to [her] school and gave her the letter, with another letter written all over my face. Later that evening Milia and I passed by her house. When I saw her, an electric shock went through my body. We all took a walk to a cliff on the Ramallah road. We sat by the rocks, and I could see in her face the marks of contentment and acceptance. We kept this pace on the next and the following days. We went for an outing in the afternoon, and then spent the evening at our house and then at hers. Yesterday she sent me a letter expressing her love, and promising to write [more details] soon.

Immediately following this episode, Khalil was overcome by guilt, expressed so often in his later correspondence. He worried that he did not deserve her, that he was being selfish in wanting her for himself, and that there must be others more deserving of her love than he. He wrote, "despite my happiness, I feel I have placed my own desires above those friends of mine who have sought her affections. I beseech you, Dawood, help me. What should I do in order not to betray their trust, and be branded among them as selfish and self-seeking?"[13]

Khalil's consuming self-doubt was not primarily the product, as it may initially seem, of self-denigration—although this element was present in his personality in considerable measure—but a result of a tension generated by some hesitation by Sultana. He had a tendency to read her affection in mere gestures, and to overreact to her silence as a mark of coldness toward him. Since we have very few direct indications of what she actually thought of his overtures, we can only surmise her mindset from his own narrative, including the utterances he attributed to her. But Sultana was not altogether silent. She did leave a few significant letters addressed to Khalil when he lived in Brooklyn, and we have Hala's reminiscences of her. In these she comes across as a reticent, intelligent, and thoughtful figure with a great sense of humor, one that was less philosophical than his, perhaps, but certainly more playful and taunting.

Her hesitation in reciprocating Khalil's sentiment seems to be primarily a result of an inherent ambiguity in their relationship. He was eight years her senior, had an unstable financial future,[14] and was about to embark on a trip whose duration, and possibly its purpose,[15] was unknown to either of them. The more he pressed her for a commitment, the more ambiguous her responses became. This, I suggest, was a major source of the continual tension that marked their overseas relationship and dominated their correspondence for the entire year.

IN THE LAND OF FAST FOOD

Sakakini was highly unconventional for his time. Although he dressed rather conservatively, he was a bon vivant, a singer, a dancer, a heavy smoker of both a pipe and the *arghileh,* and he regularly played the violin. He considered himself to be a sensualist (to use a word he used in his diaries). He loved music and poetry and wrote a great deal of the latter, apparently with moderate success.[16] Above all he enjoyed good company, long drinking sessions, and wrestling with his male friends and acquaintances. His favorite sport was to induce several men to attack him and then wrestle them simultaneously to the ground.[17] He was mesmerized by his body and spent long periods engaged in his ablutions. In his diaries, however, he comes across as a man of ambivalent and repressed sexuality. His entries are full of self-recrimination and bouts of gloom and despair. His obsession with cold-water baths in both summer and winter and his extended withdrawals from social gatherings amounted to self-flagellation. He was consumed for the rest of his life with three passionate relationships, but all three objects of his love and devotion suffered early deaths during Khalil's lifetime: his friend and youthful companion, Dawood al Saidawi; his wife, Sultana Abdo; and his only son, Sari, who died at the young age of forty-two.

Khalil Sakakini departed from Jaffa for New York on October 22, 1907, and he returned to Jerusalem on September 10, 1908. His American exile lasted less than one year, and although he traveled extensively after that year, he never returned to the United States. He had to borrow money, from Dawood and Sultana, among others, to cover the cost of the journey. He had to travel in third class, which in this case meant staying on the deck of a ship. Travel in those days was arduous, and it typically took from ten days to two weeks to get from Marseille to New York.

Sakakini offers a glimpse into these exhausting conditions in a letter he sent from London during his return trip from New York: "Third-class travel is unbelievably tiring. For nine days I could hardly sleep. I ate very little, and did not change my clothes or wash my face once. When I arrived in England I was spent from hunger, exhaustion, and lack of sleep.

I was thoroughly disgusted with myself."[18] On arrival he sent the following stanza to Milia:

> After a trip that makes you old
> I arrived at the land of gold.
> On board the ship was shaking,
> Making me regret ever departing.
> Not a soul with whom to commiserate,
> And food that leaves you with a terrible aftertaste.[19]

The United States was in the midst of a terrible recession in 1908. "Nobody has the courage to ask for work from anybody," he wrote to Dawood in one of his first letters.[20] "Only yesterday my friend Farah Antoun said to me, 'Had you asked me before you came I would have advised you not to come to this country.' . . . Every day you hear about a company declaring its bankruptcy. Messrs. Muluk, the nephews of Mr. Rafleh [Khalil's roommate in Brooklyn], last week alone lost more than 13,000 riyal [dollars]."

When he arrived in New York, he was counting on his brother Yusif, a traveling salesman in Philadelphia, to help him out, but because of the deteriorating conditions in the United States that year, Yusif was in dire straits and in need of support himself. Khalil found lodgings on Atlantic Avenue in Brooklyn (the "Syrian neighborhood") with the help of acquaintances from Jerusalem. Financial misery and loneliness hit him hard from the beginning. The atmosphere of these early months in New York was captured in a letter to Dawood, sent in the middle of the 1908 New Year revelries:

> Read this and laugh. Earlier I was crying for my current condition, but now I am laughing. I mentioned to you in my last letter that I found, after great effort, three students to teach. My income from them was four riyals [dollars] per week, assuming they all remember to show up—which is rare, for every week at least one of them disappears, losing me a riyal. With these four orphan coins I eat and wash my clothes, and pay for my room, and then I share the rest with some of my Jerusalem companions here. I wish at least it stopped here. Now all my students have disappeared during the Christmas vacation, and for two weeks I have had no income. I sent my laundry to the washerwoman and was unable to reclaim them [for lack of money], so I am left with the clothes that I am wearing. Two days ago I started washing my own clothes.
>
> That was easy. But yesterday, the last day of the year, I only had ten cents in my pocket. I went with Nicola al Barghout to the market and bought bread (nine cents), and we came back and ate it with tea. While America was bidding farewell to the year and the coming of another one,

we sat around the table in a daze, then we went to bed and fell on our faces.

[New Year's Day] What shall I do? I wrote to my brother Yusif in Philadelphia. He must be in worse shape than me since he never replied. So now I am trying fasting, and I said to myself, "best to stay in bed all day." Hanna Farraj and the lads came and said, "Get up! Let's roam the streets. Today is a great day in America." I apologized. They left and Nicola stayed. I then got up and dressed and gave him [the remaining] penny and asked him to buy bread, "to break the fast." When he came back I divided the loaf between us, but he had barely put the morsel in his mouth when he choked with emotion. He left the room hurriedly. I called him and tried to encourage him. He said, "I am not crying for myself, but for you, Khalil, as I see you unable to find food." . . .

I thought of joining the army, except that they take you for three years, and the recruit is unable to leave before that duration. I think all of this is a lesson to me, for I grew up in a comfortable and protected atmosphere. Money was never of any value for me.[21]

This last sentence about money, as well as his reference to his luxurious upbringing (the Arabic term is *mun'aman mutrafan*, a state between luxury and comfort), must have struck Dawood as odd, since the whole purpose of the trip was to make money in order to pay his debts, and to set up a house for his intended marriage to Sultana.

He summed up his attitude toward New York and the United States in a letter sent to Sultana in July of 1908:

Sultana, my love,
I left Rumford Falls after spending one month working [in the paper mill]. It felt like a century. I came to Boston and was met by Mikhael Sayegh and your cousin Bandeli. Mikhael works for half a day and hardly makes three-fourths of a riyal [dollar]. Your cousin goes out every day to sell [carpets] but hardly makes enough money to cover his travel expenses. I doubt he will make it even if he spent his whole life in this country. I nearly urged him to return home [to Palestine], except that I do not wish to interfere in what is not my business.

In the evening I bade them farewell. . . . Mikhael's wife was about to deliver her baby. I took the train for about an hour [to Providence?], then I took the boat to New York. Everyone I encounter presses me to go back home, for this country is not for the likes of me. Except that every time I am about to resolve the matter, I remember my oath to you to make every effort to make something of myself here. I would then come back and bring you and Milia to visit America. The truth, my love, is that America is worth seeing, but is not fit to be a homeland [la taslah an takun watanan] for us, for it is a nation of toil, and there is no joy in it. I have one hope left, and that is to go back and try my luck back home. I trust conditions are better now that the sultan has ratified the constitution.[22]

Sakakini's stay in Brooklyn was dominated by his relationship to Farah Antoun, the editor of the Syrian exile journal *al-Jami'ah,* and the translation work he did for Columbia University Orientalist scholar Professor Richard Gottheil.[23] He made extra money on the side by teaching Arabic to American students (mostly from Columbia) and the wives and daughters of Arab shopkeepers and merchants, who were illiterate in their mother tongue. For Antoun he edited and wrote articles and proofread the journal's galleys. As he gained confidence, he also became engaged in polemics on behalf of Antoun against his conservative opponents.

Sakakini belonged to the first wave of Arab immigration to the United States, which began in the 1870s and was halted by the radical antianarchist phobias of the 1920s. Like most of his compatriots from the Arab East, he carried Ottoman citizenship and identified himself as Syrian, and occasionally as Palestinian. Before the Great War, the Syrian community (i.e., the Lebanese, Syrians, and Palestinians) settled in Manhattan's Lower West Side in what became known as "Little Syria." (Ironically, in the 1970s this area became the plaza of the World Trade Center.) Most of these families lived around Washington Street and worked in the garment industry. As they began to make money, they added to their ranks bankers, publishers, and importers of linen, lace, and lingerie.[24] They moved their residences from the Lower West Side to Brooklyn's Atlantic Avenue. There they established the South Ferry neighborhood, which included sections of Brooklyn Heights and Cobble Hill.

Like Sakakini, many of these immigrants commuted daily from Manhattan by taking the ferry from Whitehall Street to Atlantic Avenue.[25] Khalil's descriptions of his movements in New York gleaned from his diary entries and letters are cryptic and often amusing in their naïveté. He lodged in an unnamed neighborhood of Brooklyn full of "Syrian" and Greek cafés and restaurants. One later discovers that this is Atlantic Avenue. Every day he took the elevated train or a boat to New York—meaning Manhattan—where he spent most of his day either on the Lower West Side, in the vicinity of Columbia, or midtown, in the editorial offices of *al-Jami'ah.* Quite often he would cross the bridge (the Brooklyn Bridge, perhaps?) on foot and walk to Washington Street or Greenwich Village. Sometime in early 1908, after an underground tunnel was dug connecting Brooklyn to Manhattan, Sakakini began to take subterranean transport. To describe this mode of transportation, he uses the Arabic transliteration of "subway."

When Sakakini moved to Maine, moreover, he gave his family the impression that the factory at which he was working was somewhere not far from New York City. When referring to acquaintances in distant Michigan and Chicago, he described them as living in the "inland country" *(dakhil al Bilad)*. Rumford Falls was predominantly inhabited by "Frenchmen" and "Frenchwomen," he claimed, many of whom could not speak English. Sakakini does not indicate who these Frenchmen were, but he seems to think that they were European immigrants rather than Quebecois or Acadian natives of the region.

Throughout his travels in New York and New England, Khalil moved within the confines of Arab immigrant circles. At the turn of the nineteenth century, most of these were shopkeepers, salesmen, and peddlers. He generally found them uncouth and dull, and he continued to remark how he missed his intellectual circle in Jerusalem:

> The Syrians in this country are in general a disgusting crowd, both morally and in their mannerisms, [even though] they tend to show a great deal of respect toward me. Recently I have been attending some of their social get-togethers. I took my violin and played some Arabic tunes, and they went crazy [with delight]. What a miserable lot! What if Miss Mannana [Dawood's sister] shows up here? I will not be exaggerating if I tell you that even among the Americans you will not find a woman of her education and sophistication.[26]

American culture remained alien to Sakakini. Like many of his compatriots in the pre–World War I era, he had an "us versus them" attitude toward American society. There was no pretense that American culture was a melting pot.[27] Many Arabs continued to dress as they did in their native countries and carried on with their usual customs, including smoking an *arghileh* in public cafés, as can be seen from numerous photographs from Brooklyn and Little Syria from that period.[28] Throughout his stay in New York, Khalil ate in Syrian restaurants, shopped in Arab or Greek stores, and read the Arabic press. He considered Brooklyn neighborhoods cold and inhospitable. Khalil records at least five instances in which his friends—and on one occasion his brother, Yusif— were attacked by what he called "American street gangs." Only once did he complain to the police about the attack, only to find them uncooperative. The police even threatened to arrest them all.[29]

Toward the end of his stay Khalil finally showed a faint interest in the American cultural and literary scenes. He began to read the *Evening Standard* and to visit the Metropolitan Museum of Art. On two occasions Farah Antoun prevailed upon Khalil to accompany him to a theater on Broadway, but Khalil found the musical noisy and a waste of time.

In his taxonomy of early Arab intellectuals living in the United States, Michael Suleiman lists Sakakini—the most radical pedagogue of the period—among the conservatives. He certainly seems so when compared to socialist thinkers like Farah Antoun and Tolstoyan naturalists like Michael Nu'aimi, both contemporaries of Sakakini in New York.[30] This judgment is in part a reflection of Sakakini's inability to engage himself in any positive reflection on the American scene, but it also reflects his perverse, almost peasantlike reaction to the conquest of public space by women. In a 1908 trip to the Coney Island beachfront with his friend Elias Haider, Sakakini was shocked and disgusted by the playfulness of men and women frolicking on the shoreline in swimsuits.[31]

Despite his antipathy to American mores, Khalil made many sharp and satirical observations about daily life there. "The American walks fast and eats fast," he wrote for *as-Sufur* (Cairo). "They are so fast that they have restaurants called 'Fast Food,' where you do not see chairs, as customers eat standing up. A person might even leave the restaurant with a bite still in his mouth!"[32] Because he was surrounded by Syrian and Armenian traveling salesmen, he was fascinated by their mannerisms and the way in which their work ethic reflected two different worlds.

> In the Arab world, the peddlers were happy and sang their wares. In America, however, peddlers hardly smiled and their voices were disturbing when they called for customers. They went to bed worried and anxious, and woke up the same way; such was not the case in the Levant. In comparing "our crazies and theirs," Sakakini reported that, of two madmen he knew back home, one walked day and night, the other locked himself up in a closet. In America, he found that everybody was that kind of crazy, whether in constant motion or behind a counter [closet]. In America, people worked all the time, there was no pleasure in work. Their only pleasure was in making money and more money.[33]

SULTANA'S CRUEL HEART

While in New York Sakakini would spend sleepless nights remembering outings he took with Sultana, mostly to Ein Karim, Artas, and Beit Jala, and on two occasions to Ramallah. On several occasions she spent the night at the Sakakini family house, with her family's approval.[34] Although one of the main impetuses behind his departure to America was to make enough money to set up a household for Sultana and himself, it became obvious from his pleadings with her that she was not fully committed to the idea of marriage.

Altogether Khalil wrote forty-one letters to Sultana, twenty-one of them from New York. Of these, about thirty-five survived, allowing us a glimpse at their relationship and at courtship traditions in Palestine before the Great War. Sakakini had left Palestine without a formal betrothal to Sultana, so their relationship remained a secret from both their families. Only Dawood was privy to their love vows.

Despite his pleading and several threats to sever their relationship if she did not respond, Sultana wrote to Khalil only once or twice while he was in the United States. There are three themes that recur in virtually all of his many letters: the reconstruction of every moment he spent with her in Jerusalem and during their walks in the environs of the city; his obsessive fear that he would return without enough money to make him seem worthy in her eyes; and his overwhelming feeling of unworthiness and the sense that he was denying other, more capable men from winning her favor.

Unlike his diary entries, which contain lengthy descriptions of his life in Brooklyn and his work in Manhattan, Sakakini's love letters—full of self-recrimination for having left her—are located in nostalgic space. "Explain to me, Sultana, why did you permit me to separate from you?" he wrote on November 20, 1907. "All the wealth of America, and the wonders of America, do not equal in my eyes the loss and anguish I suffer from your absence. And what if I do not make it at the end? You say it's only two years. But two years is like being away from you for a thousand years."[35]

After the New Year celebrations he accompanied a Jerusalem acquaintance, Doctor Najeeb al Jamal, to view the city from the top of a Manhattan skyscraper. Jamal informed Khalil that he would like him to intercede on his behalf to ask for Sultana's hand: "He [Dr. Jamal] began to sing the praises of your beauty and your qualities. Before him I heard similar praise coming from Issa al Issa [later the editor of the newspaper *Falastin* in Jaffa] and Afteem Mushabbik. . . . I do hope I deserve your trust and affections."

After months of incessant begging and pleading, Sultana finally replied with a single letter. It indicates a no-nonsense attitude about his misery, but also a considerable erudition and command of literary Arabic. Her style, like Khalil's, is modernist and free of the flowery language typical among contemporary Arab writers. Her writing is the perfect antidote to his sentimentalism, self-pity, and periodic eruptions of self-denigration.

Jerusalem, Monday, January 20, 1908

Dear Khalil,
I received all your letters by hand through your cousin Ya'coub [Farraj]. I thank you for your sentiments, and for your love and devotion. I was

hoping your letters would be a source of guidance to me, but unfortunately
I must confess to you that I can hardly read them more than once. For every
time I open them, I am aggravated by the wailing and crying you go
through by the sheer memory I invoke in you.

I am not dead yet, so there is no need to cry rivers of tears over me and
transform your words into eulogies! Why can't you instead smile, Khalil,
when you think of me? . . . Is there nothing pleasant or wondrous in America
that you can tell me about? I know you must have suffered a lot when you
first came to New York, but please do not make crying your main pastime.

You keep worrying that you might fail and come back with naught.
What kind of talk is this, Khalil? Why should you fail? By God, do not let
me hear you repeat this nonsense. . . . [Also,] please send me your letters directly to the bishop, or to [my] school, so that I will be the first person to
read them, rather than having them become the subject of everybody's ad-
miration en route.

. . . Do you recall our picnic in Artas, Khalil? Peace be upon that day,
for what happened has been carved in my heart indelibly. . . . I write this to
you with the moon looking at me between the olive trees, and I feel that I
am not writing to you but addressing you mouth to mouth.

. . . At your request I went with my brother Yusif the day after Christmas to have a portrait made of me at Miltyawi's [the photographer] to replace the one that you broke. I will send it immediately to you by post, and
hope that you will get it intact.

Sultana

The letter indicates that Sultana was committed to the relationship,
but that she did not want him to take her for granted. On at least two
other occasions she indicated to him that nothing was guaranteed. On
October 11, 1907, for example, she wrote to him when he was about to
embark on his trip to the United States, "I will give you my oath of love,
as long as I have control over my destiny." Then she adds cryptically,
"Blissful and happy is your condition, but there is no comfort for those
you leave behind."[36] Khalil panics. He responds immediately, "What do
you mean? Are you suggesting that if another person comes your way,
or if your folks propose a replacement, or compel you to take one, you
will succumb? I hope you do not aim at torturing me with this talk." And
then, using an Arabic pun that refers to their names, he writes, "What
prevents that I be your lover *[khalilek]* and you my mistress *[sultanati]*?
My *sultanah* have mercy on your *khalil*."[37]

After several months in the United States, Khalil's hope of earning a
stable income began to dissipate. His few steady students, mostly un-
dergraduates from Columbia University with limited finances, stopped

showing up regularly. Scholars who commissioned him to correct their manuscripts were late making their payments, and Farah Antoun's journal *al-Jami'ah* was losing money all the time. In desperation he packed his belongings and moved to Maine to work in a paper mill for a promised wage of twelve dollars a week. Since his lodging and food expenses were about six or seven dollars, Sakakini figured he could save five dollars a week.

It was not long, however, before the drudgery of work at the paper mill and physical fatigue began to take their toll. In Jerusalem he had been a respected if underpaid teacher, an upstanding member of his community with a loving circle of friends. He also had Dawood and Sultana to give him hope and solace. But Dawood was now dead, and Sultana was not responding to his letters. By the spring he had reached desperate straits. "This is the last time I address you as my love [*habibati*]," he wrote to her from Rumsford Falls on July 17, 1907.

> For that entails that I am yours and you are mine. . . . Yes, that is the oath that we took, but a miserable lout like me, unable to reach his objectives, and then transform [your] happy life into misery?? Yes, Sultana, I am destined to live in misery. Turn your eyes from me to avoid this curse. Spit me out, cut these bonds, and leave me forever. Tear up my letters, and burn all traces of my memory. Forget me. Do not mention my name, for it is too unworthy of your pure lips. If my name is mentioned before you, say, "I do not know him." But before that I beg you to forgive me for having preoccupied your heart and blocked the path to your happiness. Do not deny me your pardon, for I have lost everything: my friend, my future. . . . I have only my failure for company. And why should you put up with me. What is your crime? No, Sultana, I do not deserve you. You must choose another person [to love]. Choose somebody who will make you happy. From now on my happiness will be to hear that you are happy [with someone else]. I will be returning soon to Jerusalem, an utter failure. My punishment will be to live away from you, and to avoid the roads that you take, and the places that you frequent. I will take to the grave of my beloved [Dawood] as my solace until death comes to me, and I am forgotten by all. . . . This is my last letter to you. Farewell, Sultana.
>
> *Khalil*[38]

Khalil wrote three letters in this vein. One draft that he kept but did not send reads, "I wish I had not known you, Sultana. . . . Everybody loves you. Choose someone who loves you and who can make you happy." He then adds a note that expresses a sentiment unseen in earlier correspondence: "I write to you in a language that I would never dare address to my mother and sister. . . . It's only because you have replaced your delicate heart with one that is harder than steel and thicker than granite that I can talk to you thus."[39]

Within ten days, however, he was back on his feet. His tone was still reserved, but his confidence was restored. She was his *habiba* again. "I am preparing for my journey back home," he wrote on July 27. "I wish I could fly to you. I hope our reunion will be the beginning of a new and happy life. I will be returning, my love, burdened with grief and unhappiness, but my distress will evaporate once I see you smiling. You are my solace, my joy."[40]

AN ELUSIVE LOVE

If his memories of Sultana empowered Khalil with a hope that helped him to escape from the daily tribulations of life in New York, then Dawood Saidawi was the icon that tied him to his roots in Jerusalem. His reflections on Dawood are dreamlike, and Dawood often appeared in Khalil's actual dreams, which he recorded daily. Before he left Jerusalem, Dawood was his soul mate *(shaqiq ruhi)* and confidante. He was the one and only friend privy to his relationship with Sultana, its progress as well as its tribulations. Dawood's sudden death, communicated to him in a letter from the mysterious Miss Singer four months after his arrival in Brooklyn, was the single most devastating blow of Khalil's American sojourn.[41]

"Dawood, ya Yonathai [my Jonathan]," he wrote upon hearing of his death, "My beloved, my soul mate, my hope, my joy and happiness. How dare you leave me alone? . . . Nothing will compensate me [for your loss]. Life without you has no meaning. If you are dead now, then I am among the living dead."[42] Two months later he was still subject to extended bouts of despair and depression: "This morning, after I shaved, I was about to have breakfast when I glanced at a picture of Dawood and was overwhelmed by grief. I started crying again. Let my right hand forget me, Dawood, if I forsake you. And let my tongue be stuck to my jaws if I stop remembering you." His letters are replete with biblical incantations (e.g., "My Jonathan" and "Let my right hand") mixed with flowery borrowings from Manfalooti, the early twentieth-century Egyptian romanticist. (Both influences disappeared from his style upon his return to Palestine.)

In Khalil's American diary, Dawood remains a dominant figure in both life and death. He appears most vividly in the frequent dream episodes that Khalil narrates with enchanting detail. One month after he received news of Dawood's death, Sakakini recalls an encounter in Jaffa:

> Four months ago, in October 1907, we embraced on the Mediterranean shores. I laid my head on your chest and wept bitterly, as if I had a premonition that this moment would mark our permanent separation. I took [the ship] to the shore while you remained at the shores stoutly sending me looks of love and affection. What were you thinking then? . . . When I return to that beach tomorrow, who will console me for your absence? I will kiss the earth on which you walked. I will stand there facing you on the opposite shore—the terrain of eternal life.[43]

Following this entry a striking phenomenon occurs in the diary: in Khalil's dream narratives, the figures of Dawood and Sultana begin to merge. It is not clear what was going on in Khalil's mind, but it appears that this union was the product of a dual loss: Dawood's physical loss in death, and Sultana's increasing aloofness and detachment. In February 1908 he made the following cryptic entry: "I have spent the whole night with you. My sleep was full of anxiety. I woke up and stayed in bed all day. I remembered my mother and my [past] happiness. I could hardly withhold my tears."[44] Again, on March 7, he wrote, "I dreamt I was returning with you in the evening to our house in the [old] city. When we approached the entrance I saw the neighbor's door ajar. When we entered I kissed you."[45]

Whom did Khalil kiss in this dream? And with whom was he returning in the dark? The allusion here is oblique. Initially he seems to be referring to Sultana, but the opening line *(faqatdu habiban)* about losing his beloved suggests that he was referring to Dawood. Furthermore, Khalil never alludes to kissing Sultana in his diaries either before or after their marriage, even in his frequent dream narratives. Either he was protecting Sultana in case the diaries fell into the wrong hands, or, more likely, he was expressing a love for her that was abstract and asexual.

At this stage the reader should be warned that these diaries were written in an era when men were free to express their devotion to each other, and that such expressions were not suggestive of an erotic relationship. Furthermore, because his was a socially restrictive community, Khalil's expressions of affection for Sultana were considerably more reserved than his feelings toward her actually were. It was more permissible to express love for members of the same sex than for the opposite sex. At the same time, however, Sultana was not reciprocating his affections. The figure of Dawood, then, no longer of flesh and blood, merged with his longing for the elusive Sultana. The two objects of his adoration were united in his fantasies.

NEW YORK AS AN EPHEMERAL CITY

Virtually every diary entry recorded in Brooklyn or Rumford Falls begins and sometimes ends with a dream narrative. The majority of these dreams are set in Jerusalem and depict events such as walks with Sultana, talks with Dawood, family outings, and bizarre happenings with various acquaintances. Frequently the dreams involve death, burial, and resurrection. Many of those visitations to the Holy City involve imaginary escapades from New York, or have Khalil being transported via outer space from New York to Jerusalem. As such, New York in these dreams becomes the arena of a transitory existence.

In every dream that Khalil describes in detail, there exists a theme of jarring tension between Khalil's American persona and his status as "a son of Jerusalem." Most of these dreams juxtapose New York's monstrous industrialism and Palestine's "natural tranquility." For Khalil, the return to Jerusalem is an escape from the cruel machine of the American metropole.

In Khalil's dreams, this tension is eventually exemplified by the contrast between the oppressive conditions Sakakini experienced at the paper mill in Rumford Falls and the rustic open fields of Ein Karim and Artas. In these dreams, Jerusalem is reduced to its countryside. (In *Kadha Ana Ya Dunia*, he writes, "There is no difference here between men and machinery. The laborer moves without thought and will, and no trace of reasoning in his work. You should not be surprised that workers' souls and sentiments are dead. They work ten hours a day with little or no rest and receive no more than a dollar and a half for that. The injustice of capital has no limit. What an ugly and brutal civilization.")[46] But one should not exaggerate his anticapitalist sentiments. His criticism was directed at the soulless character of capital rather than its exploitative nature. In his dreams Khalil does not fight, he escapes.

Another related theme in these dreams is the contrast between the frigid modernity of New York and the traditional intimacy of Jerusalem social life. Those contrasts are expressed in the constant crossing and recrossing of the boundary between European and Arab dress codes.[47] Here is a typical example from his diary:

> I dreamt [last night] that I had gone back to Jerusalem wearing a European hat *[burnaita]* over my *qumbaz* [traditional Arab robe]. I became embarrassed, so I removed it and walked dishevelled. It was a hot day, and I was

passing the Russian compound next to the Italian consulate. I walked by
the new road between the houses of the Halabi family and that of Faidy al-
Alami. When I reached the end of the road I saw myself barefooted and
without the *qumbaz,* but I was covered by a white *abay* (shawl). A black
servant woman *(jariya)* confronted me and said, "What do you want?" I
replied, "I want to go home." She pointed to a fence and said, "Jump over
here." I jumped, and my white *abay* got stuck in a thorny bush at the entrance. I was so exhausted trying to free it from the thorns.[48]

The process of getting to Jerusalem always involved physical hurdles
and escape routes (from New York?). It invariably focused on jumping
walls, and on dressing and undressing in a manner that Khalil would
have hesitated to record had he been familiar with Freudian paradigms.
Just before Dawood's death, Khalil made the following entry about his
friend. (In this particular episode, as in several others, one is struck by
the vivid allusions to Jesus at the Last Supper):

Dawood and I were walking in the Old City. He was full of vigor and had a
glowing angelic smile on his face. We passed the American Colony[49] but did
not enter. Then we passed by the Tarazi store, where they [?] looked at him
as if his time has come *[dana ajaluhu].* I saw myself jumping on top of the
roofs of houses and climbing walls until I arrived at our house. I climbed
down to enter the house, but I was naked.[50]

When Khalil finally returned to Jerusalem, the dream sequences either
came to a halt, or he stopped recording them.[51]

Sakakini's failed mission in New York turned out to be only a passing
episode, and he very rarely mentioned it in his later writings. Instead, he
was quickly engulfed in different battles: the quest to reform the teaching of Arabic, the movement for Ottoman constitutional reform, and the
struggle to Arabize the Orthodox Church. Sultana received him warmly,
if not exactly with open arms. They officially became engaged by the end
of the year. They were married in Jerusalem on January 12, 1912, when
Sultana was twenty-four and Khalil was thirty-two. They had three children: Sari, who died as a young man and broke his father's heart; Hala,
who published several books about her father; and Dumia. Both Hala
and Dumia died in 2005. In all of the biographical materials about
Sakakini, his sojourn to the United States is described as a year of failure and misery.[52] That is, in all of the biographical materials except for
the writings of his daughter Hala, who makes this brief remark in her
own memoirs: "He went to [America] in the hope of finding appropriate work and eventually settling there, but he was not successful;
1907/1908 happened to be one of those depression years in America.

After an absence of nine months, during which he suffered many hardships, father returned to Jerusalem. Even this experience, though unhappy, had enriched him in many ways."[53]

Neither Hala Sakakini nor Khalil's other biographers mention in what way this trip was enriching. After reading his hitherto unpublished letters and diaries, I would suggest three ways in which his life was enriched. First, cultural life in New York, no matter how miserable Khalil found it, helped to broaden his intellectual horizons and stimulate his interests. His collaboration with Farah Antoun in particular introduced him to the writings of Nietzsche, which became, in a rudimentary way, influential for his thinking.[54] More important, his editorial work for *al-Jami'ah* made his language crisper and less flowery, as became evident when he began to edit the literary journal *al-Asma'i* in Jerusalem after his return from New York. Several years later, while he was spending dreary months in an Ottoman prison in Damascus, Khalil could look back on his years in Brooklyn with some nostalgia. "If I were to be exiled from my homeland," he wrote in the beginning of 1918, "I would choose America. Nothing would make me happier to see my son in play gear, bare headed and in shorts, jumping down the stairs of Columbia University in New York, with the wind blowing at his golden locks. . . . How happy I would be if I could be sitting with my little family having tea in an elegant home in Brooklyn or its neighboring suburbs."[55]

Finally, and most important, Khalil's American exile and the tragedies that accompanied it, Dawood's death and Sultana's vacillations, helped him to reflect on the meaning of love and loss. The first he could no longer take for granted, now that he had to fight for Sultana's affection, and the second fortified his character. Nor could he go back and find solace in conventional domesticity, for which men of his age were traditionally prepared. Instead these tribulations tested his character and his faith. The seeds of rebellion and skepticism were planted, only to bloom when he returned to Jerusalem to face the intellectual battles that he confronted on the eve of World War I: the struggle against the tyrannies of the state, the Orthodox Church (which was about to excommunicate him and bar him from marrying Sultana), and his own conservative society.

CHAPTER 8

The Last Feudal Lord

A village like no other. A city that is not urban. . . . A feudal
family that has no rural traditions. Castles and fortifications
and mansions that rise high above the peasant dwellings. . . .
Men and women attired in a manner that is at odds with their
neighbors. Foods that transcend the local cuisine. A town that
is an oasis in a desert, and a family that is uprooted from its
urbane roots and replanted in this remote mountainous
range, away from the city and the sea. . . . The visitor to this
town is astounded by his encounter with these great mansions
and its fortifications. He wonders whether he is in a village or
in a city. He is further perplexed as to why these construc-
tions appear in this particular place and not in neighboring
villages.

*Omar es-Saleh, describing nineteenth-century dwellings
in Deir Ghassaneh*

The memoirs of Omar es-Saleh, grandson of the last lord of Deir Ghassaneh, Sheikh Saleh Abdul Jaber al-Barghouti (1819–81),[1] and son of
Sheikh Mahmoud es-Saleh (d. 1919), provide us with a unique window
into the final days of the feudal lords of central Palestine in the middle
of the nineteenth century, as Ottoman regulations began to lead to the
privatization of landownership. Deir Ghassaneh was the throne village
of Bani Zeid, north of Jerusalem. Its *multazims* (tax farmers), who had
immense power over the region's peasantry, ruled over the estates of
twenty villages, which separated the northern part of the Jerusalem hills
from the Jabal Nablus.

The life of Omar es-Saleh is of great interest because, over the span of
five decades, he articulated the transition from a clear pride in local aristocratic privilege to the adoption of urban nationalist affinities and an
urban lifestyle. These Jerusalem-based affinities led him toward a number

of political shifts, such as the adoption of the path of Ottoman decentralization and a total immersion in Palestinian Arab nationalism. After joining the Istiqlal Party he became a key opponent of the leadership of Haj
Amin al Husseini, and following the 1948 war his career was closely associated with the Jordanian regime, despite his criticism of King Abdallah,
and he served as cabinet minister in two successive governments. His activity against the Zionist project and his opposition to Herbert Samuel led
to his exile to Akka in the 1920s. But Omar was also a scholar and a militant advocate of educating women in the liberal secular tradition. In
Jerusalem in 1919 he coedited *Mir'at al-Sharq,* one of the most influential
newspapers in Palestine at the time. His books include *The History of
Palestine* (with Khalil Totah, 1923), *Studies in Palestinian Customs and
Folklore* (1922), *Bedouin Law in Palestine* (1929), *al-Yazuri: the Unknown Vizier* (1948), *History of the Ummayad Califate* (n.d.), and several
works of fiction and unpublished historical manuscripts. During the Mandate he studied law and became a law professor at the Palestine Law Institute (Ma'had al Huquq), where he authored a number of legal publications, including the *Index of Laws and Statutes of Palestine* in 1931.

His memoirs vividly demonstrate that the transition from tax farming, officially abolished in 1858, was protracted, and that the lords of the
Bani Harith, Bani Zeid, and Bani Murra regions maintained substantial
privileges long after tax farming was formally terminated. These privileges included the continued collection of the tithe in the name of the
Sublime Porte, the adjudication of territorial disputes, the meting of traditional justice, the ownership of household slaves, and various administrative duties delegated by the modernizing authority in Istanbul. The
memoirs also demonstrate that the rich and complex relationships (for
example, through marriage bonds and mutual support) that linked the
feudal lords of Bani Sa'b (the Jayyusi clan), Bani Zeid, and Bani Harith,
among others, to the patrician elites of Jerusalem and Nablus were much
stronger than is often assumed. Barghouti claims in this context that his
clan's power originated in Jerusalem itself,[2] where his family was charged
with control over entry to the city through Da'ya Gate (later the New
Gate), when the Sublime Porte subcontracted to the family the collection
of taxes *(iltizam)* of a large area that covered the Bani Zeid, Bani Murra,
Bani Salem, and other areas extending as far as the Mediterranean
shores.[3] More interesting for the reader of these memoirs, however, is the
impact of these transformations on the lives of members of this rural aristocracy, who had just begun to move to the district centers and other
major cities of Palestine—in this case, Jerusalem. One should obviously

take Barghouti's narrative about his clan's history with a grain of salt. Fathi Ahmad, who wrote a history of the Bani Zeid region, correctly points out that Barghouti virtually ignores his family's main rivals for feudal power in the region, the Sihwail clan in 'Ebwein. He also considers Barghouti's claim that his family is descended from Khalid ben al Walid and his tracing of his family origins to the Jerusalem notables as pure invention.[4] But this is all beside the point. The importance of his memoirs lies in their subjective and lived narratives.

The memoirs' vivid and detailed depiction of daily life in the palace of Sheikh Saleh, Omar's grandfather, and his father, Sheikh Mahmoud, in the last days of the sultanate alone would make these memoirs a treasure trove for historians, but the significance of the memoirs goes beyond these ethnographic details. They provide us with a rare opportunity to examine a new class in the making. Omar es-Saleh is probably the only diarist who recorded the critical transformation that occurred when the scions of the major feudal lords of nineteenth-century Palestine moved from the twenty-odd throne villages to the cities of Jerusalem, Nablus, Jaffa, and Haifa, the major urban centers of the country. There a new, hegemonic urban class was emerging from the combined networks of mercantile groups, urban notables, and absentee landlords moving to the city from their rural domains. The Tuqan, Abdul Hadi, Qasim, and Jayyusi families, with whom Omar es-Saleh was intimately acquainted—as in-laws, future business partners, and political allies and adversaries—were members of this latter group.

In the first book of his diaries, Omar describes the great divide that separated the dwellings of the Baraghteh from the rest of the village's peasantry. His father's mansion, originally built in 1011 A.H., was divided into three compounds: the *salamlek,* containing the guest house, the reception area, and the dining halls; the *haremlek,* the women's and servants' quarter; and the *khazeen* (provisions) compound, which included work areas, the stables, and the food storage. Laced windows *(mashrabiyyat)* perched high above the village looking out from the upper floors allowed the women of the household to see out without being seen. On the top floor hung the *eliyyeh,* the sheikh's retreat and resting place overlooking his estates.[5]

Unlike the peasant women of the region, Barghouti women were heavily veiled and confined to the *haremlek.* Covered from top to bottom in their black *abayeh,* they were not allowed to visit relatives or pay a condolence visit except after sunset, and even then they had to be accompanied by a blood kin *(mahram).* Once inside their quarters, however, women would dress in the urban aristocratic style. The *sheikha* (the lord's wife) would wear the *tarbush* embroidered with golden coins; the tops of their headdresses were adorned with pearls. Their daily attire consisted of unembroidered light cotton or silk dresses. On their legs they wore a silver *khilkhal* (leg bracelet). Unlike urban women, however, they did not use lipstick or powder; instead, they used kohl and plucked their eyebrows (pp. 41–42). Despite these restrictions, the Barghouti women were able to accumulate small private fortunes, primarily from trading in textiles, but also by lending money at very high interest rates (p. 61)

This tradition of strict confinement was unusual even among the feudal families of Palestine (among the other families, only the Jayyusi, Rayyan, and Abdul Hadi women were similarly veiled and confined).[6] The tradition was reinforced by a strict endogamy: Barghouti women were given in marriage only to members of their own clan and to a small circle of lordly families that included the Jayyusi, Rayyan, Abu Kishek, and the Mas'udi emirs. Peasant women, by contrast, were unconstrained:

> They moved and roamed unveiled, seen by all. They worked in the fields with their menfolk and with strangers. They collected water from the local spring (*'ain*) and wood on their own. They harvested and slept under the trees, and guarded the vineyards. Men would come in on women in the cottages without knocking, and often guests would sleep in the same dwellings as [the host] women. (p. 30)

Another distinguishing feature of the lords of Deir Ghassaneh was slave ownership, a practice that continued well into the first third of the twentieth century. The slave quarters in the mansion of Omar es-Saleh housed palace guards, servants, and cooks, many of whom had lived in the household since childhood. Barghouti slaves, we are told, dressed well, carried arms, and rode horses. According to Omar es-Saleh, their status was higher than that of the local peasants, and they carried their master's name (p. 43).

OMAR ABANDONS "THE MOTHER OF THE WORLD"

In 1898, when he was only five years old, Omar was sent to the village *kuttab* to study the Qur'an and grammar. When he passed the tests (*khatm al Qur'an*) at the age of nine, his father sent him to the Alliance School, a Francophone Jewish primary school in Jerusalem. The idea was that he would study French and Turkish—the languages of those in power both locally and internationally—in preparation for his continued education in Istanbul. There he discovered the world outside his village and the novel amenities of the big city. In the first two books of the diaries—those covering his childhood and youth—Barghouti continually refers to himself in the third person:

> Alone, he would say to himself, "In Deir Ghassaneh I thought I was in the mother of the world, and the capital of capitals. When I came to Jerusalem I found it beyond my wildest expectations. I saw horse-driven carriages for hire, driving on broad asphalt avenues leading to Nablus, Jaffa, Hebron, and Jericho." . . . Initially he was fearful of riding these carriages, but his father showed him how, and then he would take it daily from Jaffa Gate to his school, paying a Turkish *matleek* for the fare, and enjoying every step of the trip.
>
> At night he was overwhelmed with the street lamps that broke the darkness and made walking the streets in the evening easier. He saw men with hats wearing their elegant formal suits. He saw beautiful women wearing fancy dress, unveiled, evoking charm and lust. He saw women covered in black, with a *mandeel* hiding their faces, walking shamelessly among men. He was amazed how these men were buying [only] a *ratl* [three kilograms] of flour, an *ouqiyyeh* [250 grams] of ghee, and a *ratl* of onions, and he was annoyed. For why would they not buy their provisions for the year, as they do in the village? He saw the streets paved with stones to prevent accumulation of mud in the winter. He was fascinated by the glass on the windows, which brought light into the room and prevented the dust from penetrating. And he thought, if these glass windows were fitted in the village homes, the boys would smash them at the first brawl.

On the verge of puberty, Omar found lodging in the Old City with Maria the Copt—a breed of woman he had never met before. She was, in his words, "a manly woman" *[imra'a nisf]*, who constantly smoked the *arghileh,* danced, and sang." Maria virtually adopted him and introduced him to the world of the city. His frequent references to her are oblique, but they are saturated with the youthful discovery of sexuality. Once a week she would bathe him and scrub him with a loofah while telling him tales of love and passion, interlaced with vulgarities that were unfamiliar to him (p. 86). She became his companion and continued to be his friend after he moved to new lodgings. Omar was constantly intrigued by the contrasts between his village and Jerusalem. He was at once repelled and fascinated by city ways. He was particularly annoyed that his father was treated as an ordinary citizen, and not as the sheikh of Bani Zeid, and he as the sheikh's eldest son. It took him a long time to get used to the milieu of restaurants, cafés, bars, and hotels where clients would pay with money for their food and lodgings. He was shocked by the open drinking of alcohol, "which only during Ramadan Muslims desist from drinking" (p. 92). But above all he was enchanted by the manners of women in the city: their tight clothes, their red lipstick, and the way they walked—"*innahu lashay'in 'ujab*" (what a wondrous thing). But he quickly acclimatized to the city, and by his second year there he was already embarrassed to be seen walking with visitors from his village (p. 94).

> The teenager [Omar himself] soon assimilated into the life of the city and began to detest his traditional clothing—*al-hatta* and the *igal*, the *kufiyyeh* and the *qumbaz* and the *abaya*. He would avoid being seen with the peasants in the market for fear of being called a *fellah*, a word that now evoked in his mind low status, rough mannerisms, dirt, and simple, naïve characters. He chose to speak with a Jerusalem accent, but only selectively. He kept his *qaf*, his *dha'*, his *tha'*, and his *dhad* [guttural letters usually softened in urban pronunciation]. He also prided himself in talking in the *fusha*. (p. 105)

Omar's schooling is a record of the modernization of pedagogy in Ottoman Palestine. His transition from the *kuttab* to the Alliance School marks his introduction to secular education. He later transferred to the Frères School, where the French curriculum was stronger, but his father was alarmed by the amount of Christian indoctrination he was subjected to there. Jewish and Muslim students rebelled and staged a strike against compulsory religion classes on Catholicism, but to no avail. He transferred again to the Anglican school St George's, where the instruction was in Arabic and English. Here the education was more liberal and open-minded, and Muslims and Jews were given instruction on their own religious texts. One of his memorable teachers there was Khalil Sakakini, the progressive educator who banned the use of violence against students (p. 109). In his fifth year of schooling he again moved, this time to Sultani Beirut, where instruction in Arabic and Turkish prepared him for the study of law in Istanbul (Dar al Funun College).

Sultani Beirut, the provincial state school, enforced military discipline. All classes in science, history, geography, mathematics, civics, grammar, and literature—except Arabic literature—were in Turkish. The students were constantly supervised by the staff, who ensured that they followed their daily routine of classes, eating meals, and praying five times a day. On Thursdays they bathed under supervision, and on Friday they were taken on a school outing, usually to Junieh or Dbayyieh. Students were issued two uniforms each year, a velvet one for winter and one of linen for summer. Curiously, students were obliged to wear their uniforms when they left the school and on holidays, but they were free to dress in their own clothes for classes. Whether this regulation was aimed at easily detecting the students when they were outside the school or was intended to generate publicity for the school is not clear. The excessive amount of praying and religious instruction to which Omar was subjected served the opposite effect of what was intended, and it seems to have alienated him from religion altogether. Yet, despite the strict discipline and his halting Turkish, Omar was happy.

BEIRUT IS NOT JERUSALEM

In Beirut the teenage Omar was exposed to Arab nationalism, the cinema, newspapers, the sea, and bordellos—more or less in that order. In 1907 the city was simmering with rebellion against Ottoman despotism and agitation for decentralization. In Omar's mind the freedom afforded by living in Beirut more than made up for the discipline imposed on him as a boarding student at Sultani Beirut. He was mocked and degraded for his poor Turkish, but he still managed to acquire a taste of the city during sick leaves he took from school. In Jerusalem he had been exposed to European imports that he had only read about in his village, but only on occasion. There he attended the theater in the company of his father at the Ma'aref Café, near Jaffa Gate. He listened to Egyptian and French music using wax cylindrical records and a gramophone at the home of Doctor Photi, the Greek physician. He got drunk on sweet wine with Maria, who also taught him how to smoke rolled cigarettes. With his cousin he went to the cinema for the first time, where he witnessed many of the viewers escaping the hall for fear of getting wet from the stormy sea on the screen (pp. 97–98).

But all of these encounters with the European experience paled in comparison with his exhilaration at the novelties of Beirut. His enchantment was in part due to the absence of his family's influence while he was at Sultani Beirut, where he traveled and lived alone. No doubt, however, it also had to do with his encounter with a cosmopolitanism that was absent in Jerusalem. In a short list in his diary, Omar itemizes what he considered to be the outstanding features of Beirut when compared to Jerusalem:

- Daily newspapers distributed each morning openly call for decentralization and establishing Arabic as the official language of [greater] Syria.

- Beirutis have a variety of dress codes that are not seen in Jerusalem or Nablus. The *kufiyyeh* is rarely seen. Instead, most men wear the *tarbush* or a hat on top of a European suit.

- Automobiles have begun to replace the horse-driven carriage everywhere.

- Restaurants and hotels are far superior to those in Jerusalem. The cuisine is much more varied, and the service is more sophisticated.

- Cafés and nightclubs contain gramophones that play the latest music from Syria, Anatolia, and Egypt. There is a rich and varied nightlife. Bordellos are regulated by the government.

- "The sea of Beirut is superior to that of Jaffa." It has a safe harbor where the customshouse receives the imports directly, and the passengers disembark in the port. In Jaffa, by contrast, passengers and goods have to be transferred from their ships to smaller boats, which carry them ashore for disembarkation. (pp. 124–26)

Omar is particularly impressed with the self-conscious urbanity of Beirut. He observes it in the Friday outings to the horse races near the Beirut forest, and in the promenades by the sea during which the middle classes flaunt their wealth through their dress and their carriages. He even sees it in the city's manicured cemeteries, which are full of flower beds and carved marble tombstones (p. 125). One should be cautious, however, when reading Omar's dramatic contrasts between Beirut and Jaffa. Muhammad Izzat Darwazeh, the great Nablus essayist and nationalist leader, had visited Beirut just a few years earlier, in 1898, when the Beirut safe harbor had not yet been built, and his description of the city was much more modest, particularly as he compared it to Nablus and Jaffa.[7]

AN IMPOSED EMANCIPATION?

Most perplexing in Omar's narrative, however, are his antifeudal diatribes, which are replete with references to the "passing order" in Palestine.[8] In discussing the objectives of the Arab Society—a secret movement he joined in his twenties (see below)—he often referred to the declining authority of *shuyukh an-nawahi* (rural potentates) in a disparaging manner: "The feudal system has demonstrated its utter failure; it has no army and no power to rule or to discipline; for the authority of the feudal lord rests on the consent of his followers—and when they defy him his power collapses" (p. 145). He frequently refers to the "reactionary feudal system" and "backward feudalism." Yet elsewhere in the memoirs Omar shows pride in his own patrimony, as well as his readiness to utilize it when it serves his interests. He exploited his privileged status to the utmost, for example, when he began to organize young fighters from the Bani Zeid region to join the Arab Society. He also referred with great pride to the exclusive marriage bonds that tied the Barghoutis of Deir Ghassaneh to the aristocracy of Jabal Nablus, particularly the Jayyusis and Qasims (p. 135). He was especially incensed when Jerusalem effendis treated his father "as if he were an equal, and did not recognize his social status and prestige" (p. 91). How does one account for this anomaly?

The explanation lies partly with his own rebellion against his father, the last representative of the passing order. Sheikh Hussein obviously belonged to the moderate opposition to the Ottomans. His leadership of the Peasants' Party, discussed below, was fully integrated into the regime's institutions and aimed at competing for proper representation in the chamber of deputies in Istanbul. He constantly opposed Omar's choices in critical moments of his youth, including his desire to study in Istanbul rather than Beirut and his joining the Arab Society and agitating against the Ottoman *mutasarrif*. Perhaps most crucially, Omar's father forced him to marry his cousin against his will. On the other hand, Omar was constantly escaping from his rural background, as is obvious in his rejection of wearing the *hatta* in Jerusalem, his adoption of a modified urban accent (while retaining the *fusha* as a mark of aristocratic distinction), and his general lifestyle. His fascination and enchantment with city life can be gleaned in his description of his first encounter with Jaffa, which stands in stark contrast with his negative impressions of Ramleh in 1904. His father took him to Jaffa's Zarifeh Hotel, which had a cabaret show that he would secretly visit at night.

> The young man [Omar] loved Jaffa. He saw in it what was absent in Jerusalem and Nablus: a thundering sea carrying ships to its harbor; a shoreline overwhelming the visitor with new smells; anchored boats and ships with their masts defying the wind. Jaffa's orange groves surrounded the city and dominated it with their intoxicating blossoms. . . . Throughout Iskandar Awad Street one sees hotels and restaurants, and everywhere singing and dancing halls, and legally established whorehouses. Of course, the abundance of cabarets and nightclubs is not uncommon in a port city, even though it may undermine the religious sentiments and mores of Arabs and Orientals. (p. 108)

This last remark is obviously perfunctory, and is meant as an observation rather than a reflection of his own attitude.

Omar's antifeudalism, therefore, should not be taken at face value. It was essentially a search for a modernism and an emancipated social setting that was denied to him in his village environment. It was a path that he articulated as a personal journey as well as a reformist agenda that he hoped would uplift the community as a whole. Invariably he expressed this reformist tendency through his support of education for women, a passion that remained constant throughout his career. Just before the war he negotiated with an English missionary from Aboud, Miss Nicolson, to open a girls' school in Deir Ghassaneh. To that end he prevailed upon his father to contribute rooms for the school, and he used another two rooms in the family mansion for the teachers' lodging. He then pressed the local *mukhtars* to sign a memorandum authorizing the payment of their salary, against the wishes of the village elders (p. 139). While criticizing the feudal system, Omar was obviously keen to maintain the privileges, status, and power that came along with his seignorial rights.

His search for personal emancipation, however, was constantly frustrated by his father's designs for him, and by his family obligations. The first major crisis occurred when his father arranged for him to marry his cousin, in an apparent attempt to distract him from his political involvements. Omar's resistance was short-lived:

> He complained against this imposition. He was still young and had not finished his schooling. For it was well known that the search for knowledge and married life do not mix. Our ancestors have wisely coined the dictum, "Learning suffocates between the thighs of women." For marriage is always followed by children, and new responsibilities. Moreover, his cousin was ignorant, uncouth, and had not been exposed to a sophisticated environment. (p. 149)

When his protestations failed, he acquiesced to the marriage, but he decided to dictate to the bride his own rules of domestic conduct: She would be his partner, not his servant; he forbade her from kissing his hand; from the first day she was to treat him as her companion; she was compelled to eat with him at the same table, and to appear next to him in public. All of these egalitarian impositions must have weighed heavily on the poor lady: they were indeed revolutionary measures for someone living in a Palestinian mountain village. It is a great loss to the reader that key sections of the diaries, in which the author discusses intimate family matters, have been removed from the published version.[9] We do know, however, that his compact with his wife did not succeed. When he moved to Jerusalem she refused to move with him, until he threatened to divorce her. When they had a child she rejected his choice for his son's name, Mis'ab, insisting on calling him Jamil. Always nagging about her life, she was especially unwelcoming to his female visitors—not a surprising attitude considering the rare glimpse of his adventures with women that we get later in his memoirs (p. 157). He adds bitterly, "She never reciprocated his respect, and she constantly maintained an attitude of anger, boredom, and disgust in his presence for reasons that she never explained" (p. 151).

WE ARE ALL OTTOMANS

After he was sent to Beirut for his schooling, Omar began to appreciate the nature of the main divide in the national movement in Syria between the Unionists and the advocates of Ottoman decentralization *(al-I'tilafiyyun)*. He became an avid reader of the opposition press, *al-Mufeed* and *ar-Raï'i al 'am,* and declared his devotion to the Arab cause.

But Omar's Arabism was ambivalent, just as his anti-Turkish tendencies were qualified. His memoirs are full of contradictions on this issue. In part this is because they were rewritten without the benefit of diaries lost during World War I, when his house was pillaged. By then anti-Turkish sentiments had been heightened by the ruthless behavior of the retreating German and Turkish officers toward their Arab recruits. The ambivalence is primarily a result, however, of Omar's intimate acquaintance with Turkish and Syrian officers who belonged to the two main contending factions of Ottoman politics, the Unionists and the Federalists, and particularly with those officers who genuinely wanted to establish a multinational constitutional state under the imperial domain of the Ottoman state.

These ambiguities in the limits of Arab nationalism are obvious in his discussion of the three political movements in which he became active as a young man. The first was the Society for Uplifting the Fellah (Jam'iyyat al Falah li-Najah al Fellah), founded by "a group of feudal leaders in Jerusalem" and chaired by Sheikh Mahmoud Saleh, his father. Its objectives were to "support the new constitution and come to the aid of the coup d'état in Istanbul" (pp. 111–12). When Sultan Abdul Hamid attempted to annul the constitution, the society mobilized thousands of armed supporters in the Jerusalem area in support of Mahmud Shawkat Pasha and the leadership of the constitutional movement in Turkey, until the sultan was arrested and exiled to Salonica. Following the coup, Palestinian

supporters of Ottoman decentralization and latent Arab nationalists became active in sending parliamentary delegates from Jerusalem (which
had three seats) to the new parliament in Istanbul. They failed, according to Barghouti, since the "Unionists controlled the local press, the institutions of government, and the intelligence units."

When the war broke out,[10] Omar, who was in Deir Ghassaneh recu-
perating from a broken leg, conspired with ten members of his clan to establish a clandestine movement, the Arab Society, whose purpose was "to
intensify the struggle against Ottoman despotism." There were four conditions for joining the group: members must be under thirty years of age;
they must own a rifle and bring in a minimum of one hundred bullets
(those who could not afford a rifle were allowed to join with a pistol); they
must be nominated by two members; and they must swear an oath of allegiance to the Arab nation. The society raised the Arab flag of Bilad ash-
Sham (greater Syria) at their headquarters, the Saleh Compound, and
within a month had 150 fighting members (p. 143). But the politics of the
Arab Society were of a dubious nature. From Omar's description, it seems
that the group emulated the traditions of *qabadayat* (neighborhood street
toughs) from the Old City, and its members essentially engaged in rural
gangsterism, training in the use of arms, imposing "taxes," and disci-
plining the opposition. The society had branches in neighboring villages,
including Beit Rima, Nabi Saleh, Aboud, and other Bani Zeid townships.
Within six months it had eight hundred active members. The fact that
both the Peasants' Party (Jam'iyyat al Fallah) and the Arab Society were
hardly mentioned in the writings on Syrian politics in the late Ottoman
movement indicate either that Barghouti was exaggerating their impact,
or—more likely—that they were local, Jerusalem-based movements.[11]

It was only when Omar joined forces with disgruntled Palestinian officers of the Ottoman army, who were active in the ranks of the al-ʿahd
(Covenant) Party—which he joined in 1912—that the Arab Society acquired a broader political perspective and a sense of national belonging.
The party's declared political objectives were much in line with other nationalist movements in Ottoman Syria:

- That Arabic be added as an official language of the state and be
  used exclusively in the Arab provinces
- That deputies to the Istanbul parliament reflect the proportion of
  Arabs in the population at large
- That half the ministers in the cabinet be Arabs, and that Arab of-
  ficials be appointed to government jobs in the Syrian provinces

- That decentralization be applied to the administration of internal affairs.

To implement these objectives the Arab Society, with the support of the al-ʿahd Party, began to call for a tax boycott followed by a call for a general insurrection. Their moment arrived when they organized a display of their military power in the procession of Nabi Saleh near Deir Ghassaneh (p. 146), with the participation of hundreds of members who converged from the Bani Zeid villages.

The main achievement of this public spectacle was to draw the attention of the Ottoman *mutasarrif* (governor) of Jerusalem and his detectives to the activities of the party. They summoned the ringleaders and arrested them. The Arab Society was banned, and Omar was co-opted by his appointment as tobacco inspector, in charge of reporting and destroying illegally planted tobacco in the Bani Zeid region. A few months later he took a job as the livestock inspector, whose job was to impose the sheep tax on sheepherders. It is illustrative of Omar's character that he portrayed this debacle and a number of other retreats in his political career as acts that he undertook to serve the community. "The *mutasarrif* aimed at getting the young man out of politics [apparently with the connivance of Omar's father] by giving him a job with a substantial salary; and while he undertook these tasks enthusiastically, he did not sever his ties with his party comrades, nor did he abandon his principles" (p. 148). As the war progressed and began to take its toll on the Palestinian conscripts, local sentiment began to take an anti-Turkish turn, and the al-ʿahd Party's activities became clandestine within the ranks of Arab officers and government civil servants. Omar was advised by his contact with the party, Syrian commander Hilmi Bey, to understate his views and to demonstrate his public loyalty to the Sublime Porte.

The vacillations in the tactics and objectives of Jerusalem political groups in that period indicate that the local elites were still locked in the Porte-centered patronage of regional feudal groups. Omar's father, and probably Omar himself, belonged to these privileged elements in the Palestinian and Syrian provinces that were still trying to find a political niche that protected their relationship to the central government while at the same time allowed them to relate effectively to local groups that sought effective autonomy from Istanbul. This persistence of the old political game under new names also explains why it was possible for Barghouti to become involved in a number of (mostly failed) political opposition groups, bouncing back to his family connections either when these forays collapsed or when he was caught. As the leadership of the constitutional movement increasingly began to take the path of Turkification, this reformist-autonomist option in the Syrian provinces became untenable.

When Omar was finally conscripted into the Ottoman army, in 1914, one of his tasks was to help mobilize villagers in the Jerusalem area, who were recruited into the army by means of inflammatory speeches against "the enemies of religion" (p. 158), which he did with a certain degree of zeal. As the war progressed, however, public sentiment in Syria and Palestine, and with it the al-ʿahd Party's objectives, moved in an openly anti-Turkish direction. Al-ʿahd began to plot clandestinely for the secession of the Arab provinces from the Empire. Jamal Pasha—according to Omar's entries in the diaries (p. 168)—brought in the Tenth Army from Izmir to suppress the potential rebellion. One of their achievements was to arrest many officers who were active in the party and execute them. At this stage Barghouti was playing the part of a political double agent. He still served as an officer on the Turkish southern front, but he was also a member of a movement that was effectively undermining the war effort. Later, when Omar was promoted to the position of procurement officer in Bir-es-Sabeʿ (Bersheva), he was given instructions to encourage Arab soldiers to desert and join Sherif Hussein's army (p. 188). He was also asked to sabotage the war effort by burning an army food depot, a task that he refused to fulfill. Instead, he gave soldiers extended leaves on forged papers.

Like many young men of Ottoman Palestine during the war, Omar was fascinated by Jamal Pasha, governor of Syria and a key leader of the Unionist movement. He was feared and hated as an opponent of the rising tide of Syrian nationalism and separatism, but at the same time admired as a ferocious military leader who, until the end of the war, attempted to keep Palestine and Syria within the Ottoman system.

At the end of the war, Omar narrated the following story about the retreating Ottoman army:

> All over Jerusalem the word spread that Jamal Pasha had negotiated a secret agreement with the Allies to rebel against the Unionists in Istanbul and to secede from the Ottoman state. In return the Allies would declare an Arab state in Palestine, Lebanon, Syria, and Iraq, of which he would be declared the head. Most people welcomed this news and tended to believe it. (p. 187)

What is important about this story is not whether it is true—which is highly questionable—but instead the fact that many Palestinians were willing to consider it and even support it. It also reflected the ambivalence of many Arab nationalist intellectuals in that period, like Omar, toward secession from Istanbul.[12] Omar's attitude toward Jamal Pasha reflects a certain complexity that is closer to the profile drawn by Ottoman revisionist historians than the prevailing attitude in Arab nationalist historiography.[13]

WAR AS AN INSTRUMENT OF MODERNITY

One of the major weaknesses of these memoirs is the author's annoying tendency to disrupt his personal narrative with political and historical interventions and commentaries that could easily have been moved to a separate volume, and which, in any case, are readily available in standard histories of the period. When Omar was a direct witness to these historical episodes, however, the reader has much to gain from his vivid recollections and personal perceptions of the events. One of the most riveting episodes in his narrative is the story of the collapse of the southern front when he was an officer in Bir-es-Sabeʿ and his resulting flight to Deir Ghassaneh, during which he tried to sneak in between the retreating Turkish and German armies and the advancing British forces. This is where the personal and the political are integrated with the best results. In his biographic essay on Omar es-Saleh, Yacoub al-ʿOdat retells the same story with one major embellishment: "In 1917, just before Jerusalem fell in British hands, [Omar al-Barghouti] was exiled to Ankara together with many young Arabs who were active in the Arab nationalist movement and who were sent to inner Anatolia to get rid of them. From his exile, Omar escaped to Jenin, and from there to Nablus . . . and to Koor, where he took refuge among the Jayyusi clan."[14]

ʿOdat got the facts wrong. He must have confused Omar with his father, who was indeed ordered into exile in Ankara but never actually arrived there (p. 201). (Omar is tight-lipped about why his father, explicitly moderate and conciliatory to the Ottomans, was exiled.) Omar's actual story is much more interesting and reads like a first-rate war adventure. It involved deserting his army post in the Negev Desert, traveling incognito to Jerusalem, where he became involved in a major debate by the city notables—meeting at Khalil Sakakini's home in the Old City—about whether Jerusalem was to be declared an open city (i.e., a noncombat zone) to be surrendered to the Allies. While hiding in Jerusalem, Omar met Fawzi al Quwakgi, the Syrian Ottoman officer who was to lead the Salvation Army into Palestine thirty years later, and

Colonel Ismat Innunu, chief of staff of the Eighth Ottoman Army and the future president of Turkey. In these debates the German commanders had the upper hand and refused to declare Jerusalem an open city. From then on, Omar was on the run. He deserted his house and belongings and tried to reach the British army in order to surrender. In the process he was shot twice and was eventually moved to a mobile British hospital in Aboud, and then to Jaffa to recuperate. In the hospital "he was visited by Mr. Dades, head of British military intelligence in the Occupied Zone. He spoke to him in Turkish and queried him about the inclinations of the Arab population. He then lectured him on the historic friendship between the Arabs and the English and asked whether he could be of any service to Omar" (pp. 208–9). Thus ends the Ottoman episode in Omar's life.

One cannot help but gain the impression that Barghouti was a survivor. This is evident from his cynicism about the Ottoman use of religion to mobilize the Palestinians when the Allies were advancing on the Egyptian front. It is also evident from his extensive use of his army and government postings to serve his career while he simultaneously advanced his ideological commitments to the Arab cause. But it is a tribute to Omar's inquisitive mind that he was able to see the long-term impact of these momentous events on the future of Palestine. Above all he was always reflecting on how the war had affected the country's social mores. He writes, "Arab society has progressed considerably from contacts with German [and Western] culture. . . . Men and women were affected by this modernism. Restrictions and divisions between individuals and groups were broken down. A new mentality emerged that was open to the offerings of the West. Without the war this change would have taken tens of years to be accomplished" (pp. 192–93).

Omar then lists some of these dramatic changes, which include both behavioral and ideological transformations. Among the behavioral changes he cites the unveiling of women, first among Christians, and then among Muslims, until the veil "was considered a reactionary habit." He also cites middle-class café societies and the drinking of alcoholic beverages, claiming that now one can hear Muslims "claim that drinking is not forbidden in religion." Among the ideological changes brought about by the war, Omar lists two outstanding phenomena. First, adherence to religion has become "purely ritual," he claims. "Today Muslims have abandoned their prayers and consider religious amulets and visits to saints' tombs and processional flags[15] as something of the past." These were the conditions in 1916. The second phenomenon was the emergence of Arab nationalism, triggered by the Turkification of the Arab provinces and the repression of Arab national pride and language.

Many of these reflections he developed in lively conversation with three of his intellectual companions: Nakhleh Zureik, Khalil Sakakini (his teacher), and Is'af al Nashashibi. During most of these debates he would "listen and not participate," presumably in deference to the status of his elders. All the time, however, he was forming his own impressions about the coming of the new era, and he had a boundless enthusiasm for the unknown.

CHAPTER 9

Ishaq Shami and the Predicament of the Arab Jew in Palestine

In his retrospective personal memoirs of the 1930s and '40s, *Ta'ir 'ala Sindiyanah: Muthakkarat* (Bird on an oak tree), the Lebanese historian Kamal Salibi discusses two groups of Jewish companions he encountered during his student days during the French Mandate in Lebanon. The first group consisted primarily of Arabic-speaking Jews from Syria and Iraq, several of whom took a prominent place in Arab nationalist and anti-imperialist intellectual circles in the 1930s and '40s; the second he identifies as Yiddish-speaking Jews from Palestine, who exhibited marked Zionist sympathies.[1] While the first group blended seamlessly into Arab social circles (many of them were middle-class and Westernized), the second, recollects Salibi, kept to their own, spoke very little Arabic, and viewed their host environment with suspicion.[2]

But this assessment does not accurately reflect the complex composition of Palestinian Jews during this period. Toward the end of Ottoman rule, native Jewish communities lived in the four "holy cities" of Palestine: Safad, Tiberius, Hebron, and Jerusalem. In the first three, Arabic and Ladino speakers constituted a substantial proportion, and perhaps a majority, of the Jewish population. Only in Jerusalem did Yiddish gain the upper hand, due to the large number of devout Ashkenazi immigrants from Russia and Eastern Europe.[3]

The life and writings of Ishaq Shami, who has been described by Arnold Band, perhaps with some exaggeration, as "one of the most significant Palestinian writers of the [twentieth century],"[4] shed an important light

Figure 6. Ishaq Shami (1888–1949). This picture
was taken after Shami abandoned his Arab *abaya*
and *qumbaz* and donned European dress, after he
left Hebron to study in Jerusalem. Jerusalem, 1913?
Photographer unknown. Photograph courtesy of
Joseph Zernik.

on one of the most contested of Levantine identities—that of the Arab
Jew. It is quite revealing that in most places today this term is considered
an oxymoron. It designates a forgotten milieu of those Mashriqi Jews
who identified themselves with the rising Arab national movement, and
who shared the same language and culture with their Muslim and Christian compatriots in greater Syria, Iraq, and Egypt as early as the Ottoman
administrative reforms of 1839. The image of the Arab Jew became more
poignant with the struggle for Ottoman decentralization and, decades
later, when Zionism began to challenge the cultural identity of Jews in the
Arab countries in favor of a separate Jewish homeland. The idea of the
Arab Jew evokes the character of the Egyptian critic and satirist Yaqoub

Sanou' from an earlier period, and Iraqi liberal and leftist writers who immigrated to Israel and Europe, including Shim'on Ballas, Sasson Somekh, Sami Michael, Nissim Rejwan, and the cineaste Ella Shohat. And, like most of those writers, Shami was never at ease with either his Jewish or his Arab identity.

The picture was more complicated in Palestine than in neighboring Arab countries. At least in Yemen, Iraq, and Syria-Lebanon, the community was largely homogeneous in ethnic and confessional terms. Internal social divisions resembled those of the Christian population in the region: between rural and urban, rich and poor. In Palestine, Jewish pilgrimage and European colonial projects (mostly the German Templars) in the late nineteenth century brought a large number of Ashkenazi immigrants from Eastern Europe and Sephardic groups from Bulgaria, Turkey, and North Africa. To these we should add the smaller group of "native" Jews who traditionally resided in the four historic holy cities. But "native" Jews were not necessarily of Iberian origins. They included also substantial Yiddish-speaking communities, which had been established in Palestine centuries earlier. Language must have played a crucial role in the formation of their identity. This is what Cooper, relying on a report prepared by A. M. Luncz in 1882, says about the spoken languages of the Jewish communities in turn-of-the-century Hebron and Jerusalem:

> Leaving aside the Karaites, a small Jewish sect which rejected Talmudic Judaism, Luncz divided the Jewish population into Sephardim and Ashkenazim: the former were subdivided into Sephardim proper, who spoke Judaeo-Spanish, and Moghrabim, who spoke Arabic; the latter differed from the Sephardim, he said, by ritual and by the fact that they spoke Judaeo-German. It is interesting to note that he found this language division to be the major distinguishing characteristic of the communities. According to Luncz, [in Jerusalem] there were 7,620 Sephardim, of whom 1,290 were Moghrabim, having come from the Maghreb or North Africa. As a rule, they were natives of the city, Turkish subjects, and fluent in Arabic.[5]

What is evident here is that although the majority of *native* Jews spoke Arabic, there was a preponderance of Ashkenazi residents whose mother tongue was either Yiddish or German.[6] In mixed cities like Safad and Hebron, however, Arabic was the common language of the Moghrabi, Sephardic, and Ashkenazi groups, as well as their essential link to their fellow Muslim and Christian Palestinians.[7]

By the turn of the twentieth century, one of the main points of contention within the resident Jewish communities was the question of

Ottoman citizenship. As long as the Jewish immigrants were granted concessions as protégés of Britain and other European powers, there were few incentives for them to become subjects of the sultan. Two factors reversed this situation: regulations stipulating that only Ottoman subjects could purchase land, and the issue of loyalty to the regime once Istanbul went to war in Crimea, and then against Britain and France in World War I. The first issue made some of the leading Sephardic families in Jerusalem a great asset to the Zionist project, since they were able to act as intermediaries in the purchase of land from absentee Arab owners and in turn pass it on to Jewish colonizing activities. With regard to the second factor, loyalty to the regime, the central issue was service in the Ottoman army. The Jewish leadership of the Yishuv was divided on this issue, with the Sephardic community favoring naturalization (and therefore, implicitly, service in the army). "Most Ashkenazim," wrote a prominent Sephardic leader, "regarded conscription into the Turkish army as adequate reason to avoid naturalization and leave the country. There were rumors that the leaders of the Yishuv had bribed Turkish officials to make departure difficult and enforce naturalization, for fear that no Jews would remain in Palestine."[8] But this battle for naturalization was largely lost, as the ferocity of the war drove thousands of Ottoman Arabs, including Jews and Christians, to evade service.

In his autobiography *Living with Jews,* Elie Eliachar suggests that, contrary to common opinion, it was the Ottoman Sephardic families in Jerusalem—both Arabic- and Ladino-speaking—and not the conservative Ashkenazim who spearheaded the move toward secular education and living outside the city walls in modern neighborhoods, and who socialized freely with their Christian and Muslim neighbours.[9] One of the main instruments of this integration was the Alliance Israelite school system, established in 1882, which introduced Jewish—and in some cases Christian and Muslim—children to secular education and competed with Russian Orthodox, Anglican, Quaker, and Catholic schools.[10] This view is confirmed by contemporary Palestinian writers such as Omar Saleh al-Barghouti, who attended the Alliance School with a number of his Muslim compatriots.[11] One should not forget, however, the impact of Nizamiyyah public schools established by the Ottoman authorities in the last third of the nineteenth century in bringing together in one classroom children who had previously gone to their own Qur'anic *kuttab* or Talmud schools *(heder).*[12]

HOW NATIVE JEWS CEASED TO BE ARABS

Writing several decades after the war, Eliachar has already adopted the Zionist distinction between Arabs and Jews as if they were binary ethnic identities. His family moved to the western suburbs from the Old City in 1902, and he had this to say about his native language: "We knew Arabic and conversed freely with our Arab neighbors, but Ladino was our mother tongue. Until the British occupation, many Ashkenazim, as well as Arabs, spoke Ladino. Hebrew, the holy tongue, was understood by Jews young and old, since it linked Ashkenazi and oriental [i.e., native] Jews in public life and business. Our teachers at the Talmud Torah schools would explain Hebrew texts by translating them into Ladino."[13]

The move from the Old City to the new suburbs—from the communal confinement of the walled city to the modern planned neighborhoods— was experienced as a rupture by most residents at the turn of the twentieth century.[14] In Eliachar's narrative, however, the opposite seems to be the case. In 1902 his family moved from the hybrid social space of the Old City to the exclusively Jewish neighborhood of Even Yisrael (and later to Beit Ya'akov, near Mahne Yehuda).[15] Wasif Jawhariyyeh, writing about basically the same period, recalls the considerable mixing of Muslims, Jews, and Christians in social and cultural activities, commercial partnerships, and even political alliances (in the Red Crescent Society, for example).[16] Eliachar is also aware of this extensive socializing, but in his retrospective consciousness it appears as a formalized ritual between confessional groups. This is especially noticeable in his description of Passover ceremonies:

> The beautiful custom of exchanging gifts between Jewish and Moslem families on the last day of Passover has been preserved to this day. Arabs sent their Jewish friends a *siniyah* (round copper bowl) laden with fresh bread, goats' butter, and honey.
> The Jews returned the *siniyah* by the same messenger, with *matzot* and homemade jam. My family maintains this old tradition to this day.[17]

A parallel reading of religious ritual in Jerusalem during Ramadan, Easter, and Passover, as recorded decades later by Jawhariyyeh and Eliachar, can illustrate how the ideological construction of the quotidian is filtered through the memories of these two writers, the first a libertarian Arab nationalist, the second a Sephardic Zionist. Although they lived side by side in contiguous neighborhoods during the same period, and they described the same events, it seems as if they were talking about two different cities.

But these distinctions between "Arab" and "Jew" were not always self-evident within the Jewish intelligentsia, and they did not go uncontested. With the establishment of the privileged position of European Zionist immigrants under the terms of the Balfour Declaration during the Mandate, many Arab and Sephardic Jews (in Palestine as in neighboring Arab countries) were placed in an untenable position. Their resistance to the imposition of Zionist identity was not primarily ideological, but cultural. The lure of Jewish nationalism was also the lure of modernity, of European liberalism, and of socialism. But these attractions also set them apart from their Arab and Levantine roots and pitted them against the independence movement in their own countries. Sociologist Yehouda Shenhav argues that the return to Zion meant little to them, either culturally or ideologically, since they were already in Zion. And for those Jews who lived in Iraq and Syria, the move to Palestine (before 1948) was seen not as a move to Zion, but as a move from one area of the Arab world to another, and thus was not considered to have any ramifications in terms of sacred geography. Even after the war, Mordechai Ben Porat, when asked to describe his relocation from Baghdad to Tel Aviv, said, "I came from an Arab environment, and I remain in constant colloquy with the Arab environment. I also didn't change my environment. I just moved from one place to another within it."[18] Citing the work of Amnon Raz-Krakotzkin, Shenhav suggests that the "negation of the diaspora" was also effectively the negation of the memory of the *galuti* (exilic, with a connotation of "ghetto mentality") Jew, including the Mizrahi Jews, and of Palestinian memory.[19]

This "negation of the diaspora," according to Shenhav, asserts the "primordiality" of Mizrahi Jews in Arab and other Middle Eastern cultures, and challenges the basic Zionist tenet that the history of the Jews was "frozen" in the years of exile:

> The primordiality thesis obliges us to ask whether the Mizrahim [i.e., Arab Jews], whose diaspora is not negated, need to return to history at all. The answer is that they do not, because theirs has been a continuous history. The Jews of the Middle East, according to this thesis, did not go through the history of Europe and therefore need not return to it. This version also disassembles the uniform, shared history of all Jews (a conception that entails the denial and repression of other cultures, notably Arab culture) that is posited by Zionist historiography.[20]

Deserting the static paradigm of the ghettoized Jew, which is borrowed from Eastern Europe and Russia and imposed on the Middle East, has significant implications, not only because it transcends the duality of East and West in relating to the Jewish condition of the Arab world, but also because it undermines the opposition of Arab and Jew as distinctive categories. In Shenhav's view, "Acceptance of this [narrative] . . . shatters the (ostensible) binary polarity between Jewishness and Arabness and posits continuity instead. In other words, it proposes a historical model that is not in conflict with Arabness and that contested the de-Arabization project of Jewish nationalism. It is a model that allows other voices to be heard, too, such as that of the writer Sami Michael: 'We viewed ourselves as Arabs of Jewish extraction; we felt even more Arab than Arabs. . . . We did not feel we belonged to a place but that the place belonged to us.'"[21]

In *Victoria,* Michael's most controversial novel, we observe the halting transition of identity of the Jewish Baghdadi working class from a ghettoized to a Zionist one forged in the Israeli *ma'abarots* (transition camps for new immigrants) of the 1950s.[22] Michael seems to suggest that in their Iraqi homeland, the Jewish upper and middle classes were relatively integrated into local Arab society, while their poorer brethren—Victoria's people—were confined to their communal neighborhoods. As they moved to Israel, their traumatic encounter with the remnants of the Palestinian Arab underclass allowed them to improve upon their questionable status in the new pecking order. Their socialization in the reconstructed Hebrew culture was achieved at the price of denigrating their Arab cultural roots. Sasson Somekh recently described this process of the conversion of the Arab Jews into Israeli Mizrahim most eloquently:

> Today I am no longer an Arabic Jew. I am 100 percent Israeli, but I came to Israel at age seventeen as a full Arab from a cultural point of view. I lived in the tent encampments of Tel Aviv and Bat Yam, and after a year, I was recruited by the Israeli Air Force. I came without knowing Hebrew, because in my home there was not even one Hebrew book—not even a Torah or *halakha* (Jewish law) books. I grew up in a secular Jewish community—the middle class in Baghdad had begun to be completely secular. No one in my family went to synagogue. That situation changed, however, when they came to Israel, along with the ambitious immigrants who wanted to get ahead. Anyone who wanted to be a successful lawyer or accountant had to accept the norms that were dictated here, and one of them was that someone who came from an Arab country had to be a little religious. That was the image, and it worked on them. We are Arabic Jews just as there are American Jews—it's a historical fact. But people did not use that definition,

because the Israeli society didn't like it. I am not afraid to use it, and there are others like me, such as the author Shimon Balas or Professor Yehouda Shenhav, who do not try to erase it, but also do not use it too much.[23]

But "use it" or not, Somekh is aware, and makes us aware, that this Arabness of the Mizrahim was so transformed in the Israeli cultural crucible that there is no easy way to go back. We can therefore speak today of cultural affinities or a symbiotic past, but a "return to the roots" would constitute an ideological project that flies in the face of the reintegration of the Mizrahim into a new Hebraic culture that stands in a new relationship to its Arab past.

This dilemma of the Mizrahi Jew, engulfed in the European culture of the Zionist project, is at the heart of Ishaq Shami's conflation of identity. Shami was born in 1888 in Hebron to a Damascene silk merchant, Eliahu Sarwi, known as esh-Shami, and a Hebronite Sephardic mother, Rifka Castel. At home his father spoke to him in Arabic and his mother in Ladino.[24]

Shami's formative years in Hebron were crucial in shaping both his secular Jewish identity and his Arab cultural affinities.[25] Eliahu Shami, according to Hebronite legend, was a strong-willed Arab patriarch who married three women. The third, the native Rifka Castel, whom he married when he was sixty, gave birth to Ishaq and his two brothers, Yacoub and Dawood. His textile trade brought him in close proximity with the peasant women of Mount Hebron, from whom Ishaq later derived his intimate knowledge of peasant conditions. For much of his youth, Ishaq wore the traditional Khalili *qumbaz* and studied both Hebrew and Arabic in the local religious school. Later, in the Hebron yeshiva, he adopted "heretical attitudes" and was asked to leave.[26] By the age of eighteen he had left Hebron with his life-long friend, David Avitzur, and enrolled in the Ezra Teachers' Training College in Jerusalem, apparently against his father's wishes.

In Jerusalem, Shami began to don Western clothes *(franji)* and discovered the ideas of the Jewish enlightenment. He received his teacher's training certificate in 1909.[27] It was through the Hebrew revivalist circle he met in Jerusalem and his friendship with S. Y. Agnon and Yitzhaq Ben Zvi that Shami became exposed to Zionist ideas. Shami was one of only a few Sephardic writers of that period to become active in Zionist circles, and he seemed to have attracted the attention of David Ben Gurion as an expert on Arab society.[28] But, unlike the well-known Jewish experts on Arab affairs in the Histadrut and the Jewish Agency (such as Yacoub

Shim'oni and Ben Zvi himself), Shami was rooted in Arab culture, and it was this dimension of his cultural identity that continued to torment him for the rest of his life. Zfira Ogden traces his agony in a series of letters he wrote from Hebron to David Avitzur. His agitation became increasingly apparent as the communal clashes between Muslims and Jews (by this period one can almost begin to identify them as a conflict between *Arabs* and Jews) intensified throughout Palestine, particularly after the clashes of 1921. Shami seemed to believe that Hebron was immune from these clashes, but his father's death, in 1927, personalized his distress:

> Now, my friend, I can reveal what has been going on inside me and expose it without a mask. One year after his death, I can say that my relationship to him was not strong enough. But his death inflamed old wounds that I had thought were about to heal. Two different worlds! But in death we forget everything. Living in poverty, need, loneliness, and these old walls of the city, blackened by soot, I feel like a mere insect. All his life was a series of pain. And in his death he was alone; not even his children accompanied his coffin.[29]

The "two worlds" referred to here have a layered meaning. They point to the schism that distanced Shami from his father's generation, as well as the wall that separated him from the Orthodox Jewish community, which he had deserted. But they also represent the distance between the world of Hebron and that of Jerusalem and the "outside" world, which was characterized by modernity and freedom. Summing up this duality around the same time, the Hebrew author Yehouda Burla wrote, "Shami is a son of Hebron, where Arab life is exposed to view, intermixed with the Jewish street like nowhere else in Eretz Israel. He can provide layers of life from the Arab existence like a man scooping up a handful of whey or cream. The Arabic language, customs, and way of life—all the features of folk literature—are as evident and palpable as they are in Hebron itself."[30]

Immediately after the clashes with the Hebron Jews of 1929, when the bulk of the community found itself compelled to leave the city, Shami's despair reached a new nadir. But it was typical of him to personalize his tragedy. Rather than blaming the situation on the increased ethnic-religious tensions in the country, he attributed them to his fate:

> Everything has lost its worth. For what is the use of anything if we are unable to reach our goals? . . . This is the secret of my tragedy: when I look back at my life, I realize that everything was distorted and wrong from the foundation. My very existence was a big mistake, beginning with the smallest matters and ending with the biggest. Due to my own faults or due to fate, it does not matter. I had the best eight years of my life in Bulgaria. I have not retained a single memory of that place that deserves to be rekindled. My life in Jerusalem before that, and in my birthplace, Hebron, and

another nine years at the bottom—of slaughter, and pillage, and poverty—
all are the same. Here you have a life of dirt and mud, without my ability to
do what it takes.[31]

Shami moved briefly to Tiberius, and then moved with his family to
Haifa, where he remained until his death. But at the height of his agony,
Hebron always loomed in his dreams as the place to which he would re-
turn, both literally and metaphorically. In 1939, the last year of the Arab
Rebellion, he was still living in Haifa and teaching. He wrote to David
Avitzur:

> Torrents of rain falling outside. My clothes are wet and my teeth are chatter-
> ing from cold, and water is flowing like rivers in the street. I am totally fa-
> tigued and walking aimlessly, looking for shelter. Suddenly the door opens,
> and a blinding light shatters the darkness. Around me I hear heavenly music,
> filling my heart with contentment. I look around me and there is a huge table
> overflowing with food, the delicious bounty of this land, set by a stack of
> carpets and silken pillows on which I saw our elderly Hebronites [khit-
> yaritna al Khalayleh], with their long white beards and red cheeks—each one
> of them holding a golden goblet, full of wine whose aroma was filling the
> room. I stood by the door for a moment. Silently they made a place for me
> and, without stopping the music, they sat me next to them.[32]

In this dream sequence it is interesting to note that his elderly Khalayleh
(he wrote the Arabic expression in Hebrew) have the combined attributes of Muslim sheikhs ("white beards and red cheeks") and Jewish elders (drinking wine from a golden goblet). They were Muslim Jews.

To the very end of his life, Shami maintained a single obsession: to
write a major book about life in Hebron, which to him meant the life of
the country as a whole. The object of his hatred was also the source of
his love and dreams. "I will tell you something about my dream," he
wrote in a letter to Avitzur. "Last week I was seized by insomnia. As I
lay awake I began to ponder a great book narrating the life of Hebron.
It should be a volume of a thousand pages and more, made up of several
chapters. Again I dream, but who knows if I can ever realize this dream.
Yes, my friend, pain often strengthens us, but sometimes it undermines
us and confiscates our creative powers."[33]

SINS OF THE FATHERS

It is very hard to categorize Shami as a writer, in part because he was an
Arab Jew writing about Palestinian themes in late Ottoman Hebrew (or,
perhaps one should say, in early modern Hebrew). Earlier in his career

he had begun writing in both Arabic and Hebrew on Arabic literary production. His early essays that still exist include contributions on Jurgi Zeidan, historical fiction, various tracts on Arab poetry, and an essay on the origins of modern Arab theater. The Jerusalem Municipal Archives also include correspondence in Arabic with a number of his colleagues, including Yehouda Burla, but apparently none of his Arabic writings are available in print.[34]

From a reading of his short stories and novella, one can say that his style is highly ethnographic, with a strong tendency toward naturalism (his work recalls Jack London's *Call of the Wild*). Many of Shami's short stories are set in his own environment, in and around Hebron, in Jerusalem, in Jericho, and in Nablus, and most of the characters in his stories are Muslim. It was this nativism that elicited from Anton Shammas singular praise: "Some seventy years ago Shami brought into the scene of modern Hebrew literature a local Palestinian validity that hasn't been matched, or challenged, since *Vengeance of the Fathers* is the only novel in modern Hebrew literature whose characters, landscapes, and narrative voice are all Palestinian."[35] Yet in this novella there is a disturbing tendency to treat religious ritual, processions, and tribal gatherings as a series of vignettes—ethnographic, if largely accurate, Orientalist tableaux—for the titillation of an external viewer.

Only in two instances does Shami deviate from this externalizing discourse and become very subjective. The first is his contrast between the crass materialism and cunning habits of the residents of the coastal plains and the basic goodness of the mountain people. Here it is clear where Shami's Hebronite affinities lie, even if we take into account the sarcastic tone:

> Those of the coastal plain—the Prophet will surely forgive them their errant ways and not injure the land on their account. They, after all, have a long way to come, and to double work, to till their own plots as well as the fields and orchards of the Jews. The Jewish *khawajas* don't even pick their own legumes: they come to the villages and offer high wages for a day's work, and even give away the gleanings. . . . The *sahil* dwellers are shrewd calculators, sharp, cunning bargainers.[36]

The mountain people, by contrast, are at peace with themselves:

> The hill dwellers can confidently leave their homes and meager farms to the children and the old folk and go off to join the celebrants [of Nebi Musa processions]. A week of little work brings in no earnings. When the work season ends in the hills, the *fellah* has little to do. Many loaf around idly even when work is available. In the hills there is no call for working hands,

and those who go off looking for work in the nearby town generally don't even earn enough to pay the price of a pita or a night's lodging at a *khan*. In bad times, when money is scarce and all sorts of creditors and tithe collectors descend on the *fellah*'s neck to suck his very blood and marrow even before his grain is ripe, the best thing is to flee to the hills and hide until the storm passes. The *mukhtars* and the sheikhs will know their job and will turn the creditors away with a curt, "Go, and return when blessings descend again."[37]

The second departure from his clinical ethnographic style occurs in a very stark and poignant episode in *Vengeance of the Fathers,* in which Shami describes the fate of Nabulsi women who went to bid farewell to the procession of men in the Nebi Musa *mawsim* leaving town toward Jericho. Shami's rich fantasia of dancing youth, horse races, and *dabkeh* circles is juxtaposed against the condition of the womenfolk, who were not allowed to accompany the horsemen and who had to turn around and head back to town. During the fantasia their spirits were lifted and they felt free to uncover their faces and ululate, but now this moment of elation is over.

> The celebration had finished so quickly: the spectacle was over, and they again felt their enslavement. Ahead of them stretched a long line of gray, monotonous working days, with no spark of joy or consolation to illuminate them. Again they would have to close themselves up in their homes and continue bearing the yoke; again they would have to suffer in silence at the hands of their rivals and mothers-in-law, to submit to having their every movement watched and used as a pretext for hints and slanderous remarks against them to their husbands. . . . Sad and dismal, . . . they made their way back mutely along the sides of the road. At the town gate they covered themselves properly again, hid the hand drums under their arms, and, dark as outcasts, moved on with a groan, slipping away like shadows into the dark, narrow alley of the town.[38]

In these moving paragraphs, Shami displays not only a feminist sensibility, but also a profound insight into the role of ritual, carnivals, and religious ceremonies in releasing the repressed libido of poor urban women. This insight, one is tempted to add, could only be gained through a close knowledge of, and empathy with, a traditional society, such as that of Hebron at the turn of the twentieth century.

Vengeance of the Fathers was subject to highly different interpretations by Shami's contemporaries, and it continues to evoke controversy in the current debate about Shami's status as early pioneer of nativist Hebrew-Arabic literature. Hannan Hever suggests that the single factor most responsible for Shami's marginalization as a writer was the series of attacks on him by the critic Yosef Chaim Brenner, who dismissed his work as belonging to the "stories of Eretz Israeli genre," meaning that he wrote folkloric ethnographies about the life of the Jews in their various national environments—in this case, Palestine.[39] The task of the new Hebrew literature, according to Brenner, was to transcend the ethnographic in favor of universalistic human norms that should depict local realities in order to discover "the manifestation of the inner life and its essence." In this task Shami failed, according to Brenner, and his failure was due to his inability to escape the confines of his environment. But it was precisely this aspect of Shami's writing that explains its significance in the eyes of Palestinian critic Issa Boullata, who notes that it evokes "earlier times free of hostilities between Palestinian Jews and Arabs."[40] He notes Shami's leisurely style, untouched by the modern preoccupation with speed. Those "who crave action in stories may be frustrated by his style, but those seeking ambience will be rewarded and indeed moved by the deep human interest of each story," he writes.[41]

It is quite intriguing to see how *Vengeance of the Fathers* continues to receive such contrasting treatment by Israeli writers. Joseph Zernik refers to this work as conveying a "blasphemous, macabre permutation of the 'Blessing of the Fathers'—one of the oldest and most central elements in Jewish prayer."[42] Zernik suggests that the story implies that the "Fathers" (i.e., Abraham, Isaac, and Jacob), the common ancestors of Muslims and Jews buried in Hebron, constitute not a blessing, but a curse, and that they are a cause of continued bloodshed among their descendants. In other words, the conflict between the Hebronites and the Nabulsis is a camouflaged allegory for Jewish-Arab (or Jewish-Muslim) fratricide. Hannan Hever, however, does not share this view. He sees Shami's story as an internal critique of Arab culture as seen from one of its practitioners. Although Shami was under pressure to produce a new, universalistic Hebrew literature, he was nevertheless keenly aware of his need to prove himself as a Sephardic Jewish writer in a Zionist European milieu. In *Vengeance of the Fathers,* as well as in many of his other stories with Arab characters, Shami produces a universalistic critique of Arab culture from the inside. Hever concludes that Shami "systematically created characters that, while central to his story, were ultimately revealed as unstable, disintegrating figures, whose attempts to face conflicts led to their own dissolution. The Arab that Shami brought to Hebrew literature is, on the one hand, what identifies his work as Jewish-Arab writing. On the other hand, it also rejects Arabism as a canonical norm of full and autonomous subjectivity. Shami, then, solved his own acute conflict by constructing a disintegrating subject."[43]

In "Jum'ah the Simpleton," the most "Hebronite" story in the collection (and, in my view, his best work), Shami was able to weave into the plot his rich knowledge of peasant lore, cropping arrangements, and grazing rights, as well as his intimate insight into the psychology of the shepherd. Here, unlike in many of his other stories, the ethnographic material is seamlessly integrated into the rest of the novel. The author emerges as a master storyteller, and the reader feels that Shami has achieved a qualitative leap in his craft. Shami does not dwell on the nobility of the lonely shepherd, nor does he glorify the embeddedness of the peasant in nature, as he does elsewhere. He tends to emphasize the viciousness of nature, the cruelty of children toward the weak and the deformed, and the hopeless existence of people at the edge of subsistence, but these themes are delicately balanced by the kindness of the elderly peasants toward those in distress. At one point, the shepherd Jum'ah the Simpleton is taunted by the town children during an epileptic fit that drives him to remove his clothes and go into an uncontrollable rage. For the older peasants, however, his madness is a sign of divinity:

> For them his fit of insanity was a visionary seizure, a gracious gift from Allah. It was plain that the hidden light of the prophet rested upon Jum'ah at that moment. They believed that the angel Gabriel had touched him with his staff, and had filled him with his spirit until it had proved too much for him, so that he was now pouring it upon the demons and the goblins who, hidden among the bushes and in the clefts between the rocks, lie in wait for the faithful.[44]

The women in the crowds were particularly agitated. His madness resonated with their anguish:

> Electric charges sparked through their bodies, as with wide eyes they watched Jum'ah's twitching and listened to his cries. Every moan of his struck a chord in their souls and filled their hearts with a sweet trepidation and a strange astonishment. The wellsprings of compassion were opened in them to the point of tears, while some of them were so moved that they tore their hair and groveled on the ground.[45]

Jum'ah's derangement has the touch of divinity in it, and it is recognized as such. His imbecility is blessed and blesses those who come to know him. His death comes after an act of redemption; he is killed by a brutal kick from the very mule he had saved from disease. He comes to his end alone in the wilderness, surrounded by his flock and the evening stars, with only Mas'oud the dog left to mourn him.

In Jum'ah's death Shami celebrates the profundity of the simple folk, who are uncontaminated by the avaricious ways of the city dwellers and the people of the coastal plains. This theme is not unique to writers of his generation. Several Arab writers also portrayed village life and glorified the peasantry; Abdel Rahman al Sharqawi comes to mind here. But Shami's treatment of this theme is doubly unique: first, because it comes from a Jewish writer who, in this instance, was not writing about Jewish life; and, second, because his celebration of the peasant did not slip into sentimental glorification. Rather, he placed it in the context of cruel nature and the incessant struggle to survive.

THE LAST OF THE LEVANTINES?

This is how David Shasha, writing in *The American Muslim,* described the Hebronite writer: "Shami, perhaps the last authentic Levantine writer among Jews of the Middle East, is the missing link between the Genizah of Goitein and the Cairo of Mahfouz. In his short stories and novella he explores the everyday lives of simple Levantines, Jews and Arabs, which bespeak simplicity and a deeply abiding understanding of the rootedness of both peoples in the region."[46] This enthusiastic assessment of Shami's work has a major flaw, common to the vast majority of retrospective appreciations of this almost forgotten writer. It attempts to place Shami's work in the context of the current conflict between Arabs and Jews. It is unlikely that Shami would have appreciated the backhanded compliment, for he wrote in an epoch and a place in which Jews *were* Arabs, or at least a substantial body of native Jews exhibited an Arabist consciousness. In contemporary narratives of the late Ottoman period, such as in the autobiographies and diaries of Khalil Sakakini and Wasif Jawhariyyeh, native Jews of Palestine were often referred to as *"abna' al balad"* (sons of the country), "compatriots," and *"yahud awlad Arab"* (Jewish sons of Arabs).[47] The Red Crescent Society of Palestine, established in 1916 in Jerusalem, brought many leading Arab-speaking Jews, including Eintabi, Mani, and Eliachar, together with their Muslim and Christian compatriots, with the aim of mobilizing Ottoman Palestinians against the Western allies.[48]

The demise of Ishaq Shami as a writer also signaled the defeat of the possibility of an Arab-Jewish cultural tradition in Palestine. Unlike the situation in Iraq or Egypt, where it was possible for native Jews to contribute to and integrate themselves into local literary and artistic production, in Palestine this opportunity was cut short immediately after the Great War and the inclusion of the project for a Jewish national home in the Mandate. It wasn't only Zionism that was responsible for this rupture, but also the social and ethnic composition of the Jewish community in Palestine. At one point it seems that the Sephardic-Oriental (native) distinctions had meanings within the indigenous communities of the Holy Land. The fact that many Sephardim spoke Ladino at home, while the Orientals (Yemenis, Iraqis, and Moghrabis) spoke Arabic was one factor. Another had do with their social status. The Sephardic aristocracy maintained a class status and genealogical claims that seem to have set them apart from all their coreligionists. Soon after the First World War these distinctions began to blur, partly due to increased intermarriage between Sephardim and Orientals (as Eliachar points out), and partly because of Hebrew revivalism. There is no doubt that the rise of Zionism was the decisive factor in this transformation, creating a new polity, a new set of relations with the Ottoman and later Mandate authorities that dwarfed the clout and access of traditional Jewish communities to power. The new cultural divide was now between the hegemonic Eastern European Ashkenazim and their poorer Sephardic coreligionists. The new term *Mizrahim* emerged and subsumed the earlier distinctions between natives, Moghrabis, Kariets, and Sephardim.

Within the rising tide of Arab national sentiment in Palestine and Syria there was a clear differentiation between the European non-Ottoman Jews and the "native Israelites." An anti-Zionist petition signed in Jerusalem in November 1918 by a number of Palestinian intellectuals makes the point that "it is our wish to live in a satisfactory manner with our brothers the Israelites, the indigenous inhabitants of the country, with complete equality between their rights and obligations and ours."[49] Yehoshuah Porath also refers to a statement made by the Syrian Congress of 1919, in which a native Jewish delegate participated. The congress claimed to represent "all the Arabs of Syria—Muslims, Christians, and Jews alike."[50] Similarly, the First Palestinian Congress meeting in February 1919 issued an anti-Zionist manifesto that rejected Zionist immigration while welcoming those Jews "among them who have been Arabicized, who have been living in our province since before the war; they are as we are, and their loyalties are our own."[51]

Ishaq Shami's predicament, however, was that he wanted to escape the repressive atmosphere of the traditional religious environment he belonged to while retaining the social bonds of the community. The web of Hebronite Arab-Muslim society, in which he was raised and to which he had made an early escape from Jewish religious repression, was too confining and too conventional for him, and he was unable to find any social or intellectual solace. It was too late for Shami, who came to his intellectual maturity in Jerusalem on the eve of the Mandate, to join forces with Palestinian secular nationalism, which had a strong religious streak in it. His adoption of Zionism was far from an embrace of Jewish nationalism, which he treats with ambivalence in his writings. One can say that his Zionism was an attempt to break away from his Jewishness, and that it was an effective vehicle for bringing him to the modernist circles of the Jerusalem literary scene.

Beyond that, Shami's writings reveal a desperate nativist undertaking, an attempt to establish his own identity in an Arab culture to which the indigenous Jew could no longer belong without finding himself at odds with his community. Shami's tragedy lies in the fact that it was the very community of native Jews that became the main target of populist wrath against Zionism. Communal clashes between Muslims and Jews in Safad, Jaffa, and Tiberius in the 1920s, and later the massacre of Jews in Hebron in 1929, took place in the context of peasant displacement by Zionist land purchases and a rising tide of nationalist agitation against Jewish migration. But it wasn't only the European immigrants who were the early targets of Palestinian Arab nationalism. It was particularly those Jewish communities that were in closest contact and most integrated with traditional Arab centers inside the country. In Hebron it was apparently peasant mobs from the rural hinterlands and not the Hebronites themselves who spearheaded the attacks, and it was established Hebronite Muslim families in the city who protected the Jews.[52] Nevertheless, in the prevailing atmosphere these distinctions must have been irrelevant to somebody like Shami, who could describe himself as both an Arab and a Jew. He was already alienated from the traditional Jewish community and its stifling orthodoxy. Nevertheless, he identified with them as his people, his Khalayleh (Hebronites). Their tragedy became his tragedy in two senses: he could not dissociate from them as victims, nor could he overcome the shattered hope that there was room for reconciliation as the two communities were driven toward irresolvable nationalist polarity.

CHAPTER 10

The Enigmatic Bolshevik
from the Holy City

Najati Sidqi (1905–79) is almost forgotten in the annals of the Palestinian national movement. Even in the ranks of the left there are few who remember him. At one point, though, Sidqi was a leading figure in Palestinian and Arab communism. A leader of the trade union movement, he represented the Palestinian Communist Party (PCP) in the Comintern, was one of the few Arab socialists to join the antifascist struggle in Spain, and contributed significantly to the political and cultural journalism of the left in Syria, Lebanon, and Palestine. Now, thanks to Hanna Abu Hanna's meticulous editing of Sidqi's memoirs—and his extensive annotations and glossary—we possess a valuable record of what went on behind the scenes of Syrian and Palestinian partisan politics, as well as a vivid account of how Arab socialists and communists lived in the Soviet Union during the Stalin era.

At various stages of his career, Sidqi maintained personal, and sometimes intimate, contacts with Joseph Stalin, Nikolai Bukharin (author of the Soviet constitution and one of the founders of the Comintern), Georgi Dimitrov (the leader of the Bulgarian communists), Dolores Ibárruri (the legendary "Pasionaria" of the Spanish Republican movement), George Marchais (leader of the French Communist Party), and Khalid Bakdash (the Kurdish leader of the Syrian Communist Party), with whom Sidqi had chronic and bitter disputes over the nature of Islam and Arab nationalism. One of these disputes occasioned a party session in Moscow at which both Dimitrov and a forty-three-year-old Mao Tse-tung acted as arbiters between them.[1] He witnessed the arrest and execution of Gregory Zinoviev and Bukharin, the fall of Madrid to Franco's forces, and the rise of the Nazi movement in Berlin. He was also an eyewitness to the entry of the British army to Palestine, the exile of King Faisal from Damascus, and the exit of the French army from Syria and Lebanon.

An important element in Sidqi's memoirs is that they expose an overlooked aspect of political life in Jerusalem. During the Mandate period, political life was generally seen as taking place in Haifa and Jaffa, with their trade union activities, radical politics, and left-wing journalism. Sidqi, however, sheds light on the earliest appearance of left-wing politics in Jerusalem, first in the context of attempts by Jewish radical groups to break with the Zionist movement, and then in the attempt by Arab socialists to infiltrate traditional gatherings such as the quasi-religious Nebi Musa processions. Sidqi also highlights the mobility of left-wing activists, and presumably other militants, who were able to move from one city to another and to smuggle themselves across the border to Syria and Lebanon with relative ease. Only four years before the memoirs begin, Syria, Mount Lebanon, Palestine, and Transjordan were all part of a single Ottoman domain, with no borders between them.

Sidqi published a fragment of his "public" memoirs in 1968.[2] Hanna Abu Hanna's more complete edition of the memoirs is supposed to expose the clandestine aspects of Sidqi's political involvement. They still, however, leave many questions unanswered and several issues unresolved, which Abu Hanna, himself a veteran of Palestinian socialism, could have clarified. For example, why did the young Sidqi join the communist movement in the 1920s when his sympathies were clearly nationalist? And why was he expelled from the movement in the 1940s? Why did his older brother Ahmad, a party militant who lived with him in Moscow, act as a state witness against Sidqi when he was arrested by the British police during the Mandate, thus becoming a crucial factor leading to his imprisonment?

Above all, Sidqi's personal life is missing from his memoirs. Abu Hanna's introduction provides a schematic biography of the diarist, but Sidqi's own account of his personal life remains enigmatic. It is as if his clandestine militant Bolshevik lifestyle kept him from disclosing his intimate thoughts for fear of posthumous exposure. Luckily, some of the missing biographic material can be gleaned from Yacoub al-'Odat's compendium on Palestinian writers, published posthumously in 1975.[3]

Sidqi was born to a middle-class Jerusalemite family in 1905. His father, Bakri Sidqi, was a teacher of Turkish (and possibly of Turkish origin) who later joined Prince Faisal in Hijaz as a lieutenant in the campaign against the Wahhabi movement. His mother, Nazira Murad, was from a prominent mercantile family in Jerusalem. Najati spent his childhood in Jeddah and Cairo, later moving with his family to Damascus when Faisal was proclaimed king. He received a modern secular education in the most prominent Ottoman schools of Jerusalem, al-Ma'muniyyah and al-Rashidiyya.[4] In the early 1920s he returned to Jerusalem, where he worked in the Department of Post and Telegraph and joined the nascent PCP, at the time dominated by immigrants from Eastern Europe, including leftist Zionists. Sidqi's recollection of the ideological program of the leftist Zionists of this period is rather amusing (and of questionable accuracy), but it does reflect the ideological mishmash on the "Arab question" that prevailed at the time:

> The left-wing labor movement represented by the Jewish immigrants in Poaleh Zion called for the establishment of a socialist Jewish state to replace the Israelite bourgeois hegemony. They did not recognize the Arab social formation. In their view, the Arabs were a socially backward people and far from suited to adopting socialist principles. The party believed that the "Arab problem" in Palestine could only be solved through naturalization [sic] and intermarriage. With time, Arabs would have been absorbed into the crucible of a socialist Jewish state.[5]

In 1921 the PCP sent Sidqi to study in Moscow at the KUTV (Communist University of Toilers of the Orient), where he became acquainted with the Turkish poet Nazim Hikmat and members of the Nehru family. At the university he wrote his thesis on the Arab national movement, from the Unionist rebellion against the Ottoman state to the formation of the National Bloc. This short dissertation, which is attached to his memoirs, sheds some light on the type of scholarship that was conducted at KUTV. It also establishes Sidqi as a minor Marxist scholar (although it is quite possible, as Abu Hanna suggests in his introduction, that the manuscript—which he collected in fragments from three different sources—is incomplete).

Sidqi's very vivid recollections of daily life in Moscow in the early years of Bolshevism represent some of the most personal sections of his memoirs. He describes the austerity of the War Communism period (when the socialist regime introduced regimentation of labor and consumption), and the ideological debates conducted by Stalin's followers and the Trotskyites after the death of Lenin. Sidqi's local party branch reprimanded him for expressing unorthodox views about the repression of small landholders and he had to recant in public. Sidqi also participated in debates that raged in the early 1920s on the future of the Soviet family and relations between the sexes under the new Soviet morality code:

> Arab students who came to Moscow in the early Soviet period were mesmerized by notions of "free love." These ideas, diffused by the Russian Revolution, released young people from many restraints. The revolution was also very hostile to the religious order, and even more opposed to inherited social conventions. Among [feminist] women there emerged a movement calling for licentiousness, and among young people there was a call for free love. For a limited period they actually experimented with these ideas, until the Soviet authorities clamped down severely on these movements. It reasserted the view that the new order does not call for the abolition of the family, but advocates the establishment of a new family under new [revolutionary] conditions.[6]

In Moscow, Sidqi married a Ukrainian communist who remains nameless, faceless, and voiceless throughout the diaries. Paradoxically, the only time we hear her in the memoirs is when she is arrested by Lebanese gendarmes during one of the family's escapes from the British authorities across the Palestinian-Lebanese border. During this episode, disguised with a veil, she only bows her head in answer to the gendarmes' questions. Similarly, Sidqi's son and daughters—one of whom became a prominent doctor in the Soviet Union—are mentioned only in passing.

Sidqi's memoirs, although lacking in personal details, show the author to be a keen and sometimes critical observer of political developments in the early evolution of the Soviet state. On a second visit to Moscow, in the mid-1930s, he was sent to Tashkent by the Comintern to observe how the "national question" was resolved in a Muslim republic, Uzbekistan. Accompanied by Khalid Bakdash ("who insisted on coming along with me"), Sidqi developed a close relationship with the Uzbeki leader Hajayef and the chairman of the Uzbeki Communist Party, Akmal Ikramov, both of whom were aligned with Bukharin's agrarian policies.[7] Through them, Sidqi became acquainted with the main theses of the right (Bukharin) and the left (Zinoviev) opposition to Stalin. Although he was clearly sympathetic to Hajayef and Ikramov—both were executed soon after he visited them—Sidqi, who had Palestine in mind, was primarily interested in how a traditional Muslim society could make the transition to modernity, industrialization, and socialism without weakening its traditional social fabric.

Having completed his academic training, Sidqi was sent to Palestine to participate in Arabizing what was essentially a Jewish party. In 1930, he was arrested by the British police and spent three years incarcerated in Jerusalem, Jaffa, and Akka. The Comintern then had him smuggled

out of the country to Paris, where he edited the Comintern's Arabic journal, *The Arab East,* which was distributed clandestinely in North Africa
and the Mashriq. Eventually, the French authorities closed the journal
and had him deported.[8] Back in Palestine, Sidqi became thoroughly involved in the debates about the composition of the party. As seen by the
Comintern, the problem was clearly how to reconstruct the leadership of
a party dominated by Jewish socialists—many of whom harbored
crypto-Zionist sympathies—to reflect the fact that Arabs formed the majority in the country. The intercommunal clashes of 1929 exacerbated
these efforts at party reorganization. Here is how Sidqi saw these events:

> The Rebellion of August 24th, 1929, shook the party severely. It was par-
> ticularly perplexing for Jewish communists. Some of them defended the
> predicament of their coreligionists, while others preferred to take a more
> neutral position. This situation created a problem in the relationship be-
> tween the Jewish and Arab comrades. Stormy meetings were held in which
> the rebellion was debated: was it a national revolt, or a sectarian massacre?
> At this point the party began to split. Some Jewish communists claimed that
> it was a massacre. Others supported the position of the Central Committee,
> which regarded it as a [mainly] national uprising against repressive British
> rule, and as [a reaction] against land seizure and the pauperization of peas-
> ants. . . . During that period I was overseeing the party branch in Haifa and
> was in close contact with the Labor Federation there. . . . I began clandes-
> tine contacts with the imam of the Haifa mosque, Sheik Izz ed-Din al
> Qassam, who had a striking, tall figure. . . . He would tell me about his
> struggles in Syria against the French in 1920, and how he sought refuge in
> Haifa since then, only to begin his fight against the British, and how they
> began to pursue him. Later, in 1935, I received the news about the martyr-
> dom of Qassam and four of his comrades near Jenin.[9]

Sidqi's description of his arrest and imprisonment in Palestine in the
early 1930s for his communist activities is the most enigmatic part of his
memoirs, for the reason mentioned above: the appearance of his older
brother, Ahmad, as the chief witness for the prosecution. Primarily on
the strength of that testimony, which was followed by Sidqi's confession,
he received a two-year sentence. Ahmad was active in the movement
under the pseudonym of Saul when he was Najati's fellow student at the
KUTV. Najati writes in his memoirs, "poor, fragile Ahmad, who seemed
to have been beaten and hounded in jail, came to the stand . . . and
began to narrate how, as my elder brother, he loved me but tried to dis-
suade me from falling prey to subversive movements. Despite his advice
that I should withdraw from the party, I persisted in my dogmatic adherence and obstinacy."[10] When asked by the judge why he volunteered

to testify against his brother, Ahmad responded that his aim was to help reduce Najati's sentence. What is baffling about this episode in the memoirs is that it appears abruptly, and out of context, in the section on Sidqi's underground period in Jerusalem. Although Sidqi mentions "Saul" as one of his comrades in the student movement in Moscow, we are never informed that he was actually his older brother. And why, of all the people who knew him during his long stay in the Soviet Union, did the police recruit his own brother to testify against him? Abu Hanna suggests that this incident underlines "a deep understanding of human frailty and filial affection on the part of Najati, without any trace of vindictiveness."[11] It also, however, shows how convoluted Sidqi's life was, and his inability to come to grips with his personal and intimate relationships.

In 1936, the Comintern sent Sidqi to mobilize Moroccan soldiers against Franco. In the early days of the fascist rebellion, it will be recalled, a significant portion of Franco's army landing in Malaga was formed of Moroccan recruits and mercenaries, whereas most of the International Brigades fighting on the side of the Republic were European leftist volunteers. It was against this background that the communist movement had an interest in approaching the Moroccans. Sidqi lived among the Republican ranks in Barcelona and Madrid, disseminating leaflets in Arabic to the North African militias of the fascist movement. (One can imagine how ineffective these leaflets would have been, given Sidqi's Palestinian Arabic and the low level of literacy among Franco's rural Moroccan troops.) At the beginning of 1937, he was sent to Algeria to set up an Arabic radio station (his own idea) to broadcast anti-Franco propaganda to the Moroccan fighters—a mission that failed for some inexplicable reason. Sidqi's description of his time in Spain is both moving and cryptic. Although his mission was to engage the Moroccan recruits in some sort of dialogue, it wasn't clear what the party's strategy toward the soldiers was, as illustrated by this entry of September 24–25, 1936:

> I was told by the Central Committee [of the Spanish Communist Party] that a group of officers from the International Brigades was heading toward Cordova, and that I had to accompany them to talk with captured Moroccan prisoners and, using a megaphone, induce those still fighting on the other side to join the Republicans, and then to distribute leaflets to them written in Moroccan Arabic. . . . We eventually reached the front line [past the Sierra Morena range]. Several officers from the IB accompanied me to meet the Republican fighters. One of their officers approached me after he was told that I am Arab and said, "Do you want to see the Moroccans?" I said yes. He took me to an embankment and directed me to an opening.

From there I could see crowds of Moroccan fighters with their headgear, readying themselves for battle. I raised the megaphone and shouted, "Listen Brothers!!!" They froze and started looking toward the embankment. I continued, "I am an Arab like you, coming from a distant Arab country. . . . I beseech you, brothers, to abandon the ranks of your [Spanish] generals, who are oppressing you in your country. Come to our side, where you will be well treated and given a daily allowance. Those of you who do not want to fight will be returned to your land and family. Viva el Frente Popular! Viva la República! Viva el presidente de España! *[sic]* Viva Marruecos!"[12]

Sidqi was basically calling for surrender in both eastern Arabic and broken Spanish. Apparently the Moroccans were not pleased, nor were his Republican comrades. "I had hardly finished my call, and by the time it was translated to the [fascist] leaders of the rebellion, all hell broke loose with every kind of weapon imaginable firing on us. I was pulled back by the Spanish commander standing next to me: 'What have you done? Did you shout missiles at them?'" Soon after that incident, the Comintern ordered Sidqi to relocate to Lebanon, where his journalistic career in the left-wing newspapers began to flourish.

It was during this period that his relations with Khalid Bakdash became so strained that Sidqi was eventually expelled from the party. Abu Hanna suggests that the main reason for the expulsion was his opposition to the Hitler-Stalin nonaggression pact in August 1939, but this is not clear from Sidqi's own narrative. In fact, the author's assessment of his differences with Bakdash's supporters is symptomatic of a striking political naïveté that prevails throughout the diaries. He claims, for example, that the pact was welcomed by the party loyalists because it signified a rapprochement between international communism and German National Socialism. Sidqi himself opposed the treaty, because he considered it "a fake agreement, meant to gain time [for Stalin]."[13] It is more likely that the opposite was true: the pro-Soviet Arab communists supported the agreement, perhaps with some hesitation, because they wanted to give the Russians a reprieve from their global isolation. It is extremely unlikely, as Sidqi claims, that they were sympathetic to the ideological affinity between the two movements.

Eventually, Sidqi came out as an Arab nationalist with socialist sympathies. His break with the Comintern and Bakdash did not turn him against the left. Rather, he pursued a successful career in literary criticism and broadcasting in Lebanon and Cyprus. By the time of his death, in Athens in 1979, he had produced a dozen books of Russian literary translations and several plays and volumes of literary criticism. One of his books, *An Arab Who Fought in Spain,* was falsely published under Bakdash's name—an episode that inflamed Sidqi against both Bakdash and the PCP. Another work, *Nazism and Islam,* which he published to mobilize traditional Muslims against the Nazi movement, was translated into English and received citations from the French and British governments. The book became a decisive factor in his expulsion from the party since—according to Sidqi—it relied too heavily on Islamic texts for the tastes of his secular party colleagues.[14]

Sidqi will probably be best remembered, however, for his popular translations that introduced Pushkin, Chekhov, and Maxim Gorky to the Arab public in the widely circulated Iqra' series, published by Dar al-Hilal in Cairo. In the 1950s he also published translations of selections from Russian, Chinese, and Spanish literary masterpieces. He translated into Arabic several works by Edgar Allan Poe, as well as short stories by Guy de Maupassant from the French. Later, in the mid-1950s, Sidqi began to publish his own short stories, including the collections *The Sad Sisters* (eighteen short stories, published in Cairo in 1953) and *The Communist Millionaire* (published in Beirut in 1963), a collection of satirical stories on Arab communists he had encountered. Neither his expulsion from the party nor his cynical attitude toward communism deterred the Soviet authorities from publishing a selection of his stories in Russian (in Moscow in 1963).[15]

Najati Sidqi's memoirs do not do justice to his spectacular presence at critical junctures of momentous events. He was in Arabia with his father at Sherif Hussein's launching of the Arab Rebellion against the Ottomans in 1916. He was a witness to the end of Ottoman rule, and the beginning of Zionist immigration to Palestine. He became an early participant in one of the great revolutionary movements of the twentieth century, immediately after the Bolshevik seizure of power. He lived in Russia through the civil war period, the Great Famine, War Communism, and the ideological debates between Bukharin, Stalin, Zinoviev, and Trotsky. He was one of the few Arabs, and even fewer Palestinians, to fight with the Republicans in Spain against the fascist forces of Generalissimo Franco. In France, he edited the Comintern organ in Arabic, *The Arab East,* which it is believed was distributed throughout the Middle East and North Africa. And, finally, in Palestine he was one of a handful of left-wingers entrusted with the Arabization of the PCP. He was imprisoned several times and severely maltreated by the British, and he lived to narrate these events. Yet reading his memoirs, one is left with the impression of how mundane it all was; it is as if Sidqi were there but did not grasp the significance of what he was doing. One gets the uncomfortable feeling that underneath it all he was a communist tourist, hopping from Moscow to Kiev, from Barcelona to Madrid, and then back to Paris and Jerusalem to check on how the lads were doing. Still, to his great credit, he left (or was made to leave) the movement to which he had dedicated his life without bitterness, and without losing hope in the justice of the cause he had propagated.

CHAPTER 11

The Vagabond Café and Jerusalem's Prince of Idleness

The return of Khalil Sakakini from his American sojourn in the autumn of 1908 was an occasion for contemplating the creation of a new kind of cultural space: the literary café, a public meeting place to accommodate the formation of his circle of literati, the Party of the Vagabonds (Hizb as Saʿaleek). For him and many like-minded intellectuals of the period, the time was ripe. The new Ottoman constitution had just been declared, and calls for decentralization, Arab autonomy, and freedom of the press and assembly were spreading throughout Syria and Palestine. Sakakini was penniless and heavily in debt. To supplement his teaching income he became a copy editor for two Jerusalem newspapers, *al-Quds* (owned by George Hanania) and *al-Asmaʾi*, a literary paper that had just been started by the al Issa family in the Old City.[1] In 1911, the al Issa brothers, Dawood and Issa, moved to Jaffa, where they launched *Falastin,* the newspaper that became an instrument of the national movement, and which often clashed with both the Ottoman and British Mandate authorities.

In this chapter I will attempt to trace the appearance and demise of a literary café, the Maqha as Saʾaleek (Vagabond Café), and its association with Sakakini's circle of Vagabonds in Ottoman Jerusalem during and immediately after World War I. Sakakini's philosophy of pleasure *(falsafat asSuroor)* and the cosmopolitan atmosphere that prevailed in Jerusalem during and immediately after the war constituted the social milieu for this café and the circle that formed there. I will also situate the

Maqha as Sa'aleek in the context of the evolution of similar cafés in Ottoman Syria and Egypt in an earlier period.

Jerusalem, similar to all medium-sized Arab cities of that period, had two kinds of public spaces in which urban residents participated in celebratory events. Major family revelries, such as weddings, births, circumcisions, and baptisms, were all celebrated within the confines of the household, while religious ceremonials took the form of street processions. These included Ramadan, Sabt enNour ("Saturday of Fire," which followed Good Friday), Nebi Musa, Purim, and al-Khader processions. Although obviously religious in character, many of those ceremonials had acquired a clearly worldly, if not mundane, character by the turn of the twentieth century. Some, like the Nebi Musa processions, were religious occasions that became almost exclusively nationalist in character. Nebi Rubeen celebrations in the south of Jaffa, in which Jerusalemites participated, had entirely lost their ostensible religious character by the end of the nineteenth century.

In earlier periods—probably around the sixteenth century—coffeehouses emerged as an Arab—or, rather, Islamic—response to the taverna; that is, it was a place for secular socialization that did not serve proscribed substances.[2] Ralph Hattox argues that the absence of a restaurant tradition in early modern Middle Eastern towns, with the exception of the traditional merchants' *khans,* made the coffeehouse a necessary instrument for receiving guests outside the more intimate confines of the home. The domestic atmosphere of the home was too restricting, and the new public space of the café would allow the host to suspend issues of rank and prestige. "This would imply," according to Hattox, "a subtle shift in the relationship of host and guest, and a break, if only symbolic, with old values."[3] It was this break that created a café atmosphere that was both informal and potentially dangerous. The danger did not come from coffee as a drink (which was attacked early on by some *ulama* as potentially intoxicating),[4] but from the atmosphere associated with the coffeehouse, and the recreational activities that were soon to be hosted in it.

By the late Ottoman period, Levantine coffeehouses served a predominantly transient population. Initially they served three different types of clientele.[5] In areas surrounding public buildings (land registries, courts, police stations), the cafés received petitioners, applicants, and people waiting for official redress of grievances. Here one could usually find a *katib adiliyyah,* a public scribe who would fill out official forms and petitions for a fee. In the mid-nineteenth century, a second type of café began to proliferate in provincial center squares where carriages and motor vehicles picked up and discharged passengers. In port cities there evolved a third type of café, which served mainly sailors, travel agents, and customs officers. The last two types evolved to serve several economic and social functions, including serving as a place for porters, stevedores, and other itinerant workers to find work. They also served as a poste restante location, where letters and packages could be dropped and later retrieved by their recipients.

But it was because the café allowed for spontaneous—and often anonymous—encounters that it began to serve a wider recreational and entertainment function. The recreational aspects of cafés were enhanced by the consumption of alcohol, small-scale gambling (cards, dominoes), the performance of music (they contained the earliest phonographs and radios), the presence of prostitution, and the sale and consumption of tobacco and hashish.[6] The relative anonymity of the café milieu permitted the emergence of political and literary groups, whose members found them convenient for unscheduled meetings and discovered they allowed an easy escape when necessary.[7] The transgressive nature of coffeehouses was particularly felt in port areas, such as Jaffa, Alexandria, and Beirut, where the consumption of proscribed substances (alcohol and later hashish, which was initially more tolerated) combined with the clients' tendency toward political dissent gave cafés their early subversive reputation. In Palestine, Jaffa's Manshiyyeh Quarter was an ethnic border area (between Jaffa and Tel Aviv) in which such cafés proliferated. Café Baghdadi was one of several cafés on Shabazi Street observed by the Mandatory police:

> Without a doubt this place is the main attraction of Shabazi Street. All hours of the day it is crowded with very shady characters who sit and gamble, playing all manner of card games and dominoes. Here, too, the "chalk and slate" system of scoring is favored, although on a few occasions players have been apprehended in flagrante delicto passing money. Many women, undoubtedly prostitutes, gather in this café and hang about, passing from table to table.[8]

In a study of public morality in turn-of-the-century Beirut, Jens Hanssen argues that the 1840s were a turning point in the public perception of cafés and their clients. Until the mid-nineteenth century, most coffeehouses were located inside the walled city by the port area, where merchants, soldiers, and sailors gave them a disreputable, if not dangerous, reputation.[9]

Once Ottoman city planning and street lighting were introduced, increased security meant that coffeehouses could move outside the city walls, particularly in the Zaytuneh, Ras Beirut, and Corniche areas. Now that cafés and other recreational centers were patronized by members of the patrician families, they suddenly became respectable. In his social history of coffeehouses, Ralph Hattox rejects the distinction made between respectable and shady cafés and suggests that the main dividing line was between bars and cafés. While the former were associated with gambling and drunkenness, "the coming of the coffeehouse signaled the beginning of an entirely new phenomenon. Perfectly respectable people went out at night for purposes other than piety."[10] In Cairo and Istanbul the public café tradition had a much older pedigree. Jabarti chronicled the coexistence of wine taverns and coffeehouses during the late eighteenth century, before the French Expedition. During Ramadan, coffeehouses were major centers for public entertainment and *arghileh* smoking. What seems to have given cafés an aura of respectability here, as in Istanbul, was their patronage by Al Azhar scholars and sheikhs, each group frequenting their own coffeehouse.[11]

The main distinction between different types of late Ottoman cafés was between popular cafés *(maqahi sha'biyyah)* and modern cafés *(maqahi franjiyyah)*, which had the distinction, from the turn of the twentieth century, of catering to a mixed male and female clientele. To these Abdel Mun'im Shmais adds the artistic café-cabaret *(maqha al-'awalem)*, which began to proliferate in Cairo during (and possibly before) the French Expedition, and spread from there to Alexandria, Beirut, and Jaffa.[12] He makes a further distinction between *'awalem* cafés, where one could see a stylized form of belly dancing and which had an aura of respectability, and *ghawazi* cafés, where more vulgar *(suqi)* dancing was performed for a lower-class clientele.[13] Literary cafés seem to have originated with the *hakawatiyyeh*, or narrators of popular ballads. Jawhariyyeh lists several of this type of café in Jerusalem's Old City, where classical ballads such as the Tale of Antara and Sirat Abu Zeid al Hilali were performed during his boyhood (1904–10).

The demise of these balladeers in all likelihood resulted from the spread of literacy and the invention of the radio and phonograph, which were always placed in a prominent place in popular cafés. In Cairo, Beirut, and Jaffa, literary cafés seem to have been the domain of journalists and copy editors, who used the café to meet with their sources, exchange views, and write their articles.[14] Poets, lyricists, songwriters, and—later—screenwriters frequented these same establishments.[15]

Naturally, the café scene in Palestine was considerably less diverse than it was in Egypt, but it followed the same trends. In Jaffa and

Jerusalem a multiplicity of new newspapers were launched after the implementation of the constitution of 1908, taking advantage of the new Ottoman press laws. Public cafés and newspapers became linked together in the public imagination. Around World War I it was customary for a reader to stand on a platform in the coffeehouse and read the daily news and commentary to other customers. In a recent study on the diffusion of literacy and reading in Palestine, the historian Ami Ayalon discusses the role of the public café in this marriage between newspapers and coffeehouses. He suggests that coffee and tea acted as stimulants for reading and discussion, while the proprietors of coffee- and teahouses increased the number of their patrons by subscribing to a number of journals. In Istanbul the café–reading room *(kiraat-hane)* constituted a new institution.[16] Jabbur al Dweihi cites Sirafim and Sivanaki as the two most popular of these cafés during the Tanzimat period.[17] In Palestine there was an added dimension of cafés: they served as reading rooms where political propaganda could be disseminated:

> Newssheet reading became a common feature of café life on the eve of the First World War and still more during the war itself, when they represented an essential source of reports on the rapid events unfolding on the front. Thus Ilyas Hamati—who as a teenager used to work in a *qahwat al-bahr* (sea café) in Acre prior to the war—remembered cafés as a "gathering place of the educated that used to read the newspaper *Falastin.*" The conquering British army used them as places for spreading propaganda, and they even opened new coffeehouses especially for that purpose. One intelligence officer reported that "all the telegrams and newspapers" were placed in them.[18]

OTTOMAN CAFÉS IN JERUSALEM

The café also constituted an arena for mundane social interaction and leisure activities, precisely because it was secular space that was not associated with economic exchange or religious celebrations. Unlike the restaurant, which was also a novelty for Palestine, it did not have a utilitarian function, such as consuming food. It was designed purely for social pleasure. In Ottoman Jerusalem, the café equivalent was the *odah,* the exclusive bachelor pad that served the entertainment purposes of young, unmarried men from upper-class families.[19]

In his memoirs, Wasif Jawhariyyeh describes several cafés and teahouses in Jerusalem and its environs, whose numbers mushroomed in the period between the Constitutional Revolution of 1908 and the years before the war. He identifies the most outstanding cafés that he frequented:

- The Seraii Café in the Suq al Attareen (Perfumers' Market), over-looking Aqabet al Takiyyah. This café, which was surrounded by a huge mulberry tree, served supplicants who were waiting for government papers from the Department of Justice, the land registry *(tapu)*, and the population registry *(da'irat al nufus)*. Next to the café, in the yard, was a holding cell, known as the cage *(qafas)*, where accused prisoners were temporarily held before their indictment.[20] Many of the café's clients were relatives waiting for the disposition of their arrested kin's case.

- Qalonia Café and Bar, run by Froso Zahran. Frequented by Ottoman officers, it housed a gambling section in the back.[21]

- The Mukhtar's Café, originally located above the bank Crédit Lyonnais, just outside Jaffa Gate. This was originally the Vagabond Café, before the buildings outside Jaffa Gate were destroyed by Colonel Storrs in the 1920s.

- Jraisheh Café and Garden, a municipal café near the Jraisheh springs. It was subcontracted annually to Jerusalemite restaurateurs. In 1915 the café was run by Jiryis Jawhariyyeh, who managed it until his death in 1918.[22]

- Café and Bar Jawhariyyeh. Opened by Khalil Jawhariyyeh in 1918, the café served Lebanese *araq* and *mezze* with iced water (thanks to the recent introduction of electricity to the city). Here, as elsewhere, light meals were available in what was otherwise exclusively a café atmosphere. Located near the Russian compound on Jaffa Road, the café hosted a number of musicians, such as Muhammad al-'Asheq and Zaki Murad, and had a cabaret show that featured Badi'a Masabni and her husband, Najib al-Rihani.[23]

A few years later Najati Sidqi, the Jerusalem socialist writer and (later) communist militant, described the radical atmosphere at the Postal Café just after the war. Owned by a Russian Jew, the café was located behind Barclays Bank, near Jaffa Gate.

> Every afternoon I used to sit in this café, where we used to encounter its cosmopolitan clientele. Among these were a tsarist officer with a white beard who claimed that he was a captain of a Russian battleship before the Bolsheviks seized his boat in Odessa; a young clerk working for the municipality, whose father was Russian and his mother was Arab; an immigrant painter who used to sketch the café customers for a few *qurush*; an elegant lady who kept talking about her properties in the Ukraine; and many young

men and women immigrants who would chat and drink sodas. The discussion was always on the same themes: Jewish migration, Arab resistance, Jabotinsky's insurrection, the battle of Tel Hai in northern Palestine, the rebellion in Jaffa [1921], and the clashes between Arabs and Jews. These discussions included ideological debates, which were translated to us in the vernacular. From them we became familiar with the basic tenets of socialism, anarchism, and Bolshevist doctrines.[24]

Although cafés began to proliferate throughout the city at the turn of the century, it was those establishments located at the periphery of the new neighborhoods around the area of Musrara, Jaffa Gate, and the vicinity of the Russian compound that provided the cosmopolitan milieu for an intellectual and artistic resurgence. This area soon became the abode of the café-bar and the café-cabaret, where music was enjoyed with alcoholic drinks. These locations and their association with music and alcohol had a lot to do with their ethnically and religiously mixed character. They were the nodes where the Christian, Muslim, Jewish, and Armenian populations could interact, creating a confessionally shared space and neutralizing the diktat of social prohibitions. They became centers where Russian, Greek, and Balkan pilgrims congregated during the Easter celebrations. With the pilgrims came affordable alcohol (cheap vodka, Cypriot brandy, and Greek cognac) and anonymous street crowds that encouraged the suspension of the strict conventions of Jerusalem public life.

Among the most famous of all Jerusalem cafés was the Qahwat al Mukhtar, later christened the Qahwat as Sa'aleek (Vagabond Café) by Khalil Sakakini and his intellectual circle. Established in 1918 in an enclave inside the Jaffa Gate by the *mukhtar* of the Orthodox community in the Old City, Issa Michael al-Toubbeh, it became known as the Mukhtar's Café. It started as a resting place for Greek, Cypriot, and Russian Easter pilgrims, as well as a general meeting place for the Orthodox community in the Old City. In his memoirs, his son Jamil Toubbeh recalls the café's genealogy:

> My father owned a café adjacent to the Jaffa Gate, abutting the southern wall of the city. Known as al Mahal (The Place), it was a sort of meeting locus for some of Jerusalem's most renowned intellectuals and humorists. These middle-aged and older residents of metropolitan Jerusalem felt as much at home in this environment as they did in their own homes. The Old City gave them an essential link to their past, their culture, their religion, and their history. Their discourse at al Mahal, over puffs on *arghilehs* and sips of Lebanon's renowned firewater, still rings in my ears. The environment of the café also tolerated occasional blasphemous language away from

the cultural revolution that was changing the character of both Jerusalem and Palestine.[25]

Sakakini had just come back from his exile in Damascus, where he was freed from Ottoman imprisonment by the army of King Faisal. Following the collapse of Faisal's Arab government in Syria, he returned to Jerusalem, where he resumed his journalism career. He wrote regularly for al Muqtatif, and al Hilal in Cairo, and for al Siyaseh al Usbu'iyeh in Jerusalem.[26]

The original owner of the café, Issa al-Toubbeh, had corresponded with Sakakini when the latter was still in New York and joined him in his struggle for the Arabization of the Orthodox Church. Toubbeh was a writer himself and shared Sakakini's literary tastes. In a compendium of Ottoman newspapers he is listed as the owner and publisher of a handwritten circular, al Ahlam (Dreams), which began to appear in September 1908.[27] Immediately after the war, when Toubbeh became the mukhtar of the Old City's Orthodox community, he moved his café to its present location inside Jaffa Gate, next to the Imperial Hotel. The café soon began to serve as a point of reference for Orthodox visitors coming to the city during the Easter pilgrimages, particularly from Russia, the Balkans, Greece, Cyprus, and the Arab countries. It was from Mukhtar's Café that the Sabt enNour procession usually departed for the Holy Sepulcher on the day after Good Friday, with the mukhtar leading.[28] Issa al-Toubbeh became a notary and advisor to the Orthodox community and acted as a mediator with the Greek Patriarchate to resolve its daily problems. It was this combination of involvement in literary circles and in the Arabization of the Orthodox church that attracted Sakakini to Toubbeh and his café. He began to meet here regularly with his literary group, which later became known as Halqat al Arbi'a (The Wednesday Circle). Its members included Adel Jaber, Is'af al Nashashibi, Issa al Issa (editor of Alif ba'), Issa al Issa (publisher of Falastin), Ishaq Musa al Husseini, Khalil Nakhleh, and, from abroad, Ahmad Zaki Pasha and Khalil Mutran.[29] It was this group that formed the core of the Party of the Vagabonds.

In his memoirs Sakakini explains the origins of his party:

During the early years of French rule over Syria [the Mandate authorities] expelled several nationalists to Palestine. Among these was the well-known writer Ali Nasir adDin, who joined the Sa'aleek group. When he was finally allowed to return to Damascus, he requested from the Vagabonds of Palestine an affidavit that would allow him to represent them in Syria. We sent him our manifesto [faraman]. Somehow the Vagabonds' manifesto fell into the hands of some journalist from [the newspaper] Falastin, which published it. When

Figure 7. Members of the Vagabond Party, many of them teachers at the Dusturiyyeh National College, in Jerusalem in 1919. From the left, sitting: Khalil Sakakini, Achille Seikaly, and Adel Jaber. From the left, standing: George Khamis, Hanna Hammameh, Musa Alami, and Anton Mushabik. Photo by Khalil Raad. © IPS Beirut.

> Nasir adDin arrived in Beirut, he was arrested on the spot and expelled for the second time to the island of Irwad on the strength of the affidavit, which made him a member of the Vagabond Party. We tried in vain to intercede on his behalf.[30]

The Vagabond Party and their café, at this point still called the Mukhtar's Café, came to light in 1921, when the Bethlehem Club wanted to honor Sakakini for his educational and literary contributions. Sakakini sent an apology on the grounds that the "bylaws of the Vagabond Party, to which I have the privilege of belonging for the past three years, forbids its members from accepting any honorary citations." He went on to say, "They insisted on celebrating my virtues, but I looked in vain in myself and could not find anything worth celebrating."[31]

Khalil's involvement with the Vagabond Party did not mean that he was "above politics," as the rhetoric of the group may suggest, but rather that he developed two personas, one reflecting his immersion in the public struggles of the day, and the other involved in creating a new cultural space in late Ottoman Palestine. Of the former we know that he belonged to one political party—the Party of Union and Progress, which represented Ottoman decentralization the Arab provinces—a party to which he had been recruited by Sheikh Tawfiq Tabanja and two other Turkish officers in the autumn of 1908. His main contact in the party was Isma'il al-Husseini. He describes, with a sense of comic relief, how he was blindfolded and swore on the Bible and a loaded pistol that he would "defend the nation and the constitution till death."[32]

The oath must have been made under duress, for two months later we see Sakakini joining another group, the Society of Arab Brotherhood (Jami'at al Ikha' Al Arabi), which included Musa Shafiq al Khalidi, Nakhleh Zureik, and Faidy Afendi al-Alami. But the group could also have been a local branch of the Party of Union and Progress.[33] That same year he also contributed to the founding of the Society of Orthodox Amity (Jam'iat al Ikha' al Urthodoxi), to which he was to devote the bulk of his energies and enthusiasm in the next few years. Sakakini felt strongly about his links to the Orthodox community and the campaign to Arabize the Greek Church—a movement that had little to do with religion and much to do with wresting communal control from the Greek clerical hierarchy. "If the [Orthodox] community aims at demanding its rights from the Brotherhood of the Holy Sepulcher today, my objective goes further. Namely, to have the Brotherhood expelled from this country and cleanse the Jerusalem Seat of their corruption. My aim is to bring to an end to Greek [ecclesiastical] tyranny."[34]

But this struggle for a new "Arabized" identity within the Orthodox community was taking place within the larger context of nationalism (a movement that involved his Muslim, and sometimes his Jewish, acquaintances), as well as within a wider—and in many ways more profound—humanist dimension that transcended nationalism, and which was eventually to triumph in Sakakini's ideational preferences. It was to this framework—exemplified in the Sa'aleek group—that Khalil began to devote his energies.

In 1925 Sakakini published the Manifesto of the Vagabonds (Faraman al Sa'aleek), which contained eighteen articles and one appendix.[35] It was clear from its language and leanings that it reflected his philosophy of pleasure *(falsafat asSuroor),* whose roots go back to his early association with Farah Antoun in New York (1907–8). He managed to synthesize in the manifesto his popular interpretation of Nietzsche's notion of power with a streak of his own personal philosophy of hedonism.[36] Initially his philosophy, as he expressed it in a letter to his young child, borders on authoritarian worship of power. "The strong shall inherit the earth," he wrote from his Damascus prison. "The right of the strong is self-evident and is based on a strong mind and a strong body." In order not to be misunderstood as a Social Darwinist, he added, "When I say that man should be powerful, I mean that he should restore himself to that inner [potential] strength that he was born with."[37]

But by the time he formulated his manifesto, seven years after his return from New York, he had modified his position. The manifesto announces—obviously tongue in cheek—that "All men and women are members of this party, whether they like it or not, unless they violate its principles." He also claims, "The party has no president, no chair, no treasurer, and no headquarters; its members meet in the street, where all vagabonds are brothers," and "the party does not recognize titles, and the only forms of personal address used are *Anta, Antuma, antum, anti, antuma,* and *antunna,* one for one, two for two, and plural for plural. No [to your] excellency *[janab],* no [to your] honor *[hadrat],* no patron, and no servant."[38] Furthermore, "Idleness is the motto of our party. The working day is made up of two hours. Every holiday, including those dedicated to the memory of obscure saints, is a legitimate occasion for taking time from work in order to indulge in eating, drinking, and merriment. We thus raise the doctrine of Yahya Ibn Khalid, who counseled his son as follows: *My son, do not fail to seize your fair share of idleness in this life.*"[39] The manifesto does not lack basic moralizing: "Our party sees black as black, and white as white. There is no left or right, and we do not recognize people as elevated or demoted,"[40] and "our party is ruthless in its criticism—we do not favor a friend, nor do we compromise over what is true and just."[41]

WHO WILL SUCCEED ME AS THE PRINCE OF IDLENESS?

This mixture of populist egalitarianism and sardonic moralism in the party's manifesto camouflaged what was essentially a narcissistic streak in Sakakini's character, a tendency that was eminently suited to the emerging café culture of the new class of literati and *salariat* flaneurs in Mediterranean cultures. The new culture of the public café suited Sakakini. He expressed his narcissistic philosophy of pleasure in several of his diary entries. He began recording these reflections on April 13, 1918, and continued after his return to Jerusalem:

> I have the greatest pity for those who do not experience pleasure in their daily lives. . . . I wake up having had the greatest joy during my sleep; I start my exercises with a great deal of sensuality; I bathe my body and find the greatest bliss in engulfing my body in cold water; I eat as if the greatest reward comes from eating—even if it is a dry piece of bread; I smoke my *arghileh* and think that happiness lies in smoking; I read and write and enjoy what I have recorded; I take a walk and find great delight in walking; I sit and talk with my friends and find contentment in socializing with them. Even when I have problems, I find a great enjoyment in overcoming my travails. I face catastrophes with fortitude and experience a strange satisfaction from confronting them.[42]

Sakakini's enforced exile in Damascus (1917–18) gave him ample opportunity to develop his narcissism into a philosophy of pleasure. This was also the period when his skepticism of religion turned into an implicit atheistic stance. There is no doubt that this turn in his mindset was enhanced by his conflict with the Orthodox Church and the (failed) attempt by the Greek clergy to ban his betrothal to his beloved Sultana. In one significant entry in his Damascus diary he records the following conversation with his German student, a Mr. Bern, who was a missionary:

> We are both preachers. He preached the teaching of Jesus Christ, and I preached my philosophy.
> He asked me: "Do you pray?"
> "No."
> "Do you beseech God to forgive your trespasses?"
> "No."
> "Do you not thank God for his bounty?"
> "No."
> "Do you not depend on God's support?"
> "No."
> And with this his puzzlement increased, until he was assured that my fate is in hell indeed.[43]

He derived his philosophy of pleasure from the medieval manuscript *Character and Morality (Tahdhib al Akhlaq)* by Ibn Miskawaih, to whom Sakakini attributed the notion that "Sorrow is neither necessary nor natural. We should immerse ourselves in life and cherish it by celebrating our nights. . . . We should indulge in music and singing. If disasters come our way, we should receive them courageously and prevent grief from consuming us."[44] From this philosophy of pleasure Sakakini created a code of conduct that involved a rigorous regime of play (exercise for one hour every morning), cold showers (twice a day), diet (vegetarian), sleep (long siestas after the midday meal), and socializing in public places. Above all, Sakakini advocated a systematic approach to leisure.

> The old conventions stipulated a day of rest per week, regulating work for the rest of the days. I say: one day is not enough. At the minimum we need two days a week, to which we must add a third day once a month. Furthermore, any kind of employment requires three periods of rest: two weeks at the beginning of the year; two weeks at the end of spring; two and a half months in the summer. . . . Workdays should be no more than four hours a day, and workers should take a ten-minute break every working hour, as in the new school system.[45]

Instead of religious pilgrimages, Sakakini advocated tourism: "Go to the nearest port and take a trip to a new land; this will give you health and revive your youth, and enhance your knowledge."[46]

In Damascus, Sakakini had the opportunity to live his philosophy in the company of Jerusalem exiles. On January 10, 1918, he was released on bail by order of Jamal Pasha (the Younger), and he was allowed to obtain lodgings in the Qasaa neighborhood while Emir Faisal's army was advancing on the city from the south. His company included Musa Alami, Tawfiq Jawhariyyeh (Wasif's brother, who was serving in the Ottoman army), Ahmad Sameh al Khalidi, Rustum Bey Haidar, Dr. Tawfiq Canaan, and his teacher, Nakhleh Zureik.

The Vagabond Café had a short life during the Mandate years. Literary cafés were rare in Jerusalem, as well as in Palestine. In his discussion of coffeehouses in Nablus in 1907–14, Muhammad Izzat Darwazeh noted that, despite their profusion, they were mostly popular hangouts for men who smoked *arghileh,* played cards and dominoes, and drank coffee and tea. More elaborate socializing took place in the neighborhood *diwans,* where storytelling and political debates took place.[47] As in Jerusalem, some Nablus coffeehouses staged *qara qoz* (shadow plays) for adults and *sanduq al 'ajab* (magic lantern shows) for children.[48] Unlike in Beirut, Damascus, and Cairo, where literary cafés served as a venue for intellectual debates and belonged to competing political groups, in Palestine during the Mandate, cultural and confessional clubs took over this role. The Vagabond Café was therefore a striking exception in a provincial capital like Jerusalem. Its appearance and decline can be attributed primarily to the magnetic personality of Khalil Sakakini and his ability to create a new cultural space through sheer energy and determination.

In 1926 Sakakini resumed his position as inspector general of education in Palestine. During the tenure of Herbert Samuel, he had refused to serve in public office as a form of protest against Samuel's support of the Zionists. Now the demands of his new job meant that he had to dissociate himself from the Vagabond Party, and his visits to the Mukhtar's Café became rare. He wrote to a friend in Egypt lamenting the end of his "age of idleness" *(asr al batalah)*.

> Tomorrow is my last day in the age of idleness, and what a magnificent period it was. Tomorrow the Vagabond Café will be deserted. Our fabulous sessions will meet no more. The Brotherhood of Amity (Ikhwan al Safa) will seek me and not find me. Until now I have never left my home without spending a [substantial time] in bathing, playing, reading, writing, singing, and smoking. From today on I will leave in black [attire], going straight to work, greeting nobody on the way.
>
> Who will succeed me as the champion of idleness in [Palestine]?[49]

The demise of the Vagabond Café, however, was not caused exclusively by the departure of the "prince of idleness." There were other factors involved, too. In the 1920s most newspapers and journals moved to either Jaffa or Haifa. The Jerusalem intelligentsia became heavily involved in nationalist politics through the newly formed parties, or in the municipal politics of the city. Café culture continued to flourish, but now they served mostly as sites for socializing and musical performance rather than as the domain of literary societies.

Notes

1. INTRODUCTION

1. This introductory analysis of social history draws on my longer essay, "Palestinian Society," which appeared in *The Encyclopedia of the Palestinians,* ed. Philip Mattar (New York: Facts on File, 2000), to which one may refer for elaborations and references.

2. THE MOUNTAIN AGAINST THE SEA?

1. Albert Hourani, *The Emergence of the Modern Middle East* (Berkeley: University of California Press, 1981).

2. Ibid., p. 175.

3. Saad E. M. Ibrahim, "Over-Urbanization and Under-Urbanism," *International Journal of Middle East Studies* 6, no. 1 (1975): 32.

4. Ibid.

5. Çaglar Keydar, Y. Eyüp Özveren, and Donald Quartet, eds., "Port Cities of the Eastern Mediterranean: 1800–1914," *Review* 16, no. 4 (Fall 1993).

6. UNLU circular dated September 25, 1990, issued by the Unified Command of the Intifada in Gaza Strip. Note that this circular—as in many other cases—was issued by the secular forces and not by Hamas. For similar leaflets issued by the Islamic movement, see "al-Hijab and the Great Challenge" (Hamas, March 1990) and "A Call to the Mothers of the Intifada" (Gaza, undated [ca. December 1989]).

7. Alain Corbin, *The Lure of the Sea: The Discovery of the Seaside in the Western World 1750–1840* (Los Angeles: University of California Press, 1994), pp. 4–5.

8. Charles Sprawson, *Haunts of the Black Masseur* (New York: Pantheon, 1992), pp. 45–68.

9. Ibid., p. 68.

10. Ibid., p. 69.

11. Corbin, *The Lure of the Sea,* p. 14.

12. Ibid., p. 17.

13. Ibid., pp. 270–73.

14. Ibid., pp. 276–77.

15. Keydar, Özveren, and Quartet, eds., "Port Cities of the Eastern Mediterranean," pp. v–vii.

16. Y. Eyüp Özveren, "Beirut," *Review* 16, no. 4 (Fall 1993): 482–84.

17. Ibid., p. 483.

18. Ibid., p. 482; and André Raymond, *Arab Cities in the Ottoman Period: Cairo, Syria, and the Maghreb* (Aldershot, UK: Ashgate/Variorum, 2002), p. 132.

19. Yusef Haikal, *Ayyam al-Siba* (Amman: n.p., 1995), p. 67; Hisham Sharabi, *Zhikrayat Madina* (Stockholm: Andalus, 1992).

20. Said Yusef Dajani, *Kay la nansa "Yafa"* (Amman: n.p., 1991).

21. Philip Baldensperger, "Religion, Feasts, and Processions," *Palestine Exploration Fund Quarterly* (1920): 163–65.

22. Ibid., p. 164. The Alsatian Baldensperger, who attended the feast, called the celebration "frivolous."

23. Ahmad Abdul Rahim, "Rubeen," in Imtiaz Diab and Hisham Sharabi, eds., *Yafa: Itr Madina* (Jaffa: The perfume of a city) (Cairo: Dar al-Fata al-Arabi, 1991), pp. 115–18; Dajani, *Kay la nansa "Yafa"*; Elias Rantisi, "Mawsim Rubeen," in *Yafa: Itr Madina,* pp. 71–73.

24. Abdul Rahim, "Rubeen," p. 115.

25. Rantisi, "Mawsim Rubeen," p. 71.

26. Dajani, *Yafa wa Thawrat 1936,* p. 131; Rantisi, "Mawsim Rubeen," p. 71.

27. Dajani, *Yafa wa Thawrat 1936,* pp. 131–32; Abdul Rahim, "Rubeen," p. 115.

28. Dajani, *Yafa wa Thawrat 1936,* p. 132; Abdul Rahim, "Rubeen," p. 115.

29. Dajani, *Yafa wa Thawrat 1936,* p. 131.

30. Abdul Rahim mentions that on one occasion, when a mixed performance of a play featuring Fatmah Rushdi was organized, a riot almost broke out ("Rubeen," p. 115).

31. The photographs appear in *Yafa: Itr Madina,* a volume of memoirs edited by Imtiaz Diab and Hisham Sharabi.

32. Author interview of Muhammad al-Batrawi, January 22, 1995. Batrawi is writing a social history of Isdud, his hometown, and its environs.

33. Author interview of al-Batrawi.

34. Salim al-Mubayyid, *Malamih al-Shakhsiyyah al-filistiniyya fi Amthaliha al-Sha'biyya* (Amman: al Shuruq, 1995).

35. Ibid., pp. 76–77. Women seeking husbands would recite the following in their rituals: "Oh sea, I come to beseech you / for unwanted I have become / all the girls have found their catch / while I roam around your shores."

36. Zaki al-'Eileh, *Turath al-Bahr al-Filistini* (Jerusalem: n.p., 1982), pp. 70–76.

37. Rema Hammami, "Between Heaven and Earth: Transformations in Religiosity and Labor among Southern Palestinian Peasant and Refugee Women, 1920–1993," Ph.D. diss., Temple University, 1994.

38. Ibid., p. 115.

39. Ibid., p. 114.

40. Ibid., p. 116.

41. Ibid., pp. 134–35.

42. Ibid., p. 136.

3. FROM EMMA BOVARY TO HASAN AL-BANNA

1. Philip Benedict, ed., *Cities and Social Change in Early Modern France* (London: Routledge, 1992), pp. 24–25.

2. Julian Barnes claims that one year after the publication of *Madame Bovary*, cabbies were available for public sex in Hamburg. They were called, appropriately enough, Bovarys. Julian Barnes, *Flaubert's Parrot* (New York: Knopf, 1985).

3. Gustave Flaubert, *Madame Bovary*, trans. Eleanor Marx-Aveling (New York: Everyman's Library, 1966), p. 108.

4. Zahra, like Emma Bovary, moves to a small town on the outskirts of the capital (Abidjan?) with her new husband, Majid; see Hanan al-Shaykh, *Hikayat Zahra* (Beirut: Dar al-Adab, 1999), p. 42. The assumption that the market town is in West Africa is based on the author's description of the nightclub scene on p. 31.

5. Raymond Williams, *The Politics of Modernism: Against the New Conformists* (London: Verso, 1989).

6. Jonathan Raban, *Soft City* (London: Fontana, 1981), pp. 157–83.

7. For a discussion of this phenomenon in Tunisia, see Nicholas Hopkins, "Popular Culture and State Power," in *Mass Culture, Popular Culture, and Social Life in the Middle East,* ed. Georg Stauth and Sami Zubaida (Frankfurt: Campus Verlag, 1987), pp. 225–40.

8. Shlomo Deshen, "Social Control in Israeli Urban Quarters," in *The Changing Middle Eastern City,* ed. Helen Rivlin and Katherine Helmer (Binghamton: State University of New York Press, 1980), p. 161.

9. Ibid., p. 162.

10. Quoted by Clifford Geertz, "Toutes Directions: Reading the Signs in an Urban Sprawl," *International Journal of Middle East Studies* 21, no. 3 (1989): 291–306.

11. Fuad Khuri, *Tents and Pyramids: Games and Ideology in Arab Culture from Backgammon to Autocratic Rule* (London: Saqi Books, 1990).

12. R. L. Singh and R. P. B. Singh, eds., *Place of Small Towns in India* (Varanasi: International Centre for Rural Habitat Studies, 1979), p. 12.

13. V. K. Tyagi, *Urban Growth and Urban Villages* (New Delhi: Kalyani Publishers, 1982), p. 4.

14. See URBAMA, *Petites villes et villes moyennes dans le monde Arabe,* 2 vols. (Tours: URBAMA, 1986). See especially the contribution of Robert Escallier on the Maghreb, pp. 3–32.

15. Singh and Singh, eds., *Place of Small Towns in India,* p. 12.

16. Bert Swanson et al., *Small Towns and Small Towners* (Beverly Hills, CA: Sage Library of Social Research, 1979), pp. 14–15.

17. G. H. Blake, "The Small Town," in *The Changing Middle Eastern City,* ed. G. H. Blake and Richard Lawless (London: Croom Helm, 1982), p. 210.

18. Ibid., p. 216.

19. Jean-Francois Troin, "Petite villes et villes moyennes au Maroc: Hypothèses et réalités," in URBAMA, *Petites villes et villes moyennes dans le monde Arabe*, pp. 69–81.

20. Fuad Khuri, "Ideological Constants and Urban Living," in *The Middle East City: Ancient Traditions Confront a Modern World*, ed. Abdulaziz Saqqaf (New York: Paragon House, 1987).

21. John Gulick, "Village and City: Cultural Continuities in Twentieth-Century Middle East Cultures," in *Middle Eastern Cities*, ed. Ira Lapidus (Berkeley: University of California Press, 1969), pp. 122–58.

22. Ibid., pp. 124–37.

23. See Elizabeth Wilson, *The Sphinx in the City: Urban Life, the Control of Disorder, and Women* (Berkeley: University of California Press, 1991).

24. Khuri, "Ideological Constants and Urban Living."

25. Ibid.

26. Khuri, *Tents and Pyramids*, p. 126.

27. Ibid., pp. 51–52.

28. Ibid., p. 126.

29. Ibid., p. 127.

30. Ibid.

31. Ibid.

32. See the discussion by Sa'd edin Ibrahim on Cairo at the end of the Khuri article.

33. Sami Zubaida, "Components of Popular Culture in the Middle East," in *Mass Culture, Popular Culture and Social Life in the Middle East*, ed. George Stauth and Sami Zubaida (Boulder, CO: Westview Press, 1987), p. 153.

34. Ibid.

35. Ibid. Zubaida elaborates on this argument in his book *Islam, the People, and the State* (London: Routledge, 1989), pp. 83–98.

36. Khuri, *Tents and Pyramids*.

37. The population of Isdud was evicted during the war of 1948. Majdal's Arab residents were forcibly transferred to Gaza in the 1950–51 period. See Benny Morris, *1948 and After: Israel and the Palestinians* (Oxford: Clarendon Press, 1990).

38. Salim Tamari, "Social Transformations and Future Prospects in the West Bank and Gaza," Occasional Papers, UNCTAD, Geneva, 1994, pp. 6–9.

39. Ann Mosely Lesch, "Gaza: Forgotten Corner of Palestine," *Journal of Palestine Studies* 151 (1985): 44.

40. CBS, *Statistical Abstract of Israel*, 1988, and The West Bank Data Project (WBDP), *The West Bank and Gaza Atlas* (Jerusalem, 1988), pp. 28–29. This section is a modified version of my essay "Shopkeepers, Peddlers, and Urban Resistance," in *Proceedings of the International Conference on Urbanism and Islam*, vol. 2 (Tokyo: Tokyo University Publications, 1989), pp. 171–75.

41. UNIDO, *Survey of the Manufacturing Industry in the West Bank and Gaza Strip*, June 1984; WBDP, *The West Bank and Gaza Atlas*, p. 43.

42. Shlomi Khayyat, *Ramallah: 1985 Masterplan* (Jerusalem, 1985), p. 32.

43. G. H. Blake, "The Small Town," in *The Changing Middle Eastern City*, ed. G. H. Blake and Richard Lawless (London: Croom Helm, 1982), pp. 214–16.

44. WBDP, *The West Bank and Gaza Atlas*, p. 28.

45. Shlomo Gazit, *The Stick and the Carrot: Israel's Rule in the West Bank* (Nicosia: Beisan Publishers, n.d.) (Arabic edition), pp. 294–95, 417–18.

46. Khayyat, *Ramallah*, p. 32.

47. A relevant discussion of peasant proletarianization without urbanization during the Mandate period can be found in Shulamit Carmi and Henry Rosenfeld, "The Origins of the Process of Proletarianization and Urbanization of Arab Peasants in Palestine," *Annals of the New York Academy of Sciences* 220 (1974): 470–85.

48. Tamari, *The Social Transformation of Palestinian Society*.

49. In the case of East Jerusalem, they were regional migrants from the Hebron district.

50. This has been true not only for towns, but also for villages. See Atef Sa'ad, "Diary of al-Zawiya Village: Concrete Social Transformations," *at-Tali'a*, August 31, 1989.

51. Saleh Abdul Jawwad, "La genèse et development du mouvement de libération nationale: Le fath," Ph.D. diss., Paris X, Nanterre, 1986, in reference to Jalazon (Ramallah) and Yibnah (Rafah); and Rosemary Sayegh, *From Peasants to Revolutionaries: A People's History* (London: Zed Press, 1979).

52. Abdul Latif al-Barghouti, *Qamus al-Lahjat al Filastiniyyah al Amiyyah* (Al-Bireh: In'ash al Usra Society, 1997).

53. Marianne Heiberg, *Palestinian Society in Gaza, West Bank and Arab Jerusalem: A Survey of Living Conditions* (Oslo: FAFO, 1993).

54. Ibid., pp. 84–88.

55. Ibid., p. 82.

56. Ibid., p. 93.

57. For a discussion of rural status hierarchies, see Suad Amiry, "Space, Kinship, and Gender: The Social Dimension of Peasant Architecture in Palestine," Ph.D. diss., University of Edinburgh, 1987.

58. Heiberg, *Palestinian Society in Gaza*, pp. 239–41.

59. Tamari, "The Soul of the Nation: The Urban Intellectuals and the Peasants," in *Middle East Studies* 5 (1982).

60. "Marriage committees" undertook mass arranged marriages between poor single men and women in public ceremonies. Bassam al-Salhi, *The Political and Religious Leadership in the Occupied Territories: 1967–1993* (Ramallah: Dar al-Quds, 1993) (in Arabic), pp. 192–97.

61. Ibid., p. 198.

62. Rema Hammami, "Women, the Hijab and the Intifada," *Middle East Report* 164/165, Intifada Year Three (May–August 1990): 27–28.

63. Ibid., p. 28.

64. Erica Lang and Itimad Mohanna, *Dirasah an al-mar'ah wa-al-'amal fi mukhayyam al-Shati' lil-laji'in fi Qita' Ghazzah* (al-Quds: al-Multaqa al-Fikri al-'Arabi, 1992), p. 14.

65. Hamas, "Dirasah 'n al-Amn: Dhahirat al-'malah" (The issue of collaboration), Asqalan Prison pamphlet, May 1991, p. 5. Quoted by Saleh Abdul Jawwad, *The Theoretical and Applied Position of the Islamic Movements Toward Collaborators* (Jerusalem: Al-Markaz al-Filastinin lil-Dirasat, 1993) (in Arabic), p. 14.

66. Ibid., p. 6.

67. Ibid., p. 12.

68. Sylvie Mansour, *Jeel al-Intifada* (Beirut: Institute of Palestine Studies, 1998); and Ahmad M. Baker, ed., *Impact of the Intifada on the Psychological Status of Palestinian Children in the Occupied Territories* (n.p., 1989), pp. 48–53.

69. Yizhar Be'er and Saleh 'Abdel-Jawad, *Collaborators in the Occupied Territories: Human Rights Abuses and Violations* (Jerusalem: B'tselem Publications, 1994).

4. BOURGEOIS NOSTALGIA AND THE ABANDONED CITY

An earlier, Arabic version of this chapter appeared as "Ad-Dhakira al-Mu'adhabah," in *al-Karmil* (Ramallah) 54.

1. These impressions are based on my attendance at the major Nakba activities that took place in March, April, and May 1998 in Ramallah, Jerusalem, and Bethlehem. The most prominent activities were organized by the Khalil Sakakini Center in Ramallah, the Popular Art Center in Al-Bireh, and the local universities. The reader can obtain a list of these events from the Khalil Sakakini Center, published as "Commemoration of Nakba Events: Lectures, Films and Exhibitions," Ramallah, 1999.

2. Testimony by Hajj Hussein Abdel Rahman Al-Hilmi, from Silwad, Khalil Sakakini Center, May 2, 1998.

3. At the end of 2000, Palestinian and Israeli negotiators were wrestling over the interpretation of UN Resolution 194, which allows those refugees who "will live at peace with their neighbors to return to their homes," in final status talks. More than Jerusalem and settlements, the refugee issue proved to be the decisive factor in the collapse of the Camp David and Taba negotiations.

4. The Arabic magazine *al-Karmil* started publishing them in spring 1997 ("Shahadat" [Testimonies], *al-Karmil* 51) and continued doing so until the summer of 1998 ("Dhikarat al-Makan" [The memory of the place . . . the place of the memory," *al-Karmil* 56/57). See specifically Shafiq Al-Hoot, "Jaffa: The City of Stubbornness"; Hasan Khader, "Al-Ghurba: Absence from the Homeland"; Mohammed Ali Taha, "Time of the Lost Childhood"; and Elias Sanbar, "Return to the Homeland."

5. Ghassan Zaqtan, "Nafi Al-Manfa" (The negation of exile), *al-Karmil* 51 (Spring 1997): 141–45.

6. Ibid., pp. 144–45.

7. Zakariyya Mohammed, "al-Adhm wal-Dhahab" (Bone and gold), *al-Karmil* 51 (Spring 1997): 125–40.

8. Hasan Khader, "Hal Kunta Huna?" (Were you there?), *al-Karmil* 51 (Spring 1997): 115–24.

9. Ibid.

10. Murid Barghouti, *Ra'aytu Ram Allah*, Kitab al-Hilal, series 558 (Cairo: Dar al-Hilal, 1997).

11. Murid Barghouti, "Al-Iqama fil-waqt" (Living in time), *al-Karmil* 51 (Spring 1997): 156–64.

12. Ibid., p. 158.

13. The reader can review this discussion in an electronic forum run by Haitham Sawalhy and Andre Mazzawi, which first appeared at www.yafa.org and is now at www.jaffacity.com.

14. That this reality can shift suddenly in the perception of native Jaffites, both Jews and Arabs, can be seen in a revealing survey of attitudes in the city in the aftermath of the bloody events that took place during the first week of the second intifada, in October 2000. See Lily Falili and Ori Nir, "City of Strangers," in *Haaretz*, November 27, 2000.

15. The best example of this tradition can be found in Imtiaz Diab and Hisham Sharabi, eds., *Yafa: Itr Madina* (Jaffa: The perfume of a city) (Cairo: Dar al-Fata al-Arabi, 1991). See especially "Mawsim Rubeen," by Elias Rantisi, pp. 70–73.

16. See Hanna Malak, *Zhikrayat al-'ailat al-Yafiyyah* (Jerusalem: Commercial Press, 1993), and *al-Juthur al-yafiyyah* (Jerusalem: Commercial Press, 1996).

17. See Yusef Haikal, *Ayyam Al-Siba* (Days of my youth) (Amman: n.p., 1995); Ahmad Dajani, *Yafa wa Thawrat 1936* (Jaffa and the 1936 Rebellion) (Amman: n.p., 2001); and Zaki al Masri, *Hadith al-Dhikriyat, 1936–1994* (Ramallah: n.p., 1994).

18. See Musa Budeiri, "The Last Plane from Jaffa," unpublished essay, 2002.

19. "Samira Tells the Story of Her Family," the Electronic Forum, www.yafa.org.

20. "Exchange," in ibid.

21. These terms, which mean "strangers" and "newcomers," respectively, have immense significance in mapping marriage strategies and business partnerships among Palestinians.

22. Andre Mazzawi, "Memories and Counter-Memories: Production, Reproduction and Deconstruction of Some Palestinian Memory Accounts about Jaffa," paper presented at the Middle East Studies Association annual conference, San Francisco, December 1997. Some of the quotations below have been translated back into English from Arabic and may differ slightly from the original English.

23. Quotation from Dajani, *Yafa wa Thawrat 1936*, p. 69.

24. Diab and Sharabi, eds., *Yafa: Itr Madina*, pp. 14 ff.

25. Mazzawi, "Memories and Counter-Memories."

26. Ibid., p. 21; and Yusef Haikal, in Diab and Sharabi, eds., *Yafa: Itr Madina*, pp. 55–56.

27. Mazzawi, "Memories and Counter-Memories," pp. 18–20.

28. Some of this work can be seen in an anthology of writings edited by Jamil Hilal and Ilan Pappé, eds., *Across the Wall* (London: I. B. Tauris, forthcoming).

29. See "Destroyed Palestinian Village Series," Documentation and Research Center, Birzeit University, published over a twelve-year period (1982–94).

30. Here I am referring to the mainstream writers of this era. No doubt there were authors who were able to transcend the spirit of the era in which they lived (see the remarks below about Jabra and Kanafani).

31. In his two autobiographical books, *The First Well* (1995) and *Princesses' Street* (2005), both published by the University of Arkansas Press (Fayetteville).

32. In *Return to Haifa*, his most important novel.

5. A MUSICIAN'S LOT

1. See Yehoshua Ben-Arieh, *Jerusalem in the 19th Century: The Old City,* vol. 1 (New York: St. Martin's Press, 1984), pp. 390–401.

2. Ayse Oncu and Petra Weyland, *Space, Culture and Power: New Identities in Globalizing Cities* (London: Zed Press, 1997), pp. 8–9. See also Michael P. Smith, *Transnational Urbanism: Locating Globalization* (Malden, MA: Black-well Publishers, 2001), pp. 136–40.

3. Benedict Anderson, "Exodus," *Critical Inquiry* 20, no. 2 (1994).

4. F. W. Dupee, Afterword to *Sentimental Education,* by Gustave Flaubert (New York: New American Edition, 1972), p. 427.

5. Jawhariyyeh refers to the Gregorian and Julian calendars, respectively. It was common in this period to use both in Palestine. Both Muslim and Christian farmers used the Julian calendar in marking the agricultural cycle.

6. Wasif Jawhariyyeh began writing his memoirs systematically in 1947 at the Agricultural Development Society in Jericho on the basis of notes he had writ-ten earlier. He continued writing in Beirut during the 1960s. That he began writ-ing in the 1940s can be gleaned from his comment on the Mascobiyyeh during the Ottoman period. He mentions in passing that "today these quarters serve as the center of British intelligence" (ms. page 220). In addition to the three-volume manuscript, he has left behind a collection of musical notes and notations, a com-pendium of poetry, and a large collection of popular proverbs and their inter-pretation. His late daughter Yusra Arnita, who died in March 2000, used the latter collection in her book on Palestinian folklore.

7. Wasif served as an Ottoman naval officer on the Dead Sea, working as a "grain soldier" by day and an "'oud officer" by night.

8. It was salvaged from its hiding place in the family's Botta Street house in West Jerusalem after the 1967 war.

9. *Andalusiat* and *muwashshahat* are classical musical forms (melodies and songs) that originated in Islamic Andalusia and were imported to North Africa and Syria after the sixteenth century. *Taqatiq* are ditties that often (but not al-ways) accompany dance routines.

10. See Wasif Jawhariyyeh, "Tarkib al-Nota al-Ifranjiyya 'ala Awtar al-'oud" in "Musical Notebook," manuscript, Institute of Jerusalem Studies, Jerusalem, pp. 9–10.

11. Wasif Jawhariyyeh, diary manuscript, IPS Library, Beirut (hereafter cited as WJ Ms.), p. 41. The published version of this manuscript is Wasif Jawhariyyeh, *Al Quds al 'Uthmaniyyeh,* vol. 1 (Jerusalem: IJS, 2003).

12. Ibid., p. 19.

13. For four *majidis* (eighty Ottoman *qirsh*). To appreciate the value of Wasif's first 'oud, a *ratl* (three kilograms) of lamb meat was valued at the time at 7.5 pias-tres. The amount of money paid for the 'oud, then, was equivalent to thirty-two kilo-grams of meat. That would be equivalent to $320 at today's prices in Jerusalem (year 2000)—certainly a huge sum for a family of modest means at the time. See WJ Ms., "A Price List of Basic Commodities in Ottoman Jerusalem: 1900–1914," p. 101.

14. Wasif had saved 20 piastres from his work and borrowed the rest from his father's friend Hussein al-Husseini. WJ Ms., p. 87.

15. Ibid., p. 17.

16. Ibid., pp. 125–26.

17. Ibid., pp. 145–46.

18. "My master Omar was widely recognized as a grand master in the performance of the *muwashah,* a genre that is almost extinct today in the Arab world, except perhaps in Aleppo. Omar used to tell me about his teacher, Ali Darwish, who was a world authority in this genre." WJ Ms., pp. 221–23. Wasif's characterization of *muwashshahat* as being extinct was premature, since it witnessed a major rebirth in the 1960s.

19. Muhammad was a *futtuwa,* a street gang member entrusted with the protection of his neighborhood. The Arabic term used by Wasif is *min Ashawis mahallat bab al-Amud'*—plural of *ashwas,* which literally means "tough guy" or "brave man." It is not clear what "initiation into manhood" means here, but the context indicates that he was being introduced to the ways of the street. As for *odah,* see the discussion in WJ Ms., p. 321.

20. WJ Ms., pp. 335–36.

21. Ibid., p. 335.

22. Although Wasif was clearly a protégé of the Husseini family, he does not indicate that he was a sympathizer of the Palestine Arab Party, which they founded in the 1930s. When his patron Hussein al-Husseini died, he allied himself with Ragheb al-Nashashibi, the protagonist of Haj Amin, without identifying himself with the Nashashibi-led Defense Party (founded in 1934). These shifts should not be read as a mark of Jawhariyyeh's opportunism, especially because both families conceived of Wasif as an artist and musician and had no political expectations of him.

23. See Rochelle Davis, "Ottoman Jerusalem," in *Jerusalem 1948: The Arab Neighbourhoods and Their Fate in the War* (Jerusalem: Institute of Jerusalem Studies, 1999), pp. 10–29.

24. Yehoshua Ben-Arieh, *Jerusalem in the 19th Century: Emergence of the New City* (Jerusalem: Yad Izhak Ben-Zvi, 1986), pp. 152–72.

25. In this they resemble the freethinking reflections of Khalil Sakakini from the Mandate period, particularly in *Kadha Ana Ya Dunia* (Beirut: al-Ittihad al-'Amm lil-Kuttab wa-al-Suhufiyin al-Filastiniyin, al-Amanah al-'Ammah, 1982).

26. WJ Ms., p. 197. It is unclear whether Wasif obtained such recollections from his father, from a diary kept by Jiryis, or by recording them from memory.

27. For a discussion of these contested loyalties, see Rashid Khalidi, "Competing and Overlapping Loyalties in Ottoman Jerusalem," in his *Palestinian Identity: The Construction of Modern National Consciousness* (New York: Columbia University Press, 1997), pp. 63–88. See also James Gevin, *Divided Loyalties: Nationalism and Mass Politics in Syria at the Close of Empire* (Berkeley: University of California Press, 1998), pp. 141–95; and, for a "revisionist" perspective, see Hasan Kayali, *Arabs and Young Turks: Ottomanism, Arabism, and Islamism in the Ottoman Empire, 1908–1918* (Berkeley: University of California Press, 1997), pp. 81–115.

28. WJ Ms., p. 226.

29. Wasif Jawhariyyeh, "Musical Notebook," untitled, undated, and unpublished, 576 pages. This handwritten manuscript, dedicated to the Ottoman sultan

and signed "Wasif Jawhariyyeh—Quds Sharif," was clearly written in the Ottoman period. It is divided into five sections: 1) *Muwashshahat* and *Anashid*, 2) *Madhahib* and *Adwar*, 3) Love Songs, 4) Ballads and Quartets, and 5) *Taqatiq* and Erotic Songs. References to this work are hereafter cited in the text by the manuscript page number.

30. There is a play on words here, since *adhana* means both "our ears" and "to injure."

31. WJ Ms., p. 162.

32. Both were well-known Syrian actors and comedians. Eventually Rihani married Badi'a Masabni, and together they formed a comedy team in Cairo. Rihani appeared in several Egyptian films during the 1930s.

33. Fakhri Nashashibi was a leading figure in the pro-British Defense Party and led the opposition to Haj Amin al Husseini. He was assassinated in Baghdad in the early 1940s.

34. All three were leading Egyptian composers and singers during the World War I era. Da'ud Husni was Jewish.

35. The author calculates that this amount equaled the annual salary of a judge during that period.

36. Edward Said, *Out of Place: A Memoir* (New York: Knopf, 1999), p. 6.

6. LEPERS, LUNATICS, AND SAINTS

1. It is not easy to find sources for this bizarre episode of the war, and its history is transmitted mainly through oral narratives. For substantiation the reader is referred to the January 2001 newsletter of the Southern Province of the Moravian Church in North America. The article "Care for Former Leprosy Patients of Star Mountain" includes a brief history of the leprosarium, and then the following reference to the war of 1948:

> After the First World War, Great Britain took over the government of Palestine. Therefore the British Mission Board of the Moravian Church was held responsible for the leprosarium. The nurses still were sent from Emmaus. During the Jewish–Arab war of 1948 the part of Jerusalem southeast of the Old City became Israeli territory. The Arab patients and the staff from abroad had to leave the hospital. The lepers found a place in the very old Turkish leprosarium in Silwan, where care and treatment of sick people were insufficient. Some of the nurses remained in East Jerusalem and continued to take care of their patients in Silwan.

For the role of Tawfiq Canaan in the leprosarium, see Khalid al Nashif, "Tawfiq Canaan: Taqweem Jadeed," *Majallat al Dirasat al Filastiniyyah* 50 (Spring 2002): 77–78.

2. Niels P. Lemche has suggested that in the biblical narrative Canaan and the Canaanites must be read as an ideological construct of the Other (i.e., as non-Jews) rather than as a reference to an actual ethnic group. "The Canaanites [of Palestine] did not know that they were themselves Canaanites. Only when they had, so to speak, 'left' their original home . . . did they acknowledge that they had been Canaanites" ("The Canaanites and Their Land," published by the *Journal for the Study of the Old Testament*, supplement no. 110, The Sheffield Academic Press, 1999, p. 152). The author suggests that in the Deuteronomistic

history, "the Canaanites are allowed only to act inside the framework of the historical reconstruction and cannot depart from the role allocated to them. [We are] entitled to say that the description of these Canaanites has little to nothing to do with the ancient pre-Israelite inhabitants of Palestine. On the contrary, the Canaanites may be considered a kind of ideological prototype of an ethnic phenomenon which was very much a reality in the period when the historical narratives were reduced to writing" (ibid., pp. 164–65). He concludes by rejecting the concept of the Canaanites' religion, since it seemed to have existed only as a normative negation of what the Israelite scribes thought Jewish religion should be, preferring the term *West Semitic religion,* which includes both Canaanite and Israelite religion. Lemche writes, "it is also natural to reject the idea of specific Canaanite cultural traits as being distinctly different from ancient Israelite ones." He ends by making the following intriguing statement: "The 'disappearance' of the Canaanites of the Old Testament can be seen as an indication of a problem which has been endemic to the study of the ancient Oriental world, namely, the application of modern ethnic concepts in oriental studies" (ibid., p. 171). He does not suggest that the Canaanites did not exist as a people, but he does argue that they did not exist as a culture distinct from other socioreligious groups such as the Israelites and that, furthermore, we cannot impose modern ethnic constructs on the biblical period.

3. "Nativism," in *The Columbia Encyclopedia* (New York: Columbia University Press, 1995).

4. In Frantz Fanon, *Black Skin, White Masks* (New York: Grove Press, 1967).

5. Mehrzad Boroujerdi, *Iranian Intellectuals and the West: The Tormented Triumph of Nativism* (Syracuse, NY: Syracuse University Press, 1996), p. 14.

6. Ibid., pp. 14–15.

7. Ibid., p. 17.

8. Ibid., pp. 18–19. The quotation is from Edward W. Said's *Culture and Imperialism* (New York: Knopf, 1993).

9. Sean Baker, "American Nativism, 1820–1945," at http://are.as.wvu.edu/baker.htm. See also Michael Holt, "Nativism," Abraham Lincoln Historical Digitization Project, 2002, at http://dig.lib.niu.edu/ps-nativism.

10. Mahmoud Mamdani, *When Victims Become Killers: Colonialism, Nativism, and the Genocide in Rwanda* (Princeton, NJ: Princeton University Press, 2001).

11. JPOS 1, no. 1 (October 1920).

12. JPOS 1, pp. 113–15.

13. Yitshak Ben Zvi, "Historical Survey of the Jewish Settlement in Kefar Yasif," JPOS 5 (1925), pp. 204–17.

14. I use the term *Canaan's circle* with some caution. There is no doubt that of the writers mentioned here Canaan was the most prolific and the most widely known, but the group was not a cohesive one and did not formally constitute itself as a school of thought. What made them a circle is a number of shared attributes: they published the bulk of their work in the JPOS in the 1920s and 1930s and saw the Palestine Oriental Society as their main platform; they were amateur ethnographers (Stephan was the only member who had some training in archaeology); they clearly acknowledged Canaan as their intellectual superior,

based upon their frequent citations of his work; and finally, and perhaps most significantly, they all sought to anchor their observations of peasant lore in biblical and other primordial patrimonies.

15. I have discussed the "discovery" of the peasantry as a depository of native culture by urban intellectuals in "Soul of the Nation: Urban Intellectuals and the Peasants," *Middle East Studies* 5 (1982).

16. See Tawfiq Canaan, Introduction to *Mohammedan Saints and Sanctuaries in Palestine* (Jerusalem: The Syrian Orphanage Press, 1927).

17. Canaan could sometimes be quite crude about his conception of the eternal peasant. In 1931 he wrote, "A study of the effect of the two antagonistic phenomena in nature, light and darkness, on the life of the present inhabitants of Palestine—*who are in many respects as primitive as their ancestors of two thousand years ago*—may explain certain allusions in the bible" ("Light and Darkness in Palestine Folklore," JPOS 16 [1931]: 15, my emphasis). He later adds, "The oil lamp is as simple, as crudely made as it was thousands of years ago. Until about fifty years ago it was still, as in Old Testament times, an indispensable utensil in every household."

18. Tawfiq Canaan, Introduction to *Mohammedan Saints and Sanctuaries in Palestine*.

19. The earliest and most persistent advocates of the "living Bible" theory are found in the pages of the *Palestine Exploration Quarterly*, published by the Palestine Exploration Fund. The most typical examples of this trend can be seen in Elizabeth Anne McCaul Finn, *Palestine Peasantry: Notes on Their Clans, Warfare, Religion, and Laws* (London: Marshall Bros., 1923).

20. Both Dalman and Granqvist were well known to Canaan's circle, and their works, particularly those of Dalman, were regularly reviewed in the JPOS. See, for example, Canaan's reviews of Dalman's *Arbeit und Sitte in Palastina*, in JPOS 14 (1934), and of Granqvist's *Marriage Conditions in a Palestinian Village*, in JPOS 12 (1933) and JPOS 17 (1937).

21. Tawfiq Canaan, *The Palestine Arab House: Its Architecture and Folklore* (Jerusalem: The Syrian Orphanage Press, 1933).

22. A review of the work of Palestinian folklorists can be found in Nimr Sirhan, "Mawsu'ah," *The Encyclopedia of Palestinian Folklore*, 2nd ed., vol. 1 (Amman: Al Bayadir Press, 1989), pp. 116–32. The review contains an extensive section on Canaan and his work. Of all the post-1948 folklorists, Salim Mubayyid is the ethnographer closest in his writings to the Canaan circle. In his *Al Jughraphia Al Fulkloriyya lil Amthal al Sha'biyya al Filastiniyya* (Folkloric geography of Palestine) (Cairo: The Egyptian Book Commission, 1986), he focuses on the Byzantine Aramaic origins of the modern calendar of peasants in the mountain areas, and on the Egypto-Coptic roots of coastal traditions, especially practices related to the sea and seafaring (pp. 261–84). Mubayyid was the first writer to use the term "little continent" to refer to the immense regional variations in Palestinian topography (see p. 15).

23. Muhammad Adib al-Amiry, *Arabs in Palestine* (London: Longman, 1968).

24. See comment by Zakariyya Mohammad in *al-Ayyam*, April 28, 1998.

25. Zakariyya Mohammad, "Canaanite Ideology," in *Deek Al Manara* (Ramallah: Muwatin, 2003), pp. 32–33.

26. According to Tawfiq Canaan, on the eve of the British Mandate he sent a letter to the military commander of the British forces in Jerusalem in response to the inclusion of the Balfour Declaration in the terms of the Mandate. In that letter he claimed that Palestine should not belong to the Arabs or Jews, but to himself and his family, as he was the sole descendant of the ancient Canaanite nation.

27. Cited in Yaacov Shavit, *The New Hebrew Nation: A Study in Israeli Heresy and Fantasy* (London: Frank Cass, 1987), p. 122.

28. Ibid.

29. Ibid.

30. See Meron Benvenisti, *Sacred Landscape: The Buried History of the Holy Land Since 1948* (Berkeley: University of California Press, 2000), pp. 62–63; and Yitshak Ben Zvi, *She'ar Yashar* (Jerusalem: Yad Yitshak Ben-Zvi, 1966), pp. 422–23. The earlier work is David Ben Gurion and Yitshak Ben Zvi, *Eretz Israel in the Past and in the Present* (1918), in Yiddish, cited in Shavit, *The New Hebrew Nation*.

31. Tawfiq Canaan, "Haunted Springs and Water Demons in Palestine," JPOS 1 (October 1920), p. 153. Later he writes, "we know that planets, in whose hands human fortune and misfortune lies, were divided by all Semitic races of antiquity, and still by the Palestinians, into good and bad planets" (ibid., p. 154).

32. Canaan, "Unwritten Laws Affecting the Arab Women of Palestine," JPOS 11 (1931), p. 203.

33. Canaan, "Arabic Magic Bowls," JPOS 16 (1936), p. 79.

34. Canaan, "Haunted Springs," p. 156.

35. Stephan H. Stephan, "Modern Palestinian Parallels to the Song of Songs," JPOS 2 (1922), pp. 199–278.

36. Stephan H. Stephan, "Lunacy in Palestinian Folklore," JPOS 5 (1925).

37. Stephan, "Modern Palestinian Parallels to the Song of Songs," p. 199.

38. Ibid.

39. Ibid., p. 224. Some of the songs he collected came from Syria and Egypt, and a few from Iraq. Stephan remarks on the cultural environment that separated ancient biblical lore from modern Palestinian folklore: "Strictly speaking, no songs of the towns are really autochthonous, as seems to be the case with the Canticles. The relative lack of independence in the lyric literature of modern Palestine when compared with that of ancient Israel is naturally due to the fact that it now has the same language and culture as the surrounding lands, while ancient Palestine was cut off by differences of language from regular interchange of songs with its neighbours." Then he adds a statement that makes his argument even more relevant to the current debate about nativism: "We must not exaggerate this independence, after the discovery of a catalogue of Assyrian erotic lyrics showing a close similarity in metaphors and expression to the songs of the Canticles, especially since Meek has demonstrated that the Canticles contain many quotations from lyrics belonging to the cult of Tammuz" (ibid.).

40. Ibid., pp. 201–2. I have not included here the citations from the Old Testament and from the repertoire of popular songs included by the author.

41. Ibid., p. 218.

42. Ibid., p. 199.

43. Ibid., p. 203.

44. Stephan, "Lunacy in Palestinian Folklore," p. 2 (see also footnote 4).

45. Ibid., p. 5.

46. Ibid., pp. 6–7.

47. Ibid., p. 7. In much of this discussion of medical maladies Stephan refers to earlier works by Canaan.

48. Canaan, Introduction to *Mohammedan Saints and Sanctuaries,* p. 311.

49. Ibid., p. 310.

50. Ibid., p. 312.

51. See ibid., p. 312, n. 5.

52. *Al Kulliyah* (Beirut) 3/5 (March 1912) (part 1); and 3/6 (April 1912) (part 2).

53. These amulets and cups are now permanently housed in the Canaan Collection at Birzeit University Library. They are catalogued in Wisam Abdallah, ed., *Ya Kafi Ya Shafi: The Tawfiq Canaan Collection of Amulets* (Birzeit: Birzeit University Press, 1999). See especially the section by Gisella Hilmeke, "Amulets," pp. 27–35.

54. "Studies in the Topography and Folklore of Petra," JPOS 9, pp. 136–218; 10, pp. 178–80. The articles were published in 1930 as a book by Bayt al Maqdis Press, Jerusalem.

55. An Arabic edition was published by the Palestinian Ministry of Culture in Ramallah in 1999.

56. Canaan, *Mohammedan Saints and Sanctuaries,* p. v.

57. Ibid.

58. Ibid., p. vi.

59. Ibid., p. 219.

60. Ibid., p. 280.

61. Ibid. He also discusses male and female saints with biblical origins, pp. 237 ff.

62. Ibid., p. 280.

63. Ibid., p. 246.

64. Ibid., p. 247.

65. Ibid., p. 254.

66. Ibid., p. 267.

67. Ibid., p. 310.

68. Ibid., p. 312.

69. Only Omar Saleh al-Barghouti bridged the two currents in his writings. He was both an active contributor to JPOS, a friend of Tawfiq Canaan, and a fierce opponent of the Husseinis within the nationalist movement. See his *al Marahel* (Beirut: Al-Anwar, 2001) (published posthumously).

70. Canaan's essays have appeared in *Heritage and Society* (published by the Palestine Folklore Society), in a number of translations by Musa Allush, and in translations by Nimr Sarhan. Several entries about him and his work appear in the *Encyclopedia of Palestinian Folklore.* Birzeit University published two monographs about Canaan's work (in *Birzeit Research Review* in 1983, and a book about his amulets in 2001). *Mohammedan Saints and Sanctuaries in Palestine* was translated by the Palestinian Ministry of Culture and published in 1999 with a long introduction about Canaan by Hamdan Taha. Unfortunately, none of his

German works on popular medicine has been translated into Arabic or English, and this remains one of the major gaps in Canaan's accessibility to his readers.

71. Abdul Latif al-Barghouti, *Qamus al Lahjat al Filastiniyyah al Amiyyah* (Al-Bireh: In'ash Usra Society, 1992).

72. "Why Was the Name Yabus Chosen?" undated brochure published by the Yabus International Music Festival, Jerusalem.

73. "Why Was the Name Yabus Chosen?"

7. SULTANA AND KHALIL

1. The diaries of Khalil Sakakini (henceforth KSD), an eight-volume series in Arabic, began with the publication of volume 1 in March 2003. The diaries are being published jointly by the Khalil Sakakini Center, in Ramallah, and the Institute of Palestine Studies, in Beirut and Jerusalem, and edited by Akram Musallam. As of 2008, six volumes had been published.

2. Author communication with Zakariyya Mohammad, January 15, 2003.

3. Abdul Hamid Yasin et al., *Zhikra al Sakakini* (Jerusalem: Modern Library, 1957), pp. 88–89. For a more detailed exposition of his educational methods, see Yusif Ayyub Haddad, *Khalil Sakakini: His Life, Ideas, and Patrimony* (in Arabic) (Nazareth: As Sawt, 1985), pp. 223–27.

4. Ishaq Musa al Husseini, "Khalil al Sakakini," in Yasin et al., *Zhikra al Sakakini*, p. 93.

5. Haddad, *Khalil Sakakini*, pp. 69–71.

6. Husseini, "Khalil al Sakakini," pp. 60–63.

7. Sakakini in Hala Sakakini, ed., *Kadha Ana Ya Dunia: The Diaries of Khalil al-Sakakini* (Jerusalem: Commercial Press, 1954).

8. Husseini, "Khalil al Sakakini," p. 61.

9. Until the diaries became available the only available source on Sultana was her daughter's memoirs, Hala Sakakini, *Jerusalem and I: A Personal Record*, (Amman: Economic Press, 1987), pp. 1–10.

10. Ibid., p. 3.

11. "A father's advice to his daughter," in Hala Sakakini, personal archives, Jerusalem, 2000, pp. 23–24.

12. Ibid., p. 4.

13. Letter to Dawood al Saidawi, October 10, 1907, Jerusalem, in Hala Sakakini, ed., *Kadha Ana Ya Dunia*.

14. We find out, for example, that he borrowed money from her for his trip. On a few occasions she also gave a few pounds to his mother when she heard that both Khalil and his brother Yusif, who was a traveling salesman in Philadelphia, were unable to send her any support.

15. The biographic notes on Khalil Sakakini published by the Sakakini Center in Ramallah suggest that he went to the United States to pursue a university education (see www.sakakini.org). This claim, however, is not supported by his diaries or correspondence, in which it is clear that he intended to make a substantial amount of money in the same manner as other immigrants from greater Syria: peddling and trade. Once in America he did consider a teaching post at Columbia University, but aside from the private lessons he gave to students of

Arabic at the university and some manuscripts that he edited, he never came close to university employment.

16. This is the opinion of Ishaq Musa al Husseini, in his "Khalil Sakakini."

17. Mansour Fahmi, "Muhammad Kuzd Ali and Khalil Sakakini," in Yasin et al., *Zhikra al Sakakini,* p. 108.

18. KSD, letter to Sultana, August 22, 1908, London.

19. KSD, letter to Milia, November 14, 1907, New York.

20. KSD, letter to Dawood Saidawi, January 1, 1908, New York. This letter is also printed in Hala Sakakini, ed., *Kadha Ana Ya Dunia.*

21. Ibid.

22. KSD, letter to Sultana, July 27, 1908, New York and Rumford Falls.

23. Richard J. H. Gottheil (1862–1936) was the chair of the Department of Rabbinic Literature and Semitic Languages at Columbia University during Sakakini's visit. During his tenure, a wide range of Semitic languages and courses were introduced at the school, and the library was vastly expanded. His relationship to Sakakini was amiable, but it is obvious from the Sakakini diaries that Gottheil was oblivious to his employee's financial plight. He assumed, wrongly, that Sakakini's work for him on Arabic manuscripts was a labor of love. At one point Gottheil tried to help Khalil sell postcards of the Holy Land to other faculty members at Columbia. (KSD and "Jewish Studies at Columbia before Salo Baron," at www.columbia.edu). Eventually he paid Sakakini twenty-five dollars for his work, but only after Sakakini pleaded with him.

24. "History of Arab New York," an online review on *Gotham Gazette,* August 22, 2002, www.gothamgazette.com/commentary/107.history_arab.shtml.

25. Ibid. See also Philip Kurata, "Arab Americans of New York," *Washington File,* June 25, 2002. "In addition to economic factors," writes Kurata, "a major impetus for Arab immigration in the early 20th century was the passage of an Ottoman law in 1908, making military service compulsory for Christians and Jews, who previously had been exempt. . . . The Lower West Side became the 'mother colony' of all the Arab immigrant communities that eventually were established in the United States."

26. KSD, January 1, 1908, New York.

27. Philip Kurata writes: "What did Brooklyn think of these immigrants? One New York newspaper said, 'There is not a more industrious or capable representative of the East than the Syrian.'" (See note 25, above.)

28. See Jonathan Friedlander, "Rare Sights: Images of Early Arab Immigration in New York City," in Kathleen Benson and Philip Kayal, *A Community of Many Worlds: Arab Americans in New York City* (Syracuse, NY: Syracuse University Press, 2002).

29. KSD, Easter Sunday, April 26, 1908. It seems, however, that in this particular instance Yusif himself was drunk and was abusive toward the police when he asked for protection.

30. Michael Suleiman, "Impressions of New York City by Early Arab Immigrants," in Benson and Kayal, *A Community of Many Worlds,* p. 44.

31. KSD, August 2, 1908.

32. Khalil Sakakini, "The Way Americans Live," *as-Sufur,* Cairo, 1918; reprinted in Khalil Sakakini, *Ma Tayassar,* vol. 1 (Jerusalem: The Modern

Press, 1943), pp. 95–98; also quoted in Suleiman, "Impressions of New York City."

33. Suleiman, "Impressions of New York City," and Sakakini, *Ma Tayassar,* p. 96.

34. See KSD, letter to Sultana, November 20, 1907.

35. Ibid.

36. KSD, letter from Sultana, January 20, 1908.

37. Ibid.

38. KSD, letter to Sultana, July 17, 1908.

39. KSD, letter to Sultana, undated [July 1908?].

40. KSD, letter to Sultana, July 27, 1908.

41. KSD, January 25, 1908.

42. Ibid.

43. KSD, February 22, 1908.

44. KSD, February 10, 1908.

45. KSD, March 7, 1908.

46. Hala Sakakini, ed., *Kadha Ana Ya Dunia,* p. 22.

47. This is what Ishaq Musa al Husseini wrote about Sakakini's dress before World War I: "He used to wear traditional Arab clothing: *qumbaz* and white *abay* in the summer, and a yellow woolen *abay* in the winter, with a *tarbush* for headgear" ("Khalil al Sakakini," p. 17). But how do we explain his Western dress in photographs taken in 1905–6? Either he used them for official travel documents, or he varied his dress depending on the occasion.

48. KSD, February 29, 1908.

49. The Swedish American hospice and school that was eventually converted into a hotel in the Sheikh Jarrah neighborhood.

50. KSD, January 30, 1908.

51. Sakakini resumed recording his dreams several years later, in the 1920s.

52. The best biography of Sakakini is Yusif Ayyub Haddad, *Khalil Sakakini: His Life, Ideas, and Patrimony.* See also Ishaq Musa al Husseini, *Khalil al Sakakini, Al Adib al Mujaddid* (Jerusalem: Centre for Islamic Studies, 1989), pp. 20–24.

53. Hala Sakakini, *Jerusalem and I: A Personal Record,* p. 4.

54. Husseini, *Khalil al Sakakini, Al Adib al Mujaddid,* p. 23.

55. Hala Sakakini, ed., *Kadha Ana Ya Dunia,* diary entry of January 4, 1918, pp. 124–25.

8. THE LAST FEUDAL LORD

I would like to thank Suad al Amiry and Rema Hammami for their critical comments on an earlier draft of this chapter.

1. These dates, which are not certain, are derived from oral sources cited by Fathi Ahmad in *Tarikh al-rif al-Filastini fi al-'ahd al-'Uthamani: mantiqat Bani Zayd namudhajan* (History of rural Palestine in the Ottoman period) (Ramallah: Shuruq, 1992).

2. These claims and many others are challenged by several historians, including Ihsan an Nimer. For a sustained critique and an alternative perspective

on the origins and status of the Barghouti family, see chapter 6, "Tribal Conflict in the Bani Zeid Region," in ibid., pp. 175–217.

3. Omar Saleh al-Barghouti, *al Marahel* (Beirut: Al-Anwar, 2001), p. 33. The memoirs were edited by Rafif al-Barghouti and published by Al Mu'assasah al Arabiyya LilDirasat wal Nashr (Beirut and Amman, 2001). The book has 739 pages, twenty-four photographs, and five appendices. References to pages in this volume are hereafter given in the text in parentheses. A sad reflection of prevailing conditions is that it is virtually impossible to buy this book unless the reader goes to Lebanon, since the book is not available in Jordan (where it is banned) or in Palestine (where it cannot be imported), the two countries where one would find most of its potential readers.

4. Fathi Ahmad, *Tarikh al-rif al-Filastini fi al-'ahd al-'Uthamani: mantiqat Bani Zayd namudhajan.* Ahmad published these comments before *al Marahel* was published. He was referring to Barghouti's *History of Palestine* (written jointly with Khalil Totah), but the publication of *al Marahel,* in my opinion, does not change the basis of this judgment.

5. For an extensive examination of Deir Ghassaneh's feudal architecture, including the Saleh palace compound, see Suad Amiry, "Space, Kinship, and Gender: The Social Dimension of Peasant Architecture in Palestine," Ph.D. diss., University of Edinburgh, 1987.

6. For a comparison of social conditions in the throne villages of central Palestine, see Suad Amiry and Rana Anani, *Amara wa Tarikh: Qura al-Karasi* (Throne villages: Architecture and history in the eighteenth and nineteenth centuries) (Ramallah: Riwaq Publications, 2003).

7. Muhammad Izzat Darwazeh, *Mudhakkarat,* vol. 1 (Beirut: Dar al-Gharb al-Islami, 1993), pp. 120–21.

8. I am using the term *feudal* here loosely to refer to the system of privileges that accrued to the rural *shuyukh* (lords) of central Palestine, most of whom were tax farmers until the passage of the Land Code of 1858. For a discussion of this issue, see Alexander Schölch, "Was There Feudalism in Palestine?" in his seminal *Palestine in Transformation, 1856–1882: Studies in Social, Economic, and Political Development* (Washington, D.C.: Institute for Palestine Studies, 1993), pp. 211–16. The page reference here is to the Arabic translation published by Jordan University Press in 1988.

9. The editor, Rafif Barghouti, Omar's granddaughter, who passed away in early 2002, courageously published all his political entries, with the result that the book was banned in Jordan. She apparently felt, however, that sensitive references to his family life and his mistresses should not appear in public.

10. Barghouti has a careless manner of (not) dating his entries, leaving it to the reader to guess what event he is describing from the context. To add further confusion to the chronology, he often describes events that took place earlier to embellish his narrative.

11. There is no mention of either movement in the memoirs of Muhammad Izzat Darwazeh, who lived and was active in Nablus-based Ottoman decentralization movements in the same period.

12. A good source on Palestinian and Syrian attitudes toward Jamal Pasha and Arab sentiments toward the Ottoman question during World War I is James

Gelvin, *Divided Loyalties: Nationalism and Mass Politics in Syria at the Close of Empire* (Berkeley: University of California Press, 1998).

13. See Hasan Kayali, *Arabs and Young Turks: Ottomanism, Arabism, and Islamism in the Ottoman Empire, 1908–1918* (Berkeley: University of California Press, 1997), especially the section "Syria Under Cemal Pasha's Governorship," pp. 192–95.

14. Yacoub al-ʿOdat, *Min Aʿlam al Fikr wal Adab fi Filasteen,* 3rd ed. (Jerusalem: Dar al-Isra', 1992).

15. Here Omar is probably referring to participation in religious festivals such as Nebi Musa and Nebi Saleh.

9. ISHAQ SHAMI AND THE PREDICAMENT OF THE ARAB JEW IN PALESTINE

I am indebted to Abigail Jacobson for obtaining several documents on Ishaq Shami from the Jerusalem Municipal Archives; to Shlomo Hassoun for his insightful comments on the native Jewish community of Palestine at the turn of nineteenth century; and particularly to Joseph (Yossi) Zernick, the grandson of Daoud Shami (Yitzhaq's brother), for sharing with me his extensive knowledge and an unpublished essay on Shami family history. I am also indebted to Hisham Nafa', from Haifa, for his translations of Hebrew material from the Jerusalem Municipal Archives.

1. Kamal Salibi, *Ta'ir ʿala Sindiyanah: Muthakkarat* (Amman: Dar al Shuruq, 2002), pp. 121–22, 128.

2. In 1945 Salibi discovered correspondence between his brother Bahij and Ishaq Elias, his Jewish classmate from Baghdad in 1940–41. In these letters Elias expresses what Salibi considered to be "radical Arab nationalist" views. During the 1950s, Elias migrated to Israel and became the deputy foreign minister in Moshe Sharett's government in the new Jewish state. Ibid., p. 128.

3. Neville Mandel, *The Arabs and Zionism Before World War I* (Berkeley: University of California Press, 1976).

4. Arnold Band, Introduction to Shami's *Hebron Stories* (Lancaster: Labyrinthos, 2000), p. xiv. In this chapter I use both the Hebrew and Arabic transliterations of Shami's first name, Yitzhaq and Ishaq.

5. Robert L. Cooper and Bernard Spolsky, *The Languages of Jerusalem* (Oxford: Oxford University Press, 1991), p. 49.

6. In the group of "native" Jews I also include Ashkenazi Jews who were Ottoman citizens and whose mother tongue was Yiddish or German.

7. For an original discussion on Jewish writings in Arabic and the persistence of the use of Arabic as a religious and literary device by Arab Jews, see Nissim Rejwan, "Jews and Arabs: The Cultural Heritage," *The Israel Review of Arts and Letters,* 105 (1997).

8. Elie Eliachar, *Living with Jews* (London: Weidenfeld and Nicholson, 1983), pp. 59–60.

9. Ibid., pp. 15–16.

10. Ibid., p. 51.

11. Omar Saleh al-Barghouti, *al Marahel* (Beirut: Al-Anwar, 2001).

12. David Landau, "The Educational Impact of Western Culture on Traditional Society in Nineteenth-Century Palestine," in *Jews in Muslim Lands in the Period of Reforms, 1830–1880* (Littman Jewish Library, 2007), p. 506.

13. Eliachar, *Living with Jews*, p. 50.

14. See, for example, the description of this move in Wasif Jawhariyyeh's memoirs, Salim Tamari and Issam Nassar, eds., *al-Quds al-'Uthmaniyah fi al-mudhakkirat al-Jawhariyah: al-kitab al-awwal min mudhakkirat al-Musiqi Wasif Jawhariyah, 1904–1917* (Beirut: Institute for Palestine Studies, 2001).

15. Eliachar, *Living with Jews*, pp. 56–57.

16. Tamari and Issam Nassar, eds., *al-Quds al-'Uthmaniyah*, pp. 200–201.

17. Eliachar, *Living with Jews*, p. 56.

18. Yehouda Shenhav, "Jews from Arab Countries and the Palestinian Right for Return: An Ethnic Community in the Realms of National Memory," *British Journal of Middle Eastern Studies* 29, no. 1 (2002): 27–56.

19. Ibid. See also Amnon Raz-Krakotzkin, "Exile within Sovereignty: Toward a Critique of the 'Negation of Exile' in Israeli Culture," in *Theory and Criticism. An Israeli Forum* 4 (1993): 23–55 (part 1); and 5 (1994): 113–32 (part 2). Both were published in Hebrew.

20. Ibid., part 1.

21. Ibid., part 2.

22. Sami Michael, *Victoria* (London: Macmillan, 1995).

23. Based on an extended interview with Sheri Lev Ari, "The Last Arabic Jew," *Haaretz*, December 22, 2003.

24. Band, Introduction to Yitzhaq Shami's *Hebron Stories*, p. xii.

25. Most of this biographical material is based on Zfira Ogden, "Izhaq Shami: The Man and His Work," in *Bikorot ve Parshanut* 21 (1986), and from Joseph Zernick's introduction to a forthcoming collection of Shami's short stories *Yithaq Shami: 1888–1949*.

26. Ogden, "Izhaq Shami," p. 37.

27. Ibid., p. 38.

28. Letter dated October 1927 from Ben Gurion to Yitzhaq Shami (in Hebrew) in the Jerusalem Municipal Archives.

29. Letter to David Avitzur in Hebron, 1927, in the Jerusalem Municipal Archives; cited in Ogden, "Izhaq Shami," p. 45.

30. Letter from Yehouda Burla to David Avitzur, May 22, 1924, quoted by Ogden and cited by Hannan Hever, "Yitzhak Shami: Ethnicity as an Unresolved Conflict," *Shofar: An Interdisciplinary Journal of Jewish Studies* 24, no. 2 (2006): 124–39.

31. Letter to David Avitzur, 1930, cited in Ogden, "Izhaq Shami."

32. Letter to David Avitzur from Haifa, 1939, in the Jerusalem Municipal Archives; cited in Ogden, "Izhaq Shami."

33. Letter to David Avitzur from Haifa, 1932, in the Jerusalem Municipal Archives; cited in Ogden, "Izhaq Shami."

34. Author communication with Joseph Zernick, January 12, 2004.

35. Anton Shammas, on the back cover of Shami's *Hebron Stories*.

36. Yitzhaq Shami, *Vengeance of the Fathers*, in *Hebron Stories*, pp. 118–19.

37. Ibid., p. 119.

38. Ibid., pp. 144–45.

39. Hever, "Yitzhak Shami," p. 2.

40. Issa Boullata and Yitzhaq Shami, "Hebrew Fiction: Arabs and Jews before Balfour," alJadeed 34 (Winter 2002): 20–21.

41. Ibid., p. 21.

42. Joseph Zernik, Introduction to a new edition of Yitzhaq Shami's collected stories, forthcoming.

43. Hever, "Yitzhak Shami," pp. 10–11.

44. Yitzhaq Shami, "Jum'ah the Simpleton," in Hebron Stories, p. 31.

45. Ibid.

46. David Shasha, The American Muslim, January–February 2003.

47. See Khalil Sakakini, Yawmiyyat, vol. 1 (Ramallah: Khalil Sakakini Centre and the Institute for Jerusalem Studies, 2003); and Wasif Jawhariyyeh, al Quds al 'Uthmaniyyah (Jerusalem: IJS, 2003).

48. Jawhariyyeh, al Quds al 'Uthmaniyyah.

49. Cited by Yehoshuah Porath, The Emergence of the Palestinian Arab National Movement, 1918–1929 (London: Frank Cass, 1974), pp. 60–61.

50. Ibid., p. 61.

51. Ibid.

52. There are several accounts of the 1929 incidents, mostly from Jewish sources. Most Jewish sources tend to stress the local conditions that gave rise to these clashes, while Arab sources, such as the memoirs of Ajaj Nweihid, relate the incidents to the wider clashes between Zionism and Arab nationalism. For contrasting views, see Neri Livneh, "Hebron Diary," Haaretz, July 9, 1999; and Shira Schoenberg, "The Hebron Massacre of 1929," in The Jewish Virtual Library, www.jewishvirtuallibrary.org/. See also Ajaj Nweihid, "What Happened in Hebron?" in his Sittun 'aman ma'alQafilah al'arbiyyah (Beirut: Dar al Istiqlal, 1993), pp. 148–49.

10. THE ENIGMATIC BOLSHEVIK FROM THE HOLY CITY

1. Najati Sidqi, Mudhakkarat Najati Sidqi, ed. Hanna Abu Hanna (Beirut: Mu'assasat al Dirasat al Filastiniyya, 2002), pp. 116–17.

2. Al-Adib (Beirut), November 1968.

3. Yacoub al-'Odat, Min A'lam al Fikr wal Adab fi Filasteen, 3rd ed. (Jerusalem: Dar al-Isra', 1992). See the entry "Sidqi Najati" on pp. 351–54.

4. Ibid., p. 352.

5. Sidqi, Mudhakkarat, p. 16.

6. Ibid., p. 53.

7. Ibid., pp. 119–21.

8. 'Odat claims that Sidqi produced The Arab East (al Sharq al Arabi) under the pseudonym Mustafa al Omary. According to 'Odat, Sidqi had published twenty-six issues of the monthly journal when it was closed by the order of the prime minister, Pierre Laval, who was executed after World War II for his collaboration with the Nazis. However, Musa Budeiri, who has researched the history of the PCP, insists that a thorough search of the archives has not yielded any

evidence that *The Arab East* ever existed and that Sidqi himself could not produce a copy of the journal when Budeiri interviewed him in Beirut. Author interview with Musa Budeiri, January 4, 2002.

9. Sidqi, *Mudhakkarat,* p. 86.

10. Ibid., pp. 96–97.

11. In his introduction to ibid., pp. 6–7. The sources for Ahmad Sidqi's presence in Moscow are Abdul Qadir Yasin, "The PCP and the National Question," *Al-Katib* 120: 97; and Musa Budeiri, *The Labour Movement in Palestine* (Jerusalem: Tali'a Publishers, 1970), p. 11, n. 6. Both works, which are in Arabic, are cited in Hanna Abu Hanna's introduction, p. 12.

12. Sidqi, *Mudhakkarat,* p. 138.

13. Ibid., pp. 165–66.

14. Ibid., p. 167.

15. The reader will find a complete list of Sidqi's publications in 'Odat, *Min A'lam al Fikr wal Adab fi Filasteen,* pp. 353–54.

11. THE VAGABOND CAFÉ AND JERUSALEM'S PRINCE OF IDLENESS

1. Hala Sakakini, ed., *Kadha Ana Ya Dunia: The Diaries of Khalil al-Sakakini* (Jerusalem: Commercial Press, 1954), p. 37.

2. Ralph Hattox, *Coffee and Coffeehouses: The Origins of a Social Beverage in the Medieval Near East* (Seattle: University of Washington Press, 1985), pp. 90–91.

3. Ibid., p. 99.

4. Abdel Mun'im Shmais, *Qahawi al Adab wal Fann fil Qahira* (Cairo: Dar al Ma'arif, 1991), p. 9. See also Hattox, *Coffee and Coffeehouses,* pp. 29–45.

5. For a discussion of how those cafés evolved in Beirut, see Jabbur Dweihi and Muhammad Abu Samra, "Maqahi Beirut Bayna mahattat al Naql al 'am wa dumu' al Muthaqafeen" (Beirut's cafés: From public transport stations to the tears of intellectuals), *an-Nahar Cultural Supplement,* April 4, 1998.

6. Ibid., p. 11.

7. Jabbur Dweihi, "Al Maqaha al Adabiyyah" (Literary cafés), *an-Nahar Cultural Supplement,* April 4, 1998.

8. Cited in Deborah Bernstein, "Contested Contact: Proximity and Social Control," unpublished paper delivered at the conference "Mixed Towns," Van Leer Institute, Jerusalem, June 13, 2003. I would like to thank the author for allowing me to quote from her paper here.

9. Jens Hanssen, "Public Morality and Marginality in Fin-de-Siècle Beirut," in *Outside In: On the Margins of the Middle East,* ed. Eugene Rogan (London: I. B. Tauris, 2002), pp. 190–91.

10. Hattox, *Coffee and Coffeehouses,* p. 43.

11. Shmais, *Qahawi al Adab wal Fann fil Qahira,* p. 14.

12. Ibid., p. 28.

13. Ibid., p. 30.

14. Ibid., pp. 102–6.

15. Ibid., pp. 107–9.

16. Ami Ayalon, *Reading Palestine: Texts and Audience 1900–1948* (Austin: University of Texas Press, 2004). See also his "Modern Texts and Their Readers in Late Ottoman Palestine," *Middle East Studies* 39, no. 4 (October 2002): 17–40.

17. Dwiehi, "Al Maqaha al Adabiyyah," p. 13.

18. Ami Ayalon, *Reading Palestine.*

19. See Wasif Jawhariyyeh, *Al Quds al 'Uthmaniyyeh,* vol. 1 (Jerusalem: IJS, 2003).

20. Ibid., p. 40.

21. Ibid., p. 77.

22. Ibid., p. 35.

23. Salim Tamari, "Jerusalem's Ottoman Modernity," *Jerusalem Quarterly File* 9 (Summer 2000): 20–21.

24. Najati Sidqi, *Mudhakkarat Najati Sidqi,* ed. Hanna Abu Hanna (Beirut: Mu'assasat al Dirasat al Filastiniyya, 2002), p. 19.

25. Jamil Issa Toubbeh, *Day of the Long Night: A Palestinian Refugee Remembers the Nakba* (London: McFarland and Company, 1998), p. 35.

26. Yusif Ayyub Haddad, *Khalil Sakakini: Hayatuhu wa Atharuhu* (Nazareth: As Sawt, 1985), p. 68.

27. Listed in Jawhariyyeh, *Al Quds al 'Uthmaniyyeh,* appendix 6, p. 265.

28. Ibrahim Qandalaft, "Ta'ala ma'i ila Muqha al Sa'aleek" (Come with me to the Vagabond Café), *al Bilad,* October 30, 1960.

29. Haddad, *Khalil Sakakini,* p. 68.

30. Khalil Sakakini, *Ma Tayassar,* vol. 1 (Jerusalem: Commercial Press, 1954), p. 82.

31. Haddad, *Khalil Sakakini,* p. 71.

32. Sakakini, ed., *Kadha Ana Ya Dunia,* p. 43. On his relationship with Isma'il al-Husseini and the party, see the entry for November 14, 1908, pp. 46–47.

33. Ibid., p. 48.

34. Ibid., pp. 39–40.

35. Khalil Sakakini, *Faraman al Sa'aleek* (Jerusalem, July 7, 1925), published in Sakakini, *Ma Tayassar,* p. 84. In this document Sakakini refers to the rejection of pluralized forms of address for high-status people in deferential address. Not addressing people with their titles and calling them instead "you," in the singular, must have been quite unconventional for that period.

36. During his imprisonment in Damascus, Sakakini expounded on this philosophy of power in a letter he wrote (but never sent) to his newborn child Sari: "Power! Power is the message we must preach. Some say that power is derived from justice, and some say that justice belongs to those who are powerful. With a little contemplation we find that justice belongs to those who are powerful, meaning that those who acquire strength in mind and body are more worthy than those who are weak in body and mind. The right of the powerful is evident and is based on the soundness of body and soul and principles. By contrast, the right of the weak is dubious since it is based on a weak mind and degenerate principles, and a weak body. . . . I want Sari to absorb this philosophy and to be strong in his body and soul." Sakakini, ed., *Kadha Ana Ya Dunia,* November 24, 1917, pp. 116–17.

37. Ibid., p. 116.

38. Sakakini, *Faraman al Sa'aleek*, p. 85.

39. Ibid.

40. Ibid., p. 86.

41. Ibid., p. 88.

42. Sakakini, *Kadha Ana Ya Dunia*, p. 141.

43. Ibid., pp. 153–54 (June 20, 1918).

44. Ibid., p. 144.

45. Ibid., pp. 142–44 (April 14, 1918).

46. Ibid., p. 144.

47. Muhammad Izzat Darwazeh, *Mudhakkarat*, vol. 1 (Beirut: Dar al-Gharb al-Islami, 1993), pp. 106–7.

48. Ibid., p. 108.

49. Quoted in Haddad, *Khalil Sakakini*, p. 71.

Bibliography

Abdallah, Wisam, ed. *Ya Kafi, Ya Shafi: The Tawfiq Canaan Collection of Amulets*. Birzeit: Birzeit University Press, 1999.

Ahmad, Fathi. *Tarikh al-rif al-Filastini fi al-ʿahd al-ʿUthamani: mantiqat Bani Zayd namudhajan* (History of rural Palestine in the Ottoman period). Ramallah: Shuruq, 1992.

al-Amiry, Muhammad Adib. *Arabs in Palestine*. London: Longman, 1968.

Amiry, Suad M. A. "Space, Kinship and Gender: The Social Dimension of Peasant Architecture in Palestine." Ph.D. dissertation, University of Edinburgh, 1987.

Amiry, Suad, and Rana Anani. *Amara wa Tarikh: Qura al-Karasi* (Throne villages: Architecture and history in the eighteenth and nineteenth centuries). Ramallah: Riwaq Publications, 2003.

Anderson, Benedict. "Exodus." *Critical Inquiry* 20, no. 2 (1994).

Ben-Arieh, Yehoshua. *Jerusalem in the 19th Century: The Old City*. New York: St. Martin's Press, 1984.

Ayalon, Ami. "Modern Texts and Their Readers in Late Ottoman Palestine." *Middle East Studies* 39, no. 4 (October 2002): 17–40.

———. *Reading Palestine: Texts and Audience 1900–1948*. Austin: University of Texas Press, 2004.

Baker, Ahmad M. *Impact of the Intifada on the Psychological Status of Palestinian Children Living in the Occupied Territories*. N.p., 1989.

Baldensperger, Philip. "Religion, Feasts, and Processions." *Palestine Exploration Fund Quarterly* (1920).

Band, Arnold. Introduction to *Hebron Stories,* by Yitzhaq Shami. Lancaster: Labyrinthos, 2000.

al-Barghouti, Abdul Latif. *al-Qamus al-ʿArabi al-shaʿbi al-Filastini: al-lahjah al-Filastiniyah al-darijah*. Ramallah: Inʾash al Usra Society, 2001.

———. *Qamus al-Lahjat al Filastiniyyah al Amiyyah*. Al-Bireh: In'ash al Usra Society, 1992.

Barghouti, Murid. "Al-Iqama fil-waqt" (Living in time). *al-Karmil* 51 (Spring 1997): 156–64.

———. *Ra'aytu Ram Allah*. Kitab al-Hilal, series 558. Cairo: Dar al-Hilal, 1997.

al-Barghouti, Omar Saleh. *al Marahel*. Beirut: Al-Anwar, 2001.

Barnes, Julian. *Flaubert's Parrot*. New York: Knopf, 1985.

Be'er, Yizhar, and Saleh 'Abdel-Jawad. *Collaborators in the Occupied Territories: Human Rights Abuses and Violations*. Jerusalem: B'tselem Publications, 1994.

Benedict, Philip. *Cities and Social Change in Early Modern France*. London: Routledge, 1992.

Benvenisti, Meron. *Sacred Landscape: The Buried History of the Holy Land Since 1948*. Berkeley: University of California Press, 2000.

Blake, G. H. "The Small Town." In *The Changing Middle Eastern City*, ed. G. H. Blake and Richard Lawless. London: Croom Helm, 1982.

Boroujerdi, Mehrzad. *Iranian Intellectuals and the West: The Tormented Triumph of Nativism*. Syracuse, NY: Syracuse University Press, 1996.

Boullata, Issa, and Yitzhaq Shami. "Hebrew Fiction: Arabs and Jews before Balfour." *alJadeed* 34 (Winter 2002).

Budeiri, Musa. *The Labour Movement in Palestine*. Jerusalem: Tali'a Publishers, 1970.

———. "The Last Plane from Jaffa." Unpublished essay, 2002.

Canaan, Tawfiq. "Arabic Magic Bowls." *Journal of the Palestine Oriental Society* 16 (1936).

———. "Haunted Springs and Water Demons in Palestine." *Journal of the Palestine Oriental Society* 1, no. 1 (October 1920).

———. Introduction to *Mohammedan Saints and Sanctuaries in Palestine*. Jerusalem: The Syrian Orphanage Press, 1927.

———. "Light and Darkness in Palestine Folklore." *Journal of the Palestine Oriental Society* 16 (1931).

———. *The Palestine Arab House: Its Architecture and Folklore*. Jerusalem: The Syrian Orphanage Press, 1933.

———. "Unwritten Laws Affecting the Arab Women of Palestine." *Journal of the Palestine Oriental Society* 11 (1931).

Carmi, Shulamit, and Henry Rosenfeld. "The Origins of the Process of Proletarianization and Urbanization of Arab Peasants in Palestine." *Annals of the New York Academy of Sciences* 220 (1974).

Cooper, Robert L., and Bernard Spolsky. *The Languages of Jerusalem*. Oxford: Oxford University Press, 1991.

Corbin, Alain. *The Lure of the Sea: The Discovery of the Seaside in the Western World 1750–1840*. Los Angeles: University of California Press, 1994.

Dajani, Ahmad. *Yafa wa Thawrat 1936* (Jaffa and the 1936 rebellion). Amman: n.p., 2001.

Dajani, Said Yusef. *Kay la nansa "Yafa."* Amman: n.p., 1991.

Dalman, Gustaf. "Arbeit und Sitte in Palastina." *Journal of the Palestine Oriental Society* 14 (1934).

Darwazeh, Muhammad Izzat. *Mudhakkarat,* vol. 1. Beirut: Dar al-Gharb al-Islami, 1993.

Davis, Rochelle. "Ottoman Jerusalem." In *Jerusalem 1948: The Arab Neighbourhoods and Their Fate in the War.* Jerusalem: Institute of Jerusalem Studies, 1999.

Deshen, Shlomo. "Social Control in Israeli Urban Quarters." In *The Changing Middle Eastern City,* ed. Helen Rivlin and Katherine Helmer. Binghamton: State University of New York Press, 1980.

Diab, Imtiaz, and Hisham Sharabi, eds. *Yafa: Itr Madina* (Jaffa: The perfume of a city). Cairo: Dar al-Fata al-Arabi, 1991.

Doumani, Beshara. *Rediscovering Palestine Merchants and Peasants in Jabal Nablus, 1700–1900.* Berkeley: University of California Press, 1995.

Dupee, F. W. Afterword to *Sentimental Education,* by Gustave Flaubert. New York: New American Edition, 1972.

Dweihi, Jabbur. "Al Maqaha al Adabiyyah" (Literary cafés). *an-Nahar Cultural Supplement,* April 4, 1998.

Dweihi, Jabbur and Muhammad Abu Samra. "Maqahi Beirut Bayna mahattat al Naql al ʿam wa dumuʿ al Muthaqafeen" (Beirut's cafés: From public transport stations to the tears of intellectuals). *an-Nahar Cultural Supplement,* April 4, 1998.

al-ʾEileh, Zaki. *Turath al-Bahr al-Filistini,* Jerusalem: n.p., 1982.

Eliachar, Elie. *Living with Jews.* London: Weidenfeld and Nicholson, 1983.

Falili, Lilly, and Ori Nir. "City of Strangers." *Haaretz,* November 27, 2000.

Fanon, Frantz. *Black Skin, White Masks.* New York: Grove Press, 1967.

Finn, Elizabeth Anne McCaul. *Palestine Peasantry: Notes on Their Clans, Warfare, Religion, and Laws.* London: Marshall Bros., 1923.

Flaubert, Gustave. *Madame Bovary.* Trans. Eleanor Marx-Aveling. New York: Everyman's Library, 1966.

Friedlander, Jonathan. "Rare Sights: Images of Early Arab Immigration in New York City." In *A Community of Many Worlds: Arab Americans in New York City,* ed. Kathleen Benson and Philip Kayal. Syracuse, NY: Syracuse University Press, 2002.

Gazit, Shlomo. *The Stick and the Carrot: Israel's Rule in the West Bank* (Arabic edition). Nicosia: Beisan Publishers, 1998.

Geertz, Clifford. "Toutes Directions: Reading the Signs in an Urban Sprawl." *International Journal of Middle East Studies* 21, no. 3 (1989).

Gelvin, James. *Divided Loyalties: Nationalism and Mass Politics in Syria at the Close of Empire.* Berkeley: University of California Press, 1998.

Gulick, John. "Village and City: Cultural Continuities in Twentieth-Century Middle East Cultures." In *Middle Eastern Cities,* ed. Ira Lapidus. Berkeley: University of California Press, 1969.

Haddad, Yusif Ayyub. *Khalil Sakakini: Hayatuhu wa Atharuhu.* Nazareth: As Sawt, 1985.

Haikal, Yusef. *Ayyam Al-Siba* (Days of my youth). Amman: n.p., 1995.

Hammami, Rema. "Between Heaven and Earth: Transformations in Religiosity and Labor among Southern Palestinian Peasant and Refugee Women, 1920–1993." Ph.D. dissertation, Temple University, 1994.

———. "Women, the Hijab and the Intifada." *Middle East Report* 164/165, Intifada Year Three (May–August 1990): 24–28.

Hattox, Ralph. *Coffee and Coffeehouses: The Origins of a Social Beverage in the Medieval Near East.* Seattle: University of Washington Press, 1985.

Heiberg, Marianne. *Palestinian Society in Gaza, West Bank and Arab Jerusalem: A Survey of Living Conditions.* Oslo: FAFO, 1993.

Hever, Hanan. "Yitzhak Shami: Ethnicity as an Unresolved Conflict." *Shofar: An Interdisciplinary Journal of Jewish Studies* 24, no. 2 (2006): 124–39, and 24, no. 4 (2006): 225–30.

Hilal, Jamil, and Ilan Pappé, eds. *Across the Wall.* London: I. B. Tauris, forthcoming.

Hopkins, Nicholas. "Popular Culture and State Power." In *Mass Culture, Popular Culture, and Social Life in the Middle East,* ed. Georg Stauth and Sami Zubaida. Frankfurt: Campus Verlag, 1987.

Hourani, Albert. *The Emergence of the Modern Middle East.* Berkeley: University of California Press, 1981.

al Husseini, Ishaq Musa. *Khalil al Sakakini, Al Adib al Mujaddid.* Jerusalem: Centre for Islamic Studies, 1989.

Ibrahim, Saad E. M. "Over-Urbanization and Under-Urbanism." *International Journal of Middle East Studies* 6, no. 1 (1975).

Jawhariyyeh, Wasif. *Al Quds al 'Uthmaniyyeh,* vol. 1. Jerusalem: IJS, 2003.

Jawwad, Saleh Abdul. "La genèse et development du mouvement de libération nationale: Le fath." Ph.D. dissertation, Paris X, Nanterre, 1986.

———. *The Theoretical and Applied Position of the Islamic Movements Toward Collaborators* (in Arabic). Jerusalem: Al-Markaz al-Filastinin lil-Dirasat, 1993.

Kayali, Hasan. *Arabs and Young Turks: Ottomanism, Arabism, and Islamism in the Ottoman Empire, 1908–1918.* Berkeley: University of California Press, 1997.

Keydar, Çaglar, Resat Kasaba, and Faruk Tabak. "Eastern Mediterranean Port Cities and Their Bourgeoisies: Merchants, Political Projects, and Nation-States." *Review* 10, no. 1 (Summer 1986).

Keydar, Çaglar, Y. Eyüp Özveren, and Donald Quartet, eds. "Port Cities of the Eastern Mediterranean: 1800–1914." *Review* 16, no. 4 (Fall 1993).

Khader, Hasan. "Hal Kunta Huna?" (Were you there?). *al-Karmil* 51 (Spring 1997): 115–24.

Khalidi, Rashid. "Competing and Overlapping Loyalties in Ottoman Jerusalem." In *Palestinian Identity: The Construction of Modern National Consciousness.* New York: Columbia University Press, 1997.

Khayyat, Shlomi. *Ramallah: 1985 Masterplan.* Jerusalem: Ministry of Interior, Office of Planning, 1985.

Khuri, Fuad I. "Ideological Constants and Urban Living." In *The Middle East City: Ancient Traditions Confront a Modern World,* ed. Abdulaziz Y. Saqqaf. New York: Paragon House, 1987.

———. *Tents and Pyramids: Games and Ideology in Arab Culture from Backgammon to Autocratic Rule.* London: Saqi Books, 1990.

Landau, David. "The Educational Impact of Western Culture on Traditional Society in Nineteenth-Century Palestine." In *Jews in Muslim Lands in the Period of Reforms, 1830–1880.* Littman Jewish Library, 2007.

Lang, Erica, and Itimad Mohanna. *Dirasah an al-mar'ah wa-al-'amal fi mukhayyam al-Shati' lil-laji'in fi Qita' Ghazzah*. al-Quds: al-Multaqa al-Fikri al-'Arabi, 1992.

Lesch, Ann Mosely. "Gaza: Forgotten Corner of Palestine." *Journal of Palestine Studies* 151 (1985): 43–61.

Malak, Hanna. *al-Juthur al-yafiyyah*. Jerusalem: Commercial Press, 1996.

———. *Zhikrayat al-'ailat al-Yafiyyah*. Jerusalem: Commercial Press, 1993.

Mamdani, Mahmoud. *When Victims Become Killers: Colonialism, Nativism, and the Genocide in Rwanda*. Princeton, NJ: Princeton University Press, 2001.

Mandel, Neville. *The Arabs and Zionism before World War I*. Berkeley: University of California Press, 1976.

Mansour, Sylvie. *Jeel al-Intifada*. Beirut: Institute of Palestine Studies, 1998.

al Masri, Zaki. *Hadith al-Dhikriyat, 1936–1994*. Ramallah: n.p., 1994.

Mazzawi, Andre. "Memories and Counter-Memories: Production, Reproduction and Deconstruction of Some Palestinian Memory Accounts about Jaffa." Paper presented at the Middle East Studies Association annual conference, San Francisco, December 1997.

Michael, Sami. *Victoria*. London: Macmillan, 1995.

Mohammad, Zakariyya. "al-Adhm wal-Dhahab" (Bone and gold). *al-Karmil* 51 (Spring 1997): 125–40.

———. "Canaanite Ideology." In *Deek Al Manara*. Ramallah: Muwatin, 2003.

Morris, Benny. *1948 and After: Israel and the Palestinians*. Oxford: Clarendon Press, 1990.

al-Mubayyid, Salim. *Malamih al-Shakhsiyyah al-filistiniyya fi Amthaliha al-Sha'biyya*. Amman: al Shuruq, 1995.

al Nashif, Khalid. "Tawfiq Canaan: Taqweem Jadeed." *Majallat al Dirasat al Filastiniyyah* 50 (Spring 2002).

Nweihid, Ajaj. "What Happened in Hebron?" In *Sittun 'aman ma'alQafilah al'arbiyyah*. Beirut: Dar al Istiqlal, 1993.

al-'Odat, Yacoub. *Min A'lam al Fikr wal Adab fi Filasteen*. 3rd ed. Jerusalem: Dar al-Isra', 1992.

Ogden, Zfira. "Izhaq Shami: The Man and His Work." In *Bikorot ve Parshanut* 21 (1986).

Oncu, Ayse, and Petra Weyland. *Space, Culture and Power: New Identities in Globalizing Cities*. London: Zed Press, 1997.

Özveren, Y. Eyüp. "Beirut." *Review* 16, no. 4 (Fall 1993).

Porath, Yehoshuah. *The Emergence of the Palestinian Arab National Movement, 1918–1929*. London: Frank Cass, 1974.

Raban, Jonathan. *Soft City*. London: Fontana, 1981.

Raymond, André. *Arab Cities in the Ottoman Period: Cairo, Syria, and the Maghreb*. Aldershot, UK: Ashgate/Variorum, 2002.

Raz-Krakotzkin, Amnon. "Exile within Sovereignty: Toward a Critique of the 'Negation of Exile' in Israeli Culture." *Theory and Criticism: An Israeli Forum* 4–5 (1993–).

Rejwan, Nissim. "Jews and Arabs: The Cultural Heritage." *The Israel Review of Arts and Letters* 105 (1997).

Rogan, Eugene, ed. *Outside In: On the Margins of the Middle East*. London: I. B. Tauris, 2002.

Said, Edward W. *Culture and Imperialism*. New York: Knopf, 1993.

———. *Out of Place: A Memoir*. New York: Knopf, 1999.

Sakakini, Hala. *Jerusalem and I: A Personal Record*. Amman: Economic Press, 1987.

Sakakini, Hala, ed. *Kadha Ana Ya Dunia: The Diaries of Khalil al-Sakakini*. Jerusalem: Commercial Press, 1954.

Sakakini, Khalil. *Kadha Ana Ya Dunia*. Beirut: al-Ittihad al-ʿAmm lil-Kuttab wa-al-Suhufiyin al-Filastiniyin, al-Amanah al-ʿAmmah, 1982.

———. *Ma Tayassar*, vol. 1. Jerusalem: Commercial Press, 1954.

Sakakini, Khalil, and Akram Musallam. *Yawmiyat Khalil al-Sakakini: yawmiyat, rasaʾil wa-taʾammulat* (Diaries of Khalil Sakakini), vol. 1. ʿRam Allah: Markaz Khalil al-Sakakini al-Thaqafi, 2003.

al-Salhi, Bassam. *The Political and Religious Leadership in the Occupied Territories: 1967–1993* (in Arabic). Ramallah: Dar al-Quds, 1993.

Salibi, Kamal. *Taʾir ʿala Sindiyanah: Muthakkarat*. Amman: Dar al Shuruq, 2002.

Sayegh, Rosemary. *From Peasants to Revolutionaries: A People's History*. London: Zed Press, 1979.

Schölch, Alexander. *Palestine in Transformation, 1856–1882: Studies in Social, Economic, and Political Development*. Washington, D.C.: Institute for Palestine Studies, 1993.

Sharabi, Hisham. *Zhikrayat Madina*. Stockholm: Andalus, 1992.

Shavit, Yaacov. *The New Hebrew Nation: A Study in Israeli Heresy and Fantasy*. London: Frank Cass, 1987.

al-Shaykh, Hanan. *Hikayat Zahra*. Beirut: Dar al-Adab, 1999.

Shenhav, Yehouda. "Jews from Arab Countries and the Palestinian Right for Return: An Ethnic Community in the Realms of National Memory." *British Journal of Middle Eastern Studies* 29, no. 1 (2002).

Shmais, Abdel Munʾim. *Qahawi al Adab wal Fann fil Qahira*. Cairo: Dar al Maʾarif, 1991.

Sidqi, Najati. *Mudhakkarat Najati Sidqi*, ed. Hanna Abu Hanna. Beirut: Muʾassasat al Dirasat al Filastiniyya, 2002.

Singh, R. L. and R. P. B. Singh, eds. *Place of Small Towns in India*. Varanasi: International Centre for Rural Habitat Studies, 1979.

Smith, Michael P. *Transnational Urbanism: Locating Globalization*. Malden, MA: Blackwell Publishers, 2001.

Sprawson, Charles. *Haunts of the Black Masseur*. New York: Pantheon, 1992.

Stephan, Stephan H. "Lunacy in Palestinian Folklore." *Journal of the Palestine Oriental Society* 5 (1925).

———. "Modern Palestinian Parallels to the Song of Songs." *Journal of the Palestine Oriental Society* 2 (1922).

Suleiman, Michael. "Impressions of New York City by Early Arab Immigrants." In *Community of Many Worlds: Arab Americans in New York City*, ed. Kathleen Benson and Philip Kayal. Syracuse, NY: Syracuse University Press, 2002.

Swanson, Bert, et al. *Small Towns and Small Towners*. Beverly Hills, CA: Sage Library of Social Research, 1979.

Tamari, Salim. "Palestinian Society." In *The Encyclopedia of the Palestinians,* ed. Philip Mattar. New York: Facts on File, 2000.

———. "Shopkeepers, Peddlers, and Urban Resistance." In Proceedings of the International Conference on Urbanism and Islam, vol. 2. Tokyo: Tokyo University Publications, 1989.

———. "Social Transformations and Future Prospects in the West Bank and Gaza." Occasional Papers, UNCTAD, Geneva, 1994.

———. "Soul of the Nation: Urban Intellectuals and the Peasants." *Middle East Studies* 5 (1982).

Tamari, Salim, ed. *Jerusalem 1948: The Arab Neighbourhoods and their Fate in the War.* Jerusalem: Institute of Jerusalem Studies, 1999.

———. "Jerusalem's Ottoman Modernity." *Jerusalem Quarterly File* 9 (Summer 2000).

Tamari, Salim, and Issam Nassar, eds. *al-Quds al-intidabiyah fi al-mudhakkirat al-Jawhariyah: al-kitab al-thani min mudhakkirat al-Musiqi Wasif Jawhariyah, 1918–1948.* Beirut: Institute for Palestine Studies, 2005.

———. *al-Quds al-'Uthmaniyah fi al-mudhakkirat al-Jawhariyah: al-kitab al-awwal min mudhakkirat al-Musiqi Wasif Jawhariyah, 1904–1917.* Beirut: Institute for Palestine Studies, 2003.

Troin, Jean-Francois. "Petite villes et villes moyennes au Maroc: Hypothèses et réalités." In *Petites villes et villes moyennes dans le monde Arabe,* ed. URBAMA, 1986.

Toubbeh, Jamil Issa. *Day of the Long Night: A Palestinian Refugee Remembers the Nakba.* London: McFarland and Company, 1998.

Tyagi, V. K. *Urban Growth and Urban Villages: A Case Study of Delhi.* New Delhi: Kalyani Publishers, 1982.

Tzur, Yaron, ed. *Jews in Muslim Lands in the Period of the Reforms, 1830–1880.* Littman Jewish Library, 2007.

URBAMA. *Petites villes et villes moyennes dans le monde Arabe.* 2 vols. Tours: URBAMA, 1986.

Williams, Raymond. *The Politics of Modernism: Against the New Conformists.* London: Verso, 1989.

Wilson, Elizabeth. *The Sphinx in the City: Urban Life, the Control of Disorder, and Women.* Berkeley: University of California Press, 1991.

———. *Jerusalem in the 19th Century: Emergence of the New City.* Jerusalem: Yad Yitshak Ben-Zvi, 1986.

Yasin, Abdul Hamid, et al. *Zhikra al Sakakini.* Jerusalem: Modern Library, 1957.

Zaqtan, Ghassan. "Nafi al Manfa" (Negation of exile). *al-Karmil* 51 (Spring 1997): 141–45.

Zubaida, Sami. "Components of Popular Culture in the Middle East." In *Mass Culture, Popular Culture and Social Life in the Middle East,* ed. George Stauth and Sami Zubaida. Boulder, CO: Westview Press, 1987.

———. *Islam, the People, and the State.* London: Routledge, 1989.

Ben Zvi, Yitshak. "Historical Survey of the Jewish Settlement in Kefar Yasif." *Journal of the Palestine Oriental Society* 5 (1925).

———. *She'ar Yashar.* Jerusalem: Yad Yitshak Ben-Zvi, 1966.

Index

Text: 10/13 Sabon
Display: Sabon
Compositor: Binghamton Valley Composition
Indexer: Sharon Sweeney
Printer and Binder: Maple-Vail Book Manufacturing Group